# 5 STEPS TO A 5™

# AP Precalculus

# 5 STEPS TO A 5™

# AP Precalculus

Deborah B. Klipp

Paul Rodriguez

McGraw Hill

2 3 4 5 6 7 8 9   LOV   28 27 26 25 24

ISBN        978-1-266-71669-0
MHID        1-266-71669-6

McGraw Hill, the McGraw Hill logo, *5 Steps to a 5*, and related trade dress are trademarks or registered trademarks of McGraw Hill and/or its affiliates in the United States and other countries and may not be used without written permission. All other trademarks are the property of their respective owners. McGraw Hill is not associated with any product or vendor mentioned in this book.

*AP, Advanced Placement Program*, and *College Board* are registered trademarks of the College Board, which was not involved in the production of, and does not endorse, this product.

The series editor was Grace Freedson, and the project editor was Del Franz.

Series design by Jane Tenenbaum.

McGraw Hill products are available at special quantity discounts to use as premiums and sales promotions, or for use in corporate training programs. To contact a representative, please visit the Contact Us pages at www.mhprofessional.com.

McGraw Hill is committed to making our products accessible to all learners. To learn more about the available support and accommodations we offer, please contact us at accessibility@mheducation.com. We also participate in the Access Text Network (www.accesstext.org), and ATN members may submit requests through ATN.

# CONTENTS

**STEP 5**  ## Build Your Test-Taking Confidence

# PREFACE

Congratulations! You are an AP Precalculus student. By taking the AP Precalculus Exam, you're giving yourself the skills necessary to prepare for other college-level mathematics and science courses, whether you take those courses while in high school or at the college/university level. These courses are foundational to careers in mathematics, biology, physics, social science, health science, computer science, and data science. The knowledge you gain in this course will give you an advantage no matter what field you study in the future, whether you are interested in a STEM or non-STEM major. Non-STEM majors who don't require calculus can use AP Precalculus as a capstone math course, earning college credits.

The purpose of this book is to help you score a 5 on the AP Precalculus Exam. Along the way, your mathematics and problem-solving ability should dramatically improve. So, how do you do well on the AP Precalculus Exam? How do you earn a 5? One of the first steps is to read this book and make sure you understand the material. Do the practice problems. For many of the questions, you are also expected to use a graphing calculator to find the solution, so make sure you are comfortable using your calculator.

# ACKNOWLEDGMENTS

I am very grateful to have been given the opportunity to write this book alongside Paul Rodriguez. Thank you to Grace Freedson from The Publishing Network and Anya Kozorez from McGraw Hill for giving us the opportunity to embark on a new book for this new AP course.

I would like to thank my husband, Doug, and my daughters Melissa Klipp and Samantha Beidler, for all the support they have given me over the years while I teach and travel the country presenting and attending workshops and conferences.

*Deborah Klipp*

I would like to thank Deborah for working with me on this project as her insights and suggestions have been invaluable. Also, we could not have completed this without the efforts of Grace Freedson from The Publishing Network and Anya Kozorez from McGraw Hill. Thank you both for trusting us in writing this new book for AP Precalculus.

I would like to thank my wife, Michelle, for her patience and support while I worked late nights and traveled during my educational career. Also, I thank my parents for their love and encouragement that started me on my journey so many years ago. Finally, to my daughters, Denise Eddy and Breanna Rodriguez, for putting up with my busy schedule while I attended workshops.

*Paul Rodriguez*

# ABOUT THE AUTHORS

**DEBORAH B. KLIPP** began teaching at Mainland Regional High School in Linwood, New Jersey in 1985. After teaching math at Mainland for 25 years, she moved to Florida with her husband and two daughters. She taught math at Hillsborough Community College for five years and is currently working at Florida Virtual School. She received a Bachelor of Science in Mathematics, Computer Science minor from Pennsylvania State University and a Master of Arts degree in Education from Rowan University. She has been an AP Computer Science A reader, table leader, and question leader since 1999 and has been an AP College Board Consultant since 2001. She enjoys teaching and sharing her love and passion for math and computer science with both students and teachers. Deborah is also an author of *5 Steps to a 5 AP Computer Science A.*

**PAUL RODRIGUEZ** has completed 29 years of teaching, including 25 at Troy High School in Fullerton, California. He received a Bachelor of Science in Applied Mathematics from UCLA and a Master of Arts in Mathematics Teaching from Cal State Fullerton. Paul has worked for the College Board for 20 years, including writing for the content team for AP Precalculus and as a reader, table leader, and question leader for AP Statistics since 2004. Paul also served on the AP Statistics Test Development Committee, writing, and editing the AP exam and was the co-chair of the committee when the course and exam description was written. Paul has been an AP College Board Consultant since 2015 and enjoys the opportunity to share his love of math and passion for teaching to improve mathematics education.

# INTRODUCTION

## Organization of the Book

This book was created to help you earn a 5 on the AP Precalculus Exam. It is important that you understand how this book has been written specifically for you.

This book contains the following:

- An explanation of the highly successful Five-Step Program
- A suggested calendar based on how you want to prepare for the AP Precalculus Exam
- A series of test-taking strategies
- A diagnostic exam with solutions and explanations
- A thorough explanation of each topic tested on the AP Precalculus Exam
- Two practice exams with solutions and explanations

Mathematics is one of those fields that can be taught in many completely different ways; even the order in which things are taught can be different. Sure, there are some concepts that you must understand before you can move on to others, but the reality is, there is a lot of flexibility.

For instance, throw a dozen math teachers in a room and ask them if graphing calculators should be used or how often they should be used. Then grab a bag of popcorn and sit back and enjoy the show. Math teachers have been arguing which way is best for years. I have taught high school and college students both ways, and I believe there are valid arguments on both sides.

## Advice from Our Students

We asked our students for advice on writing this book. One thing they told us is to never explain a new topic using concepts that haven't been introduced yet. Students hate it when authors say, "Oh, I'm going to use something that I won't be explaining right now, but we'll get to it in a later chapter." We have tried really hard to design this book in a linear fashion, so I hope that we never do this to you.

One of the goals in writing this book was to strike the right balance between explaining topics in a way that *any* high school student can understand but still technical enough so students can earn a 5 on the exam. Our students recommended that we start off by explaining each concept in a simple way so that anyone can understand it, and then go into greater detail by working through examples. We hope you will appreciate our attempts at this. In other words, we've tried to make the book easy enough for average math students to understand the basics, so they are not completely lost, but then hard enough so that advanced students have the potential to earn a 5 on the AP Precalculus Exam.

## Basic and Advanced Levels

It is for this reason that we have also chosen to create two levels of questions for each of the main concepts: Basic and Advanced. As teachers, we have learned that students like to know that they understand the basics of a concept before moving on to harder questions. If a book only has really hard practice questions, then most of the average students find them impossible to do, start feeling like failures, lose interest, and eventually drop out because they can't relate to anything the book is talking about.

We've also learned that it helps to try to find something that the student can relate to and explain the concept using that. We have tried to use examples with which high school students can identify.

## The Unit Summary

Each unit begins with a unit summary. The summary explains what's covered in the unit, and it should give you a reason why you would want to learn the material covered in that unit. It also is a great tool for deciding if you need to look further at that topic.

## The Rapid Review

Each unit ends with a "Rapid Review," which is a complete summary of the important ideas relating to the concept. The lists are full of wonderful one-liners that you should understand before taking the AP Precalculus Exam. Make sure that you understand every line in the Rapid Review before taking the exam.

## The Graphics Used in This Book

 **Powerful Tip:** This graphic identifies a helpful tip for taking the AP Precalculus Exam

 **Fun Fact:** This graphic identifies fun deviations from the subject matter.

 **Warning:** This graphic points out a common error to avoid

If you have any questions, suggestions, or would like to report an error, we'd love to hear from you. Email us at 5stepsAPprecalc@gmail.com

## The Five-Step Program

This guide leads you through the five steps necessary to prepare yourself for success on the exam. These steps will provide you with the skills and strategies that are vital to the exam as well as the practice that can lead you toward the score of 5. Reading this guide will not guarantee you a 5 when you take the AP Precalculus Exam in May. However, by understanding what's on the exam, using the test-taking strategies provided for each section of the test, and carefully reviewing the concepts covered on the exam, you will definitely be on your way!

**Step One** gives you the basic information you need to know about the exam and helps you determine which type of exam preparation you want to commit to. In Step One, you'll find:

- The goals of the AP Precalculus course
- Frequently asked questions about the exam
- An explanation of how the exam is graded
- Types of graphing calculators that are allowed on the exam
- Calendars for three different preparation plans
  - Full School Year Plan (September through May)
  - One-Semester Plan (January through May)
  - Six-Week Plan (March through May)

**Step Two** introduces you to the types of questions you'll find on the actual exam and by identifying the content areas where you are weak, allows you to prioritize the areas you most need to review. In Step Two, you'll find:

- A diagnostic exam in AP Precalculus. This exam is similar to the real exam except it is organized by units and has 50 questions with most being open ended. The actual AP Precalculus Exam has 40 multiple-choice questions and 4 free-response questions.
- Answers and explanations for all the exam questions. Read the explanations not just for the questions you miss, but also for all the questions and answer choices you didn't completely understand.

**Step Three** helps you develop the strategies and techniques you need in order to do your best on the exam. In Step Three, you'll learn:

- Strategies to tackle the multiple-choice questions efficiently and effectively
- Strategies to maximize your score on the free-response questions
- What you need to bring to the exam on exam day

**Step Four** develops the knowledge and skills necessary to do well on the exam. This is organized into four key units. In Step Four, you'll review by using:

- Complete, but easy-to-follow, explanations of all the concepts covered on the exam
- Review questions—both basic and advanced levels—for each unit, followed by step-by-step explanations so you'll understand anything you missed
- Rapid Reviews for each unit that you can use to make sure you have the knowledge and skills you'll need

Important Note: We have included a "Unit 0" in this book to help you brush up on Algebra and Geometry concepts before diving into the AP Precalculus content. Also, while Unit 4 (Functions Involving Parameters, Vectors, and Matrices) may be covered in your class, this unit will not yet be tested on the AP exam, so will not be included in our review.

**Step Five** will give you test-taking practice and develop your confidence for taking the exam. In Step Five, you'll find:

- Two full-length practice exams that closely resemble the actual AP Precalculus Exam. As well as checking your mastery of the concepts, you can use these exams to practice pacing and using the test-taking strategies given in Step Three.
- Step-by-step explanations for all the exam questions so you can understand anything you missed and learn from your mistakes.
- Scoring guidelines so you can assess your performance and estimate your score in order to see if you have reached your goal.

# Set Up Your Study Plan

# CHAPTER 1

# What You Need to Know About the AP Precalculus Exam

**IN THIS CHAPTER**

**Summary:** Learn topics that are tested on the exam, what the format is, which calculators are allowed, and how the exam is graded.

**Key Ideas**

✪ The AP Precalculus exam has 40 multiple-choice questions and 4 free-response questions.
✪ Both multiple-choice questions and free-response questions are separated into two parts.
✪ In one part graphing calculators are required and in one part they are not permitted.

## Background Information

### A Brief History of the Exam

Every year thousands of new college students must take a remedial math course that does not count toward their degree. To help those students the College Board and the Advanced Placement Program convened college faculty to build a precalculus course that invites a diverse group of students to prepare for college mathematics, encourages more students to complete four years of mathematics in high school, and improves the readiness to succeed in STEM (Science, Technology, Engineering and Mathematics) courses and majors in college.

The first AP Precalculus exam will be given in May 2024.

### Goals of the Course

In AP Precalculus, students explore everyday situations and phenomena using mathematical tools and lenses. Through regular practice, students build deep mastery of modeling and functions, and they examine scenarios through multiple representations. They will learn how to observe, explore, and build mathematical meaning from dynamic systems, an important practice for thriving in an ever-changing world. Students will experience:

**Modeling Real-World Data**—Examine scenarios, conditions, and data sets to apply the mathematical tools to determine and validate appropriate function models by gaining a deeper understanding of the nature and behavior of each function type.

**Exploring Multiple Representations**—Examine functions graphically, numerically, verbally, and analytically to gain a deeper understanding of functions through multiple representations.

**Mastering Symbolic Manipulation**—Develop rigorous symbolic manipulation skills needed for future mathematics courses. A single mathematical object can have different analytical representations depending on the function type or coordinate system, and the different analytical representations reveal different attributes of the mathematical object.

**Harnessing a Dynamic World**—Engage in function building that reflects not a static view of things but embodies how things change. Every function representation characterizes the way in which values of one variable simultaneously change as the values in another variable change.

For a more detailed description of the topics covered in the AP Precalculus exam, visit the College Board AP website at https://apcentral.collegeboard.org/courses/ap-precalculus.

## Frequently Asked Questions About the Exam

### Who Writes the AP Precalculus Exam? Who Grades the Exam?

The AP Precalculus exam is designed by a committee of college professors and high school precalculus teachers. The process to build an exam takes years to ensure that the exam questions reflect the high quality and fairness that is expected by the College Board and that matches the equivalent college math course.

The free-response questions are scored by hundreds of college professors and high school AP Precalculus teachers during one week in June. These teachers, the AP exam "readers", are thoroughly trained to apply a given rubric so that all exams are graded consistently.

### Why Take the AP Precalculus Exam?

There are several benefits to taking an AP exam. If you score a 3, 4, or 5 on the exam, you can earn credit and/or placement at most colleges and universities. This saves you both time and money (and who doesn't want to save those?). If you are a student interested in a non-STEM major, you should be able to use a qualifying AP Precalculus exam score to fulfill a college math requirement, which means no need to take a remedial course in college. If you are a STEM major, you will start off at a higher level in your college coursework so that you can advance faster.

### When Is the Exam and How Do I Register for It?

The AP exams are given during the first two weeks of May. The College Board publishes a schedule each year as to which exams are given each day during those two weeks. The College Board deadline for exam registration is early in November but check with your school's AP Coordinator about the exact deadlines and procedures for registering for the exam. If you are not taking an AP Precalculus course at your school and want to take the exam on your own, you need to contact your AP Coordinator so that they can order an exam for you. The cost of the exam (whether you are taking an AP course or not) is approximately $100.

### What Is the Format of the AP Precalculus Exam?

The AP Precalculus exam has two sections:

Section I contains 40 multiple-choice questions for which you are given 2 hours to complete.

Section II contains 4 free-response questions for which you are given 1 hour to complete.

The total time allotted for both sections of the exam is 3 hours. Below is a summary of the different parts of the exam and the graphing calculator usage.

| SECTION | QUESTION TYPE | NUMBER OF QUESTIONS | EXAM WEIGHTING | TIMING |
|---------|---------------|---------------------|----------------|--------|
| I MULTIPLE-CHOICE QUESTIONS | | | | |
| | Part A: Graphing calculator not permitted | 28 | 43.75% | 80 minutes |
| | Part B: Graphing calculator required | 12 | 18.75% | 40 minutes |
| II FREE-RESPONSE QUESTIONS | | | | |
| | Part A: Graphing calculator required | 2 | 18.75% | 30 minutes |
| | Part B: Graphing calculator not permitted | 2 | 18.75% | 30 minutes |

During the time allotted for Part B of Section II, you can continue to work on the questions from Part A of Section II. However, you may not use a calculator while working on Part B.

You can't share calculators with other exam takers. If you don't want to use a calculator, then you must sign a Calculator Release Statement on exam day which will be provided by your proctor.

### How Is My Final Score Calculated?

Each question in the multiple-choice section is worth 1 point (total of 40 points). Each of the free-response questions is worth 6 points (total of 24 points).

The total raw score for both section I and section II are converted to a 5-point scale. The cut-off points for each grade (1-5) varies from year to year.

| AP SCORE | RECOMMENDATION |
|----------|----------------|
| 5 | Extremely Well Qualified |
| 4 | Well Qualified |
| 3 | Qualified |
| 2 | Possibly Qualified |
| 1 | No Recommendation |

## Which Graphing Calculators Are Allowed for the Exam?

The AP Precalculus Exam requires using a graphing calculator on Part B of Section I Multiple-Choice and Part A of Section II Free-Response. The calculators must be able to:

- Perform calculations (e.g., exponents, roots, trigonometric values, logarithms)
- Graph functions and analyze graphs
- Generate a table of values for a function
- Find real zeros of functions
- Find points of intersection of graphs and functions
- Find minima/maxima of functions
- Find numerical solutions to equation in one variable
- Find regression equations to model data (linear, quadratic, cubic, exponential, logarithmic, and sinusoidal) and plot the corresponding residuals

| BRAND | MODELS |
|-------|--------|
| Casio | FX-9750 series (G Plus, GA Plus, GII, GIII, and later) |
| | FX-9860 series |
| | CFX-9850 series |
| | CFX-9950 series |
| | CFX-9970 series |
| | FX 1.0 series |
| | Algebra FX 2.0 series |
| | FX-CG-10 |
| | FX-CG-20 series |
| | FX-CG-50 |
| | FX-CG-500 (Using a stylus is not permitted.) |
| | Graph35 series |
| | Graph75 series |
| | Graph95 series |
| | Graph100 series |
| Hewlett-Packard | HP Prime |
| NumWorks | NumWorks with Software Version 19.3 and higher |

| BRAND | MODELS |
| --- | --- |
| Sharp | EL-9900 series |
| Texas Instruments | TI-83 |
| | TI-83 Plus |
| | TI-83 Plus Silver |
| | TI-84 Plus |
| | TI-84 Plus CE |
| | TI-84 Plus CE Python |
| | TI-84 Plus Silver |
| | TI-84 Plus C Silver |
| | TI-84 Plus T |
| | TI-84 Plus CE-T |
| | TI-84 Plus CE-T Python Edition |
| | TI-89 Titanium |
| | TI-Nspire |
| | TI-Nspire CX |
| | TI-Nspire CX II |
| | TI-Nspire CX II-T |
| | TI-Nspire CM-C |
| | TI-Nspire CAS |
| | TI-Nspire CX CAS |
| | TI-Nspire CX II CAS |
| | TI-Nspire CX II-T CAS |
| | TI-Nspire CM-C CAS |
| | TI-Nspire CX-C CAS |
| | TI-Nspire CX II-C CAS |

Notes on Calculators

- You may bring up to two approved graphing calculators to the exam.
- You may not share calculators with another student.
- You may store programs in your calculator.
- Your calculator should be in radian mode, unless stated otherwise.
- You are not required to clear the memories in your calculator for the exam.
- You may not use the memories of your calculator to store exam questions and take them out of the testing room.
- You may not use TI-92 Plus, Voyage 200, and devices with QWERTY keyboards.
- You may not use non-graphing scientific calculators.

- You may not use laptop computers.
- You may not use pocket organizers, electronic writing pads, or pen-input devices.
- You may not use cellular phone calculators.

For more information regarding graphing calculators allowed, visit https://apcentral .collegeboard.org/courses/ap-precalculus/graphing-calculators.

# What Concepts Are Included in the Multiple-Choice Section?

The table below shows what topics are covered on the multiple-choice section of the test. The percentages change slightly from year to year, but the emphasis stays about the same. Keep in mind that many questions belong to more than one category, which is why the percentages don't add up to 100.

| FUNCTION TYPE | UNIT | MCQ SECTION WEIGHTING |
|---|---|---|
| General Functions (non-analytical) | Units 1 and 2 | 15–23% |
| Polynomial and Rational Functions | Unit 1 | 20–25% |
| Exponential and Logarithmic Functions | Unit 2 | 22–28% |
| Trigonometric and Polar Functions | Unit 3 | 30–35% |

# What Concepts Are Included in the Free-Response Section?

The free-response section consists of four questions.

| FREE RESPONSE TASK TYPE | UNIT FOCUS | GRAPHING CALCULATOR? | REAL-WORLD CONTEXT? |
|---|---|---|---|
| FRQ 1: Function Concepts | 1, 2 | Yes | No |
| FRQ 2: Modeling a Non-Periodic Context | 1, 2 | Yes | Yes |
| FRQ 3: Modeling a Periodic Context | 3 | No | Yes |
| FRQ 4: Symbolic Manipulation | 2, 3 | No | No |

For a more detailed description of the topics covered in the AP Precalculus exam, visit the College Board website at https://apcentral.collegeboard.org/courses/ap-precalculus.

**Important Note to AP Educators:** As per the College Board CED: Units 1, 2, and 3 comprise the content and conceptual understandings in which colleges and universities typically expect students to be proficient, in order to qualify for college credit and/or placement. Therefore, these topics are included on the AP exam. **Unit 4 consists of topics that teachers may include based on state or local requirements. As such, those topics are not currently included in this book.**

# CHAPTER 2

# How to Plan Your Time

IN THIS CHAPTER

**Summary:** The right preparation plan for you depends on your study habits, your own strengths and weaknesses, and the amount of time you have to prepare for the exam. This chapter recommends some possible plans to get you started.

**Key Ideas**
✪ Select the study plan that best suits your situation and adapt it to fit your needs.

## Three Approaches to Preparing for the AP Precalculus Exam

It's up to you to decide how you want to use this book to study for the AP Precalculus Exam. In this chapter you'll find three plans, each of which provides a different schedule for your review effort. Choose one or combine them if you want. Adapt the plan to your strengths and weaknesses and the way you like to study. If you are taking an AP Precalculus course at your school, you will have more flexibility than someone learning the material independently.

### The Full School-Year Plan

Choose this plan if you like taking your time going through the material. Following this path will allow you to practice your skills and develop your confidence gradually. This is a good choice if you want to use this book as a resource while taking an AP Precalculus course.

## The One-Semester Plan

Choose this plan if you are good with learning a lot of material in a fairly short amount of time. You'll need to be a pretty good math student who can grasp concepts quickly. This plan is also a good choice if you are currently taking an AP Precalculus course.

## The Six-Week Plan

This option is available if any one of these sounds like you:

- You are enrolled in an AP Precalculus course and want to do a final review before the exam.
- You are enrolled in an AP Precalculus course and want to use this book as a reference to refresh your skills.
- You are not currently enrolled in an AP Precalculus course, but you are a good math student and want to know what is tested on the exam.

> **When to Take the Practice Exams**
>
> You should take the practice exams *prior* to May. If you wait until May to take the practice exams, you won't have enough time to review the concepts that you do not fully understand.

## The Three Plans Compared

The chart summarizes and compares the three study plans.

| MONTH | FULL SCHOOL-YEAR PLAN | ONE-SEMESTER PLAN | SIX-WEEK PLAN |
|---|---|---|---|
| September | Diagnostic Exam<br>Units 0, 1 | | |
| October | Unit 1 | | |
| November | Unit 2 | | |
| December | Unit 2 | | |
| January | Unit 3 | Diagnostic Exam<br>Units 0, 1 | |
| February | Unit 3 | Unit 2 | |
| March | Practice Exam 1<br>Review all concepts | Unit 3 | Diagnostic Exam<br>Units 0, 1, 2, 3 |
| April | Practice Exam 2<br>Review all concepts | Practice Exam 1<br>Review all concepts<br>Practice Exam 2<br>Review all concepts | Practice Exam 1<br>Review all concepts<br>Practice Exam 2<br>Review all concepts |
| May | Review all concepts | Review all concepts | Review all concepts |

# Calendars for Preparing for Each of the Plans

## The Full School-Year Plan

### September
- Learn how the book is organized
- Determine your approach
- Take the Diagnostic Exam
- Read Unit 0
- Review linear functions
- Review polynomial addition and multiplication
- Review factoring quadratic trinomials
- Review using the quadratic formula
- Review solving right triangle problems involving trigonometry
- Review solving linear and quadratic equations and inequalities
- Review algebraic manipulation of linear equations and expressions
- Review solving systems of equations in two and three variables
- Review piecewise-defined functions
- Review exponential functions and rules for exponents
- Review radicals (e.g., square roots, cube roots)
- Review complex numbers

### October
- Read Unit 1
- Learn change in tandem
- Find average rates of change
- Identify increasing and decreasing intervals of a function
- Identify concavity, points of inflection of a graph
- Find local (relative) and global (absolute) maximum(s) and minimum(s) of a graph
- Find zeros of a function and their multiplicities
- Determine if a polynomial is even, odd, or neither
- Describe the end behaviors of polynomial functions
- Describe the end behaviors of rational functions
- Determine vertical asymptotes of graphs and rational functions
- Determine holes in graphs of rational functions
- Rewrite polynomial and rational expressions in equivalent forms
- Use long division to determine the quotient and remainder of two polynomial functions
- Use the binomial theorem to expand $(a + b)^n$
- Construct a function that is an additive and/or multiplicative transformation of another function
- Identify an appropriate function type to construct a function model for a given scenario

### November
- Read Unit 2
- Define arithmetic sequences
- Define geometric sequences
- Construct functions that are comparable to arithmetic and geometric sequences
- Describe the similarities and differences between linear and exponential functions
- Identify key characteristics of exponential functions
- Rewrite exponential functions in equivalent forms using exponential properties

- Construct models for situations involving proportional output values over equal-length input value intervals
- Construct and validate linear, quadratic, and exponential models based on a data set

### December
- Continue reading Unit 2
- Evaluate the composition of two or more functions
- Rewrite a function as a composition of two or more functions
- Find the inverse of a function
- Evaluate logarithmic functions
- Construct the inverse of an exponential function
- Identify key characteristics of logarithmic functions
- Rewrite logarithmic expressions in equivalent forms using logarithmic properties
- Solve exponential and logarithmic equations and inequalities
- Construct the inverse function for exponential and logarithmic functions
- Construct logarithmic function models
- Determine if an exponential model is appropriate by examining a semi-plot of a data set
- Construct the linearization of exponential data

### January
- Read Unit 3
- Describe key characteristics of a periodic function
- Determine the sine, cosine, and tangent of an angle using the unit circle
- Determine the coordinates of points on a circle centered at the origin
- Graph the sine and cosine functions
- Identify key characteristics of the sine, cosine, and tangent functions
- Identify amplitude, vertical shift, period, and phase shift of the sine, cosine, and tangent functions
- Construct analytical and graphical representations of the inverse of the sine, cosine, and tangent functions
- Identify key characteristics of the secant, cosecant, and cotangent functions

### February
- Continue Unit 3
- Solve equations and inequalities involving trigonometric functions
- Rewrite trigonometric expressions in equivalent forms with the Pythagorean identity, sine and cosine sum identities
- Graph using polar coordinates
- Construct graphs of polar functions
- Describe characteristics of the graph of a polar function

### March
- Take Practice Exam 1
- Evaluate your strengths and weaknesses
- Study appropriate units to correct weaknesses

### April
- Take Practice Exam 2
- Evaluate your strengths and weaknesses
- Study appropriate units to correct weaknesses

**May**
- Review Units 0–3
- Get a good night's sleep the night before the exam. Fall asleep knowing you are well prepared
- Take and ace the exam. Good luck!

## The One-Semester Plan

### January
- Learn how the book is organized
- Determine your approach
- Take the Diagnostic Exam
- Read Unit 0, 1
- Find average rates of change
- Identify increasing and decreasing intervals of a function
- Identify concavity, points of inflection of a graph
- Find local (relative) and global (absolute) maximum(s) and minimum(s) of a graph
- Find zeros of a function and their multiplicities
- Determine if a polynomial is even, odd, or neither
- Describe the end behaviors of polynomial and rational functions
- Determine vertical asymptotes of graphs and rational functions
- Determine holes in graphs of rational functions
- Rewrite polynomial and rational expressions in equivalent forms
- Use long division to determine the quotient and remainder of two polynomial functions
- Use the binomial theorem to expand $(a + b)^n$
- Construct a function that is an additive and/or multiplicative transformation of another function
- Identify an appropriate function type to construct a function model for a given scenario

### February
- Read Unit 2
- Define arithmetic and geometric sequences and construct functions
- Describe the similarities and differences between linear and exponential functions
- Identify key characteristics of exponential and logarithmic functions
- Rewrite exponential and logarithmic functions in equivalent forms using properties
- Construct and validate linear, quadratic, and exponential models based on a data set
- Evaluate the composition of two or more functions
- Rewrite a function as a composition of two or more functions
- Find the inverse of a function
- Evaluate logarithmic functions
- Construct the inverse of an exponential function
- Solve exponential and logarithmic equations and inequalities
- Construct the inverse function for exponential and logarithmic functions
- Construct logarithmic function models
- Determine if an exponential model is appropriate by examining a semi-plot of a data set
- Construct the linearization of exponential data

### March
- Read Unit 3
- Describe key characteristics of a periodic function
- Determine the sine, cosine, and tangent of an angle using the unit circle
- Determine the coordinates of points on a circle centered at the origin

- Graph the sine and cosine functions
- Identify key characteristics of the sine, cosine, tangent, secant, cosecant, and cotangent functions
- Construct analytical and graphical representations of the inverse of the sine, cosine, and tangent functions
- Solve equations and inequalities involving trigonometric functions
- Rewrite trigonometric expressions in equivalent forms with the Pythagorean identity, sine and cosine sum identities
- Construct graphs of polar functions
- Describe characteristics of the graph of a polar function

### April
- Take Practice Exams 1, 2
- Evaluate your strengths and weaknesses
- Study appropriate units to correct weaknesses

### May
- Review Units 0–3
- Get a good night's sleep the night before the exam. Fall asleep knowing you are well prepared
- Take and ace the exam. Good luck!

## The Six-Week Plan

### March
- Learn how the book is organized
- Take the Diagnostic Exam
- Read and review topics in Unit 1—Polynomial and Rational Functions
- Read and review topics in Unit 2—Exponential and Logarithmic Functions
- Read and review topics in Unit 3—Trigonometric and Polar Functions

### April
- Take Practice Exams 1 and 2
- Evaluate your strengths and weaknesses
- Study appropriate units to correct weaknesses

### May
- Review Units 0–3
- Get a good night's sleep the night before the exam. Fall asleep knowing you are well prepared
- Take and ace the exam. Good luck!

STEP 2

# Determine Your Test Readiness

CHAPTER 3    Take a Diagnostic Exam

# CHAPTER 3

# Take a Diagnostic Exam

## IN THIS CHAPTER

**Summary:** This step contains a diagnostic exam that closely matches what you can expect to find on the actual AP Precalculus exam. Use this test to familiarize yourself with the exam and to access your strengths and weaknesses as you begin your review for the exam. The questions in the diagnostic exam are presented in small groups matching the order of the units in this book. Your results should give you a good idea of how well prepared you are for the AP Precalculus exam at this time. Note the units that you need to study the most and spend more time on them.

### Key Ideas

✪ Familiarize yourself with the types of questions and the level of difficulty of the actual AP Precalculus exam early in your test preparation process.

✪ Use the diagnostic exam to identify the content areas on which you need to focus your test preparation efforts.

## Using the Diagnostic Exam

The purpose of the diagnostic exam is to give you a feel for what the actual AP Precalculus exam will be like and to identify content areas that you need most to review. The actual exam will have answer choices A-D, but some of the questions on the diagnostic exam simply require you to answer the questions without showing answer choices.

## When to Take the Diagnostic Exam

Since one purpose of the diagnostic exam is to give you a preview of what to expect on the AP Precalculus exam, you should take the exam earlier rather than later. However, if you are attempting the diagnostic exam without having studied the precalculus topics yet, you may feel overwhelmed and confused. If you are starting this book in September, you may want to read a sampling of questions from the diagnostic exam, but then save the test until later when you know more precalculus topics. Taking the diagnostic exam when you begin to review will help you identify what content you already know and what content you need to revisit; then you can alter your test prep accordingly.

Take the diagnostic exam in this step when you begin your review but save both practice exams at the end of the book until after you have covered all the material and are ready to test your abilities.

## How to Administer the Exam

When you take the diagnostic exam, try to reproduce the actual testing environment as closely as possible. Find a quiet place where you will not be interrupted. Do not listen to music or watch a movie while taking the exam. You will not be able to do this on the real exam. Set a timer and stop working when the time is up for each section. Note how far you have gotten so you can learn to pace yourself but take some extra time to complete all the questions so you can find your areas of weakness. Use the answer sheet provided for your answers.

## After Taking the Diagnostic Exam

Following the exam, you'll find not only the answers to the test questions, but also complete explanations for each answer. Do not just read the explanations for the questions you missed; you also need to understand the explanations for the questions you got right but weren't sure of. In fact, it's a good idea to work through the explanations for all the questions. Working through the step-by-step explanations is one of the most effective review tools in this book.

If you missed a lot of questions on the diagnostic exam or are just starting out learning the precalculus topics, do not stress out! Step 4 of this book explains all the concepts that will appear on the AP Precalculus Exam. Read Units 0–3 in Step 4, do the practice questions for each unit, and read the explanations so you understand what the correct answer is and why it is correct. Once you do that you will be prepared for the AP Precalculus Exam.

On the other hand, if you did well on some of the questions on the diagnostic exam and understand the explanations for these questions, you may be able to skip some of the units in Step 4. Look at the summaries and key ideas that begin each of the units in Step 4. If you're reasonably sure you understand a concept already, you may want to skip that unit's review questions or the "Rapid Review" and then move on to the next unit. A good test prep plan focuses on the areas you most need to review.

Now let's get started.

# AP Precalculus Diagnostic Exam—Answers

**ANSWER SHEET**

1. _____
2. _____
3. _____
4. _____
5. _____
6. _____
7. _____
8. _____
9. _____
10. _____
11. _____
12. _____
13. _____
14. _____
15. _____
16. _____
17. _____
18. _____
19. _____
20. _____
21. _____
22. _____
23. _____
24. _____
25. _____

26. _____
27. _____
28. _____
29. _____
30. _____
31. _____
32. _____
33. _____
34. _____
35. _____
36. _____
37. _____
38. _____
39. _____
40. _____
41. _____
42. _____
43. _____
44. _____
45. _____
46. _____
47. _____
48. _____
49. _____
50. _____

# AP Precalculus Diagnostic Exam

*Directions*: Taking the Diagnostic Exam helps assess your strengths and weaknesses as you begin preparing for the AP Precalculus Exam. The questions in the Diagnostic Exam contain both multiple-choice and open-ended questions. They are arranged by topic and designed to review concepts tested on the AP Precalculus exam. Most of the questions in the Diagnostic Exam should be done without the use of a graphing calculator.

## Chapter 5 (Unit 0)

1. Factor completely $y = 5x^3 - 65x^2 - 150x$.

2. List the following expressions in order from least degree to greatest degree.

$$\sqrt{x^3}, \ \frac{x^2}{x^{-5}}, \ x^2 \cdot \sqrt{x}, \ x^4 \cdot x^{-3}, \ (x^2)^3$$

3. Find the points of intersection for the graphs of $f(x) = x - 1$ and $g(x) = x^2 - 2x - 11$.

4. The figure to the right represents an observer standing at point $A$ watching a balloon $B$ as it rises from point $C$. The balloon is rising at a constant rate of 2 feet per second and the observer is 100 feet from point $C$. Find the distance, $d$, from point $A$ to the balloon and the angle, $\theta$, when the balloon is 50 feet in the air.

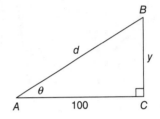

5. Solve $\sqrt{x+6} \le x$.

6. Write the equation of the function graphed below.

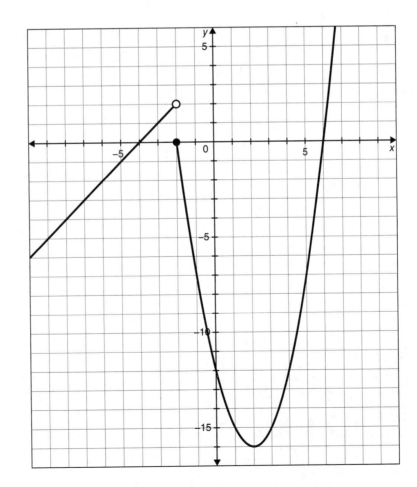

## Chapter 6 (Unit 1)

7. The graph of a function $f$ is shown in the figure below. List the intervals where the graph of $f$ is increasing and concave down.

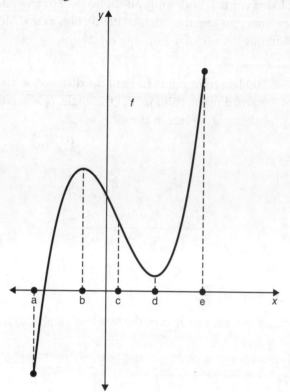

8. A function $f$ is continuous on $[-2,4]$ and some of the values of $f$ are shown in the table below.

| $x$ | $-2$ | $0$ | $4$ |
|---|---|---|---|
| $f(x)$ | $-1$ | $b$ | $11$ |

If the average rate of change from $-2$ to $0$ is the same as the average rate of change from $0$ to $4$, what is the value of $b$?

9. The following table contains values from three different functions ($f$, $g$, and $h$) for certain consecutive equal-length intervals. Which function is quadratic? Explain.

| $x$ | $0$ | $1$ | $2$ | $3$ | $4$ |
|---|---|---|---|---|---|
| $f(x)$ | $7$ | $5$ | $3$ | $1$ | $-1$ |
| $g(x)$ | $5$ | $6$ | $5$ | $2$ | $-3$ |
| $h(x)$ | $1$ | $2$ | $4$ | $8$ | $16$ |

10. A polynomial function $p$ has degree 4 with two distinct real zeros and no complex zeros. Which of the following must be true about the graph of $p(x)$?

(A) There are 3 local maximums or minimums, one of which is a global maximum or minimum.
(B) There are 3 local maximums or minimums and there is no global maximum or minimum.
(C) There is at least 1 local maximum or minimum and it is a global maximum or minimum.
(D) There is at least 1 local maximum or minimum and there is no global maximum or minimum.

11. Some of the values of a polynomial function, $p$, are shown in the table below. What is the degree of the polynomial function $p(x)$?

| $x$ | $0$ | $1$ | $2$ | $3$ | $4$ | $5$ | $6$ |
|---|---|---|---|---|---|---|---|
| $p(x)$ | $1$ | $1$ | $2$ | $4$ | $8$ | $16$ | $31$ |

12. A polynomial function is given by $f(x)=-3x^4+2x^3-5x^2+6x+7$. Which of the following describes the end behavior of $f$?

(A) $\lim\limits_{x\to-\infty} f(x)=-\infty$ and $\lim\limits_{x\to\infty} f(x)=-\infty$.
(B) $\lim\limits_{x\to-\infty} f(x)=\infty$ and $\lim\limits_{x\to\infty} f(x)=-\infty$.
(C) $\lim\limits_{x\to-\infty} f(x)=-\infty$ and $\lim\limits_{x\to\infty} f(x)=\infty$.
(D) $\lim\limits_{x\to-\infty} f(x)=\infty$ and $\lim\limits_{x\to\infty} f(x)=\infty$.

13. Consider the function $r(x)=\dfrac{2x^3+3x-7}{4x^2-x^3}$. Describe the end behavior of $r$.

14. What are the $x$-intercepts of the graph of $f(x)=\dfrac{x(x+1)(x-2)}{(x-1)(x-2)}$?

15. What are the equations of all vertical asymptotes of function $f(x)=\dfrac{x^2-7x+10}{x^2-4}$?

16. Determine the location of any holes in the graph of $r(x)=\dfrac{x^2-8x-20}{x^2+8x+12}$.

17. What is the expanded form of $p(x)=(x-2)^5$?

**18.** The point $(2,-1)$ is on the graph of $f(x)$. If the function $g$ is defined by $g(x)=3f(2x+8)+7$, where does the point $(2,-1)$ on the graph of $f$ get mapped to on the graph of $g$?

**19.** Shown in the table is the height of a ball, in feet, $t$ seconds after being tossed in the air off the side of a 100-foot hill for selected values of $t$. What function best models the data?

| $t$ | 0 | 1 | 2 | 3 | 4 | 5 |
|---|---|---|---|---|---|---|
| Height, in feet | 200 | 228.5 | 224.2 | 187.8 | 120.1 | 19.9 |

**20.** The table below shows the length, in inches (in.), and the weight, in pounds (lbs.) of 8 brown trout that were caught in a certain lake. Create a cubic model for predicting the weight of brown trout in this lake from the length of the trout to estimate the weight of a 20-inch brown trout.

| Length (in.) | 13.4 | 14.1 | 15.8 | 16.7 | 18.5 | 20.8 | 21.2 | 22.3 |
|---|---|---|---|---|---|---|---|---|
| Weight (lbs.) | 1.04 | 1.21 | 1.70 | 2.01 | 2.74 | 3.89 | 4.13 | 4.80 |

## Chapter 7 (Unit 2)

**21.** The 4th term of an arithmetic sequence is 4 and the 13th term of the sequence is 10. Find the 20th term of the sequence.

**22.** The graph of an exponential function goes through the point $(4,32)$ and $(5,128)$. Which of the following does not represent the equation of the exponential function?

(A) $f(x)=128(4)^{x-5}$
(B) $f(x)=32(4)^{x-4}$
(C) $f(x)=(2)^{2x-3}$
(D) $f(x)=128(5)^{x-5}$

**23.** Which of the following describes the graph of the function $f(x)=3\left(\dfrac{1}{2}\right)^{x}$?

(A) Increasing and concave up.
(B) Increasing and concave down.
(C) Decreasing and concave up.
(D) Decreasing and concave down.

**24.** Let $f(x)=2^{x}$ and let $g$ be defined $g(x)=f(x+3)$. What is the type of dilation (vertical or horizontal) and size of the dilation that transforms $f$ to $g$?

**25.** The number of bacteria on the third day of an experiment was 30. Six days later, the number of bacteria was 120. Write the model $f(d)$ to represent the number of bacteria present $d$ days after the experiment began.

**26.** Data were collected on the fuel economy, in miles per gallon (mpg), and the speed, in miles per hour (mph), a certain car can travel. The data was used to create a model to predict the fuel economy, $fe$, based on the speed, $s$. The resulting regression was $\widehat{fe}=-0.01s^{2}+0.86s+11.67$ and the residuals of the regression appear without pattern. One of the values in the data set had a fuel economy of 28.5 mpg when the speed was 60 mph. Calculate the model's error and describe the error in context.

**27.** Select values of a function, $f$, are shown in the table below. If the function $g$ is defined as $g(x)=x^{2}-x-1$, what is $f(g(-1))$?

| $x$ | $-2$ | $-1$ | 0 | 1 | 2 |
|---|---|---|---|---|---|
| $f(x)$ | 2 | 0 | $-1$ | $-2$ | 1 |

**28.** Given $f(x)=\dfrac{x-1}{x+3}$, find $f^{-1}(x)$.

**29.** Evaluate $\log_{9}(27)+\log(0.1)$.

**30.** Let $f$ be the function $f(x)=b^{x}$, with $b>1$. Which of the following describe the graph of $f^{-1}(x)$?

(A) Increasing and concave up.
(B) Increasing and concave down.
(C) Decreasing and concave up.
(D) Decreasing and concave down.

**31.** Let $f$ be the function $f(x)=\log_{b} x$, with $0<b<1$. Which of the following describe the graph of $f(x)$?

(A) $\lim\limits_{x\to 0^{+}} f(x)=-\infty$ and $\lim\limits_{x\to\infty} f(x)=\infty$
(B) $\lim\limits_{x\to 0^{+}} f(x)=-\infty$ and $\lim\limits_{x\to\infty} f(x)=-\infty$
(C) $\lim\limits_{x\to 0^{+}} f(x)=\infty$ and $\lim\limits_{x\to\infty} f(x)=\infty$
(D) $\lim\limits_{x\to 0^{+}} f(x)=\infty$ and $\lim\limits_{x\to\infty} f(x)=-\infty$

**32.** Rewrite $\log_4(2x) + 3\log_2(x+1)$ into a single logarithm.

**33.** Solve the equation $\log_2(2x-4) + \log_2(x-2) = 5$.

**34.** A common way to measure the size of an earthquake is the Richter scale. The function, $R(A)$ is defined as $R(A) = \log\left(\dfrac{A}{A_0}\right)$, with $A$ being the measure of the amplitude of the earthquake wave and $A_0$ equal to the amplitude of the smallest detectable wave. An earthquake was measured as 5.9 on the Richter scale and had an aftershock that was measured as 4.5 on the Richter scale. The amplitude of the original earthquake wave is how many times more than the amplitude of the aftershock wave?

**35.** Data were collected on the population size in a certain city. It was noted that the data appears exponential with the year the data was recorded as the independent variable and the population size as the dependent variable. Which of the following data sets would appear linear when graphed?

(A) The population size as the independent variable and the year the data was recorded as the dependent variable.

(B) The year the data was recorded as the independent variable and the natural log of the population size as the dependent variable.

(C) The population size as the independent variable and the natural log of the year the data was recorded as the dependent variable.

(D) The natural log of the year the data was recorded as the independent variable and the population size as the dependent variable.

## Chapter 8 (Unit 3)

**36.** Let $g$ be a periodic function with period 4 such that $g$ is increasing and concave down on the interval $[0,1]$, decreasing and concave down on the interval $[1,2]$, decreasing and concave up on the interval $[2,3]$, and increasing and concave up on $[3,4]$. Which of the following $x$-values will be the $x$-coordinate of a local maximum?

(A) 20

(B) 21

(C) 22

(D) 23

**37.** A circle is centered at the origin. Find the cosine of the angle in standard position that intersects the circle at the point $(-3, -4)$.

**38.** Evaluate $\sin\left(\dfrac{7\pi}{6}\right)$.

**39.** Given an angle of measure $\theta$ in standard position and a unit circle centered at the origin. There is a point, $P$, where the terminal ray intersects the circle. The function $f(\theta) = \cos\theta$ measures the _____ displacement from the ____-axis.

**40.** Which of the following is NOT true about the functions $f(\theta) = \sin\theta$ and $f(\theta) = \cos\theta$.

(A) Both functions have amplitude 1.

(B) Both have frequency $\dfrac{1}{2\pi}$.

(C) Both have a midline $y = 0$.

(D) Both are odd functions.

**41.** Let $f$ be the function $f(\theta) = 2\sin(3\theta - 6) + 4$. What is the period of $f$?

**42.** The amount of sunlight in a certain city was recorded for a year with 365 days. The data can be modeled by a sinusoidal function. The maximum daylight was on June 21st, the 172nd day of the year, was estimated to be 14.41 hours. The minimum daylight was on December 21st, the 355th day of the year, was estimated to be 9.91 hours. What is an appropriate estimate of the amplitude of the sinusoidal function modeled by the data?

**43.** Which of the following describes the behavior of the tangent function between consecutive asymptotes?

(A) The function decreases and the graph changes from concave down to concave up.

(B) The function decreases and the graph changes from concave up to concave down.

(C) The function increases and the graph changes from concave down to concave up.

(D) The function increases and the graph changes from concave up to concave down.

**44.** For the cosine function to have an inverse, the domain must be restricted to which of the following intervals?

(A) $\left[-\dfrac{\pi}{2}, \dfrac{\pi}{2}\right]$

(B) $[0, \pi]$

(C) $\left(-\dfrac{\pi}{2}, \dfrac{\pi}{2}\right)$

(D) $(0, \pi)$

**45.** Solve $2\sin^2 x + \sin x - 1 = 0$.

**46.** Which of the following is the graph of the cosecant function?

(A)

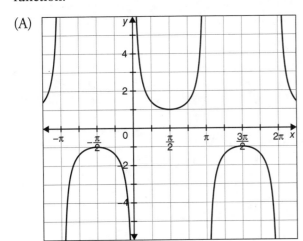

(B)

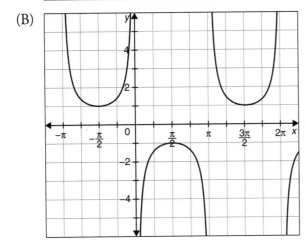

(C)

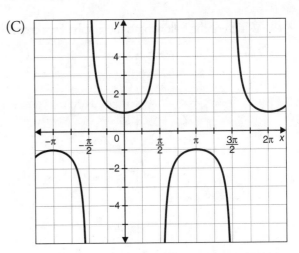

(D)

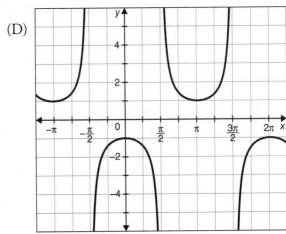

**47.** If $\sin\theta = \dfrac{5}{13}$ for $0 < \theta < \dfrac{\pi}{2}$, calculate $\cos(2\theta)$.

**48.** What is the polar form of the complex number $2 - 2\sqrt{3}i$?

**49.** Which of the following is the graph of $r = 3\cos(2\theta)$?

(A)

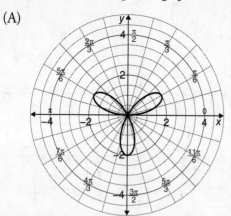

(B)

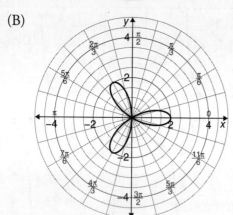

(C)

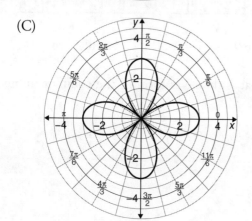

(D)

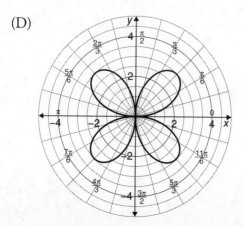

**50.** For the polar graph of the function $f(\theta) = 2 - 4\sin\theta$, the distance between $f(\theta)$ and the origin is increasing for $\dfrac{\pi}{6} < \theta < \dfrac{\pi}{2}$ because

(A) $f(\theta)$ is positive and increasing
(B) $f(\theta)$ is positive and decreasing
(C) $f(\theta)$ is negative and increasing
(D) $f(\theta)$ is negative and decreasing

# ❯ Diagnostic Exam Answers and Explanations

## Chapter 5 (Unit 0)

**1.** • The expression $5x^3 - 65x^2 - 150x$ has a common factor of $5x$, so $y = 5x^3 - 65x^2 - 150x$ is equivalent to $y = 5x(x^2 - 13x - 30)$.
   • The binomial factorization of $x^2 - 13x - 30$ is $(x+2)(x-15)$, so $y$ can be factored as $y = 5x(x+2)(x-15)$.

**2.** • Roots are fractional powers, so $\sqrt{x^3} = x^{1.5}$.
   • When dividing expressions of the same base, we subtract the powers, so $\dfrac{x^2}{x^{-5}} = x^7$.
   • When multiplying expressions of the same base, we add the powers, so $x^2 \cdot \sqrt{x} = x^{2.5}$ and $x^4 \cdot x^{-3} = x^1$.
   • When raising an expression to another exponent, we multiply the powers, so $(x^2)^3 = x^6$.
   • Therefore, the order, from least to greatest is $x^4 \cdot x^{-3}$, $\sqrt{x^3}$, $x^2 \cdot \sqrt{x}$, $(x^2)^3$, $\dfrac{x^2}{x^{-5}}$

**3.** • When the graphs intersect, their functions are equal, or $x - 1 = x^2 - 2x - 11$.
   • This is equivalent to $0 = x^2 - 3x - 10$, which factors as $0 = (x+2)(x-5)$.
   • The $x$-coordinates of intersection are $-2$ and $5$.
   • Substituting $-2$ into either equation yields $-3$ and substituting $5$ into either equation yields $4$.
   • The points of intersections are $(-2, -3)$ and $(5, 4)$

**4.** • Pythagorean Theorem can be used to find $d$.
   • $50^2 + 100^2 = d^2$. This is equivalent to $50^2 + (50 \cdot 2)^2 = d^2$, or $50^2 + 4 \cdot 50^2 = d^2$, which is $50^2(1+4) = d^2$.
   • This simplifies to $50\sqrt{5} = d$.
   • In a right triangle, the tangent of the acute angle is the ratio of the opposite side to the adjacent side, or $\tan(\theta) = \dfrac{50}{100}$.
   • This is equivalent to $\theta = \tan^{-1}\left(\dfrac{50}{100}\right)$.
   • The distance is $d = 50\sqrt{5}$, or about $111.803$ feet, and the angle is $\theta = \tan^{-1}\left(\dfrac{1}{2}\right)$, or about $0.464$ radians or $26.565$ degrees.

**5.** • We want to know when $\sqrt{x+6} \leq x$, or $x + 6 \leq x^2$, which is equivalent to $0 \leq x^2 - x - 6$.
   • First, find the critical numbers by finding when $0 = x^2 - x - 6$, or $0 = (x+2)(x-3)$ which has solutions $x = -2$ and $x = 3$.
   • Examining the solution, it is found that $x = -2$ is an extraneous solution as $\sqrt{x+6}$ does not equal $-2$.
   • The solution is $x \geq 3$.

**6.** • The function is a line for $x < -2$. The slope of the line is $1$ and goes through the point $(-4, 0)$, so $y - 0 = 1(x - (-4))$, or $y = x + 4$ for $x < -2$.
   • The function is a parabola for $x \geq -2$ that has vertex at $(2, -16)$, so $y = a(x-2)^2 - 16$.
   • The parabola also contains the point $(6, 0)$, so $0 = a(6-2)^2 - 16$, or $a = 1$.
   • Therefore, $y = (x-2)^2 - 16$ or $y = x^2 - 4x - 12$ for $x \geq -2$.

## Chapter 6 (Unit 1)

**7.** • A graph is increasing on an interval when for all $a$ and $b$ in the interval, if $a < b$, then $f(a) < f(b)$. Therefore, the graph is increasing on the intervals $[a, b]$ and $[d, e]$.
   • A graph is concave down on an interval when the rate of change is decreasing. Therefore, the graph is concave down on the intervals $[a, b]$ and $[b, c]$.
   • It follows that the graph is increasing and concave down only on the interval $[a, b]$.

**8.** • The average rate of change is the ratio of the change in the output values to the change in input values over that interval, or $\dfrac{f(b) - f(a)}{b - a}$.
   • If the average rates of change are equal, then $\dfrac{f(0) - f(-2)}{0 - (-2)} = \dfrac{f(4) - f(0)}{4 - 0}$.
   • Substituting in the given values from the table yields $\dfrac{b - (-1)}{0 - (-2)} = \dfrac{11 - b}{4 - 0}$, or $\dfrac{b+1}{2} = \dfrac{11 - b}{4}$.
   • Multiplying both sides of this equation by $4$ yields $2b + 2 = 11 - b \Rightarrow 3b = 9 \Rightarrow b = 3$.

**9.** • The table below shows the average rate of change over the listed intervals.

| intervals | [0,1] | [1,2] | [2,3] | [3,4] |
|---|---|---|---|---|
| Average rate of change for $f(x)$ | −2 | −2 | −2 | −2 |
| Average rate of change for $g(x)$ | 1 | −1 | −3 | −5 |
| Average rate of change for $h(x)$ | 1 | 2 | 4 | 8 |

• The function $g(x)$ is quadratic because the average rate of change of a quadratic function over consecutive equal-length input-value intervals can be given by a linear function, the rate of change of the average rates of change of a quadratic function is constant.
• In this case, the rate of change of the average rates of change for function $g(x)$ is a constant −2.
• The average rate of change of a linear function over any length input-value interval is constant, so $f(x)$ is linear.
• Over equal-length input-value intervals, if the output values of a function change proportionally, then the function is exponential.
• For $h(x)$, each average rate of change is twice the previous average rate of change, therefore, $h(x)$ is exponential.

**10.** • The correct answer is (C).
• It is given that the polynomial function $p$ has degree four.
• Polynomial functions of even degree will have either a global maximum or a global minimum.
• Also, between any two real zeros, there is at least one input value corresponding to a local maximum or a local minimum.
• It is unknown if the multiplicity of each of the zeros is 2 or if the multiplicity of one zero is 3 and the other zero is 1.
• In the latter case, the graph of the polynomial function has only one local maximum or local minimum and it is the global maximum or global minimum.

**11.** • The degree of a polynomial function can be found by examining the successive differences of the output values over equal-interval input values.
• The degree of the polynomial function is equal to the least value $n$ for which the successive $n$th differences are constant.

• As shown below, the 4th successive difference is constant, so the degree of the polynomial is 4.

| x | p(x) | 1st difference | 2nd difference | 3rd difference | 4th difference |
|---|---|---|---|---|---|
| 0 | 1 | | | | |
| | | 0 | | | |
| 1 | 1 | | 1 | | |
| | | 1 | | 0 | |
| 2 | 2 | | 1 | | 1 |
| | | 2 | | 1 | |
| 3 | 4 | | 2 | | 1 |
| | | 4 | | 2 | |
| 4 | 8 | | 4 | | 1 |
| | | 8 | | 3 | |
| 5 | 16 | | 7 | | |
| | | 15 | | | |
| 6 | 31 | | | | |

**12.** • The correct answer is (A).
• The degree and sign of the leading term of a polynomial determines the end behavior of the polynomial function, because as the input values increase or decrease without bound, the values of the leading term dominate the values of all lower-degree terms.
• In this case, as $x$ increases and decreases without bound, $p(x) \approx -3x^4$.
• Therefore, $\lim\limits_{x \to -\infty} p(x) = -\infty$ and $\lim\limits_{x \to \infty} p(x) = -\infty$.

**13.** • If neither polynomial in a rational function dominates the other for input values of large magnitude, then the quotient of the leading terms is a constant, and that constant indicates the location of a horizontal asymptote of the original rational function.
• In this case, both the numerator and denominator are polynomials of degree 3.
• Therefore, as $x$ increases or decreases without bound, the function tends towards −2.

**14.** • If $a$ is a real root of a function $f$, then the graph of $y = f(x)$ has an $x$-intercept at the point $(a, 0)$.
• For rational functions, the real zeros correspond to the real zeros of the numerator for such values in its domain.
• In this case, the real zeros of the numerator are 0, −1, and 2.
• However, 2 is not in the domain of the rational function, so the $x$-intercepts are $(0, 0)$ and $(-1, 0)$.

**15.** • If the value $a$ is a real zero of the polynomial in the denominator of a rational function and is not also a real zero of the polynomial in the numerator, then the graph of the rational function has a vertical asymptote at $x = a$.

• In this case, $f(x) = \dfrac{x^2 - 7x + 10}{x^2 - 4} = \dfrac{(x-2)(x-5)}{(x-2)(x+2)}$, so the zeros of the polynomial in the denominator of the rational function has zeros at $-2$ and $2$.

• The value $2$ is also a zero of the numerator, so $x = 2$ is not a vertical asymptote, but $x = -2$ is a vertical asymptote.

**16.** • If the multiplicity of a real zero in the numerator is equal to its multiplicity in the denominator, then the graph of the rational function has a hole at the corresponding input value.

• The function can be written as $r(x) = \dfrac{(x+2)(x-10)}{(x+2)(x+6)}$, so the multiplicity of the real zero $x = -2$ in the numerator and denominator is equal, so there is a hole at $x = -2$.

• Because the function can be rewritten as $r(x) = \dfrac{x-10}{x+6}$, plugging in $-2$ yields $-3$, so there is a hole at $(-2, -3)$.

**17.** • The fifth row of Pascal's Triangle is 1 5 10 10 5 1

• The binomial expansion of $(x-2)^5$ is $1 \cdot x^5 \cdot (-2)^0 + 5 \cdot x^4 \cdot (-2)^1 + 10 \cdot x^3 \cdot (-2)^2 + 10 \cdot x^2 \cdot (-2)^3 + 5 \cdot x^1 \cdot (-2)^4 + 1 \cdot x^0 \cdot (-2)^5 = x^5 - 10x^4 + 40x^3 - 80x^2 + 80x - 32$.

**18.** • The function $g$ can be written as $g(x) = 3f(2(x+4)) + 7$.

• Therefore, $g$ is a vertical dilation of the graph of $f$ by a factor of 3 and an additive transformation of $f$ that results in a vertical translation of 7.

• Also, $g$ is a horizontal dilation of the graph of $f$ by a factor of $\dfrac{1}{2}$ and an additive transformation of $f$ that results in a horizontal translation of $-4$.

• Therefore, the point $(2, -1)$ on the graph of $f$ gets mapped to $(-3, 4)$ on the graph of $g$.

**19.** • Quadratic functions model data sets or aspects of contextual scenarios that demonstrate roughly linear rates of change, or data sets that are roughly symmetric with a unique maximum or minimum value.

• The data are roughly symmetric about 1.5 and appears to have a unique maximum height.

• Also, the rates of change appear to be approximately linear.

**20.** • Entering the data into lists and using cubic regression, the cubic function can be estimated by the function $w(l) \approx 0.00035x^3 + 0.0046x^2 - 0.0835x + 0.4895$.

• Therefore, $w(20) \approx 3.4595$.

• A brown trout from this lake can be estimated to weigh about 3.4595 pounds.

## Chapter 7 (Unit 2)

**21.** • It is given that the 4th term of the arithmetic sequence is 4 and the 13th term is 10.

• Therefore, $4 = a_0 + 4d$ and $10 = a_0 + 13d$.

• Subtracting these equations yields $6 = 9d$, or $d = \dfrac{2}{3}$.

• Substituting $\dfrac{2}{3}$ in for $d$ in the equation $4 = a_0 + 4d$ yields $4 = a_0 + 4 \cdot \dfrac{2}{3}$, or $a_0 = \dfrac{4}{3}$.

• Therefore, the 20th term of the sequence is $a_{20} = \dfrac{4}{3} + 20 \cdot \dfrac{2}{3}$, or $a_{20} = \dfrac{44}{3}$.

**22.** • The graph of an exponential function goes through the point $(4, 32)$ and $(5, 128)$, so the common ratio is $r = \dfrac{128}{32}$, or $r = 4$.

• The equation of an exponential equation is $f(x) = y_i r^{x - x_i}$ based on a known ratio $r$ and point $(x_i, y_i)$.

• Therefore, one equation is $f(x) = 128(4)^{x-5}$ and the other equation is $f(x) = 32(4)^{x-4}$.

• Using rules of exponents, $f(x) = 32(4)^{x-4}$ is the same as $f(x) = 2^5((2)^2)^{x-4}$, or $f(x) = 2^{2x-3}$.

• The base for choice (D) is 5, which is not correct.

**23.** • The graph of the function contains the points $(0, 3)$ and $\left(1, \dfrac{3}{2}\right)$, therefore the graph is decreasing.

• Because the base of the exponential function is between 0 and 1 with a leading term that is positive, the function is concave up.

**24.** • $g(x) = f(x+3)$, which is equivalent to $g(x) = 2^{x+3}$.

• The product property for exponents states that $b^m \cdot b^n = b^{(m+n)}$, so $g(x) = 2^{x+3}$ is the same as $g(x) = 2^x \cdot 2^3$, or $g(x) = 8(2)^x$.

• Therefore, $g(x)$ is a vertical dilation of $f(x)$ by a factor of 8.

**25.** • The general form for exponential growth is $f(d) = ab^d$.
• The given information yields the equations $30 = a \cdot b^3$ and $120 = a \cdot b^9$.
• Dividing $120 = a \cdot b^9$ by $30 = a \cdot b^3$ yields $\dfrac{120}{30} = \dfrac{a \cdot b^9}{a \cdot b^3}$, or $4 = b^6$.
• This is equivalent to $b = 4^{\frac{1}{6}}$, or $b = (2^2)^{1/6} = 2^{1/3}$.
• Substituting this value in the equation $30 = a \cdot b^3$ yields $a = 15$.
• The size of the bacteria population can be modeled by $f(d) = 15(2)^{d/3}$.

**26.** • $\widehat{fe}(60) = -0.01(60)^2 + 0.86(60) + 11.67$, so the model predicts a fuel economy of 27.27 mpg.
• The error is $27.27 - 28.5 = -1.23$.
• Because the actual value was 28.5 mpg, the model underestimates the fuel economy.

**27.** • $g(-1) = 1$, therefore $f(g(-1)) = f(1)$.
• The table indicates that $f(1) = -2$.

**28.** • Given $f(x) = \dfrac{x-1}{x+3}$, or $y = \dfrac{x-1}{x+3}$, to find $f^{-1}(x)$ we reverse the roles of $x$ and $y$ to get $x = \dfrac{y-1}{y+3}$.
• This is equivalent to $xy + 3x = y - 1$, or $xy - y = -3x - 1 \Rightarrow y(x-1) = -3x - 1$ or $y = \dfrac{-3x-1}{x-1}$.

**29.** • $\log_9 27 = \log_9 9^{3/2}$ which is the same as $\log_9 9^{3/2} = \dfrac{3}{2}\log_9 9 = \dfrac{3}{2}$.
• Also, $\log(0.1) = \log 10^{-1}$, which is the same as $\log 10^{-1} = (-1)\log 10 = -1$.
• Therefore $\log_9(27) + \log(0.1) = \dfrac{3}{2} - 1 = \dfrac{1}{2}$.

**30.** • The correct answer is (B).
• If $b > 1$, then the graph of $f(x) = b^x$ is increasing and concave up.
• The graph of $f^{-1}(x)$ is a reflection of the graph of $f(x)$ over the line $y = x$, therefore, the graph of $f^{-1}(x)$ is increasing and concave down.

**31.** • The correct answer is (D).
• Because the base, $b$, is between 0 and 1, the inverse function is an exponential function that is positive and decreasing such that $\lim\limits_{x \to \infty} f^{-1}(x) = 0$ and $\lim\limits_{x \to -\infty} f^{-1}(x) = \infty$.

• The inverse reverses the roles of $x$ and $y$, so $\lim\limits_{x \to \infty} f^{-1}(x) = 0$ means $\lim\limits_{x \to 0^+} f^{-1}(x) = \infty$ and $\lim\limits_{x \to -\infty} f^{-1}(x) = \infty$ means $\lim\limits_{x \to \infty} f^{-1}(x) = -\infty$.

**32.** • Using the change of base formula yields $\log_4(2x) = \dfrac{\log_2(2x)}{\log_2(4)}$, or $\dfrac{\log_2(2x)}{2} = \dfrac{1}{2}\log_2(2x)$.
• Using the power rule for logarithms yields $\dfrac{1}{2}\log_2(2x) = \log_2(2x)^{1/2} = \log_2 \sqrt{2x}$.
• The power rule also means $3\log_2(x+1) = \log_2(x+1)^3$.
• Therefore, $\log_4(2x) + 3\log_2(x+1) = \log_2 \sqrt{2x} + \log_2(x+1)^3$.
• Using the product rule yields $\log_4(2x) + 3\log_2(x+1) = \log_2(\sqrt{2x}(x+1)^3)$.

**33.** • $\log_2(2x-4) + \log_2(x-2) = 5$
• $\log_2(2x-4)(x-2) = 5$
• $\log_2(2x^2 - 8x + 8) = 5$
• $2x^2 - 8x + 8 = 2^5$
• $2x^2 - 8x + 8 = 32$
• $2x^2 - 8x - 24 = 0$
• $x^2 - 4x - 12 = 0$
• $(x-6)(x+2) = 0$
• $x = 6$ or $x = -2$
• The only solution is $x = 6$ as $x = -2$ would produce $\log_2(-8) + \log_2(-6)$, both of which do not exist.

**34.** • The earthquake gives the equation $5.9 = \log\left(\dfrac{A_e}{A_0}\right)$, which means $10^{5.9}(A_0) = A_e$ with $A_e$ being the measure of the amplitude of the earthquake wave.
• The aftershock gives the equation $4.5 = \log\left(\dfrac{A_a}{A_0}\right)$ which means $10^{4.5}(A_0) = A_a$ with $A_a$ being the measure of the amplitude of the aftershock wave.
• Therefore, $\dfrac{A_e}{A_a} = \dfrac{10^{5.9}(A_0)}{10^{4.5}(A_0)}$, or $\dfrac{A_e}{A_a} \approx 25.12$.
• The amplitude of the original earthquake wave is about 25 times that of the aftershock wave.

**35.** • The correct answer is (B).
• When the $y$-axis of a semi-log plot is logarithmically scaled, data that demonstrates exponential characteristics will appear linear.

## Chapter 8 (Unit 3)

**36.** • The correct answer is (B).
   • The function $g$ is increasing on $[0,1]$ while decreasing on $[1,2]$.
   • Therefore, the point on the graph with $x$-coordinate equal to 1 is a local maximum.
   • Because the period of the function is 4, the local maximum will repeat every 4 units from 1, or $1+4k$, where $k$ is an integer.
   • Of the numbers listed, only 21 is of the form $1+4k$, where $k$ is an integer.

**37.** • The cosine of the angle in standard position that intersects the circle is the ratio of the horizontal displacement of $P$ from the $y$-axis to the distance between the origin and point $P$.
   • The horizontal displacement is $-3$ and the distance from the origin to $P$ is 5 by using Pythagorean's Theorem for the right triangle with legs of length 3 and 4 as shown.
   • Therefore, $\cos\theta = -\dfrac{3}{5}$.

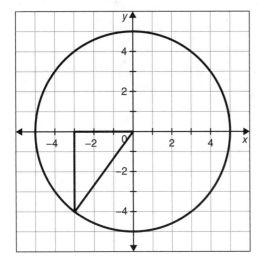

**38.** • The $\sin\left(\dfrac{\pi}{6}\right)$ is $y$-coordinate of the point of intersection between the unit circle and the terminal side of the angle $\dfrac{\pi}{6}$ in standard position, which is $\dfrac{1}{2}$.
   • Using symmetry with respect to the origin, the $y$-coordinate of the point of intersection between the unit circle and the terminal side of the angle $\dfrac{7\pi}{6}$ in standard position is $-\dfrac{1}{2}$.

**39.** • Given an angle of measure $\theta$ in standard position and a unit circle centered at the origin.
   • There is a point, $P$, where the terminal ray intersects the circle.
   • The function $f(\theta) = \cos\theta$ measures the horizontal displacement from the $y$-axis.

**40.** • The correct answer is (D).
   • The graph of $y = \sin\theta$ has rotational symmetry about the origin and is therefore an odd function.
   • The graph of $y = \cos\theta$ has reflective symmetry over the $y$-axis and is therefore an even function.

**41.** • The period of the function
   $$f(\theta) = a\sin(b(\theta+c))+d \text{ is } \left|\dfrac{1}{b}\right|2\pi \text{ units.}$$
   • Therefore, the period of
   $$f(\theta) = 2\sin(3\theta-6)+4 \text{ is } \left|\dfrac{1}{3}\right|2\pi.$$

**42.** • The average of the maximum and minimum amount of sunlight in a certain city was 12.16, so an estimate of the midline is $y = 12.16$.
   • The amplitude is the vertical distance from the maximum to the midline or the midline to the minimum, which is $14.41-12.16 = 2.25$ or $12.16-9.91 = 2.25$.

**43.** • The correct answer is (C).
   • The graph of the tangent function, shown below, is always increasing.
   • Between $\left(-\dfrac{\pi}{2},0\right)$ the graph is concave down and between $\left(0,\dfrac{\pi}{2}\right)$ the graph is concave up.

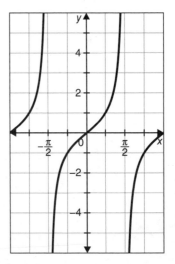

**44.** • The correct answer is (B).
- The cosine function has a maximum at $(0,1)$, a minimum at $(\pi,-1)$ and takes on all $y$-values between 1 and $-1$ for $x$-values between 0 and $\pi$.
- To be invertible, the function domain of the cosine must be restricted to $[0, \pi]$.

**45.** • $2\sin^2 x + \sin x - 1 = 0 \Rightarrow (2\sin x - 1)(\sin x + 1) = 0$, therefore $2\sin x - 1 = 0$ or $\sin x + 1 = 0$.
- For $2\sin x - 1 = 0 \Rightarrow \sin x = \dfrac{1}{2}$.
- From the unit circle, $x = \dfrac{\pi}{6}$ or $x = \dfrac{5\pi}{6}$.
- For $\sin x + 1 = 0 \Rightarrow \sin x = -1$.
- From the unit circle, $x = \dfrac{3\pi}{2}$.
- Because the sine function has period $2\pi$, other solutions will occur when an integer multiple of $2\pi$ is added to any of these solutions.

**46.** • The correct answer is (A).
- The cosecant function is the reciprocal of the sine function with vertical asymptotes where $\sin(\theta) = 0$.
- The sine function is 0 at even multiples of $\pi$. Also, $\sin\left(\dfrac{\pi}{2}\right) = 1$, so $\csc\left(\dfrac{\pi}{2}\right) = 1$.

**47.** • From the double angle formula, $\cos(2\theta) = \cos^2\theta - \sin^2\theta$.
- From the Pythagorean identity, $\sin^2\theta + \cos^2\theta = 1$.
- Therefore, $\cos(2\theta) = 1 - 2\sin^2\theta$.
- It is given that $\sin\theta = \dfrac{5}{13}$, so $\cos(2\theta) = 1 - 2\left(\dfrac{5}{13}\right)^2$, or $\cos(2\theta) = \dfrac{119}{169}$.

**48.** • The complex number $2 - 2\sqrt{3}i$ is the expression of the rectangular coordinate $(2, -2\sqrt{3})$.
- Therefore, $r = \sqrt{x^2 + y^2}$, or $r = 4$.
- Because $x > 0$, $\theta = \arctan\left(\dfrac{y}{x}\right)$, or $\theta = -\dfrac{\pi}{3}$ which is equivalent to $\theta = \dfrac{5\pi}{3}$.
- The polar form of $2 - 2\sqrt{3}i$ is $\left(4\cos\dfrac{5\pi}{3}\right) + i\left(4\sin\dfrac{5\pi}{3}\right)$.

**49.** • The correct answer is (C).
- The function $r = 3\cos(2\theta)$ is a rose curve with four petals and contains the point $(3,0)$.

**50.** • The correct answer is (D).
- $\sin\dfrac{\pi}{6} = \dfrac{1}{2}$, therefore, $f\left(\dfrac{\pi}{6}\right) = 2 - 4\sin\dfrac{\pi}{6} = 0$.
- Also, the sine function is increasing from $\dfrac{\pi}{6} < \theta < \dfrac{\pi}{2}$, so $f(\theta) < 0$ and is decreasing.

STEP 3

# Develop Strategies for Success

CHAPTER **4** Strategies to Help You Do Your Best on the Exam

# CHAPTER 4

# Strategies to Help You Do Your Best on the Exam

## IN THIS CHAPTER

**Summary:** This chapter supplies you with strategies for taking the multiple-choice and the free-response sections of the AP Precalculus exam. The strategies will help you earn all the points you deserve.

### Key Ideas

- ✪ Read each question carefully.
- ✪ Do not spend too much time on any one question. Time yourself accordingly.
- ✪ For multiple-choice questions, sometimes it is easier to work backward by trying each of the given choices. You will be able to eliminate some of the choices quickly. There is no penalty for guessing.
- ✪ For free-response questions, always show sufficient work so that your line of reasoning is clear.
- ✪ Write legibly.
- ✪ Always use mathematical notations instead of calculator syntax.
- ✪ If the question involves decimals, round your final answer to 3 decimal places unless the question indicates otherwise.
- ✪ Trust your instincts. Your first approach to solving a problem is usually the correct one.
- ✪ Get a good night's sleep the night before.

# Strategies for the Multiple-Choice Questions

- There are 40 multiple-choice questions for the AP Precalculus exam. These questions are divided into Section I – Part A, which contains 28 questions for which the use of a graphing calculator is *not* permitted; and Section I – Part B, with 12 questions, for which the use of a graphing calculator is required. The multiple-choice questions account for 62.5% of the grade for the whole test.
- You have 80 minutes in Section I – Part A and 40 minutes in Section I – Part B. Do not spend too much time on any one question. Time yourself accordingly. This is why taking as many practice exams as you can in a timed setting is critical. You will know how to allocate your time when you take the actual AP Precalculus exam in May.
- There is no penalty for incorrect answers, so answer each question. Make sure you eliminate the choices that don't make sense before guessing. If you are running out of time, quickly make guesses for the questions you couldn't get to.
- Be careful to bubble your answer in the correct spot in the grid, especially if you skip a question.
- Read the question carefully. If there is a graph or chart, look at it carefully. Pay close attention to the *x*- and *y*-axis units of measurement.
- Sometimes, its easiest to work backward by trying each of the given choices as the final answer. Often, you can eliminate some of the answer choices quickly.
- If a question involves decimal numbers, do not round until the final answer, and at that point, the final answer is usually rounded to 3 decimal places. Look at the number of decimal places in the choices to guide your work.
- Trust your instincts. Your first approach to solving a problem is usually the correct one.

# Strategies for the Free-Response Questions

- There are 4 free-response questions in Section II. Part A consists of 2 questions which require the use of a graphing calculator, and Part B with 2 questions which do not permit the use of a calculator. The free-response questions account for 37.5% of the grade for the whole test.
- You have 30 minutes in Section II – Part A and 30 minutes in Section II – Part B.
- Monitor your time carefully. You might want to look at both questions in the part before beginning the first one, so you have enough time to answer both.
- During Part B, you are permitted to continue work on the problems from Part A, but you will not have a graphing calculator during that time.
- If you do work that you think is incorrect, simply draw an "X" through it instead of spending time erasing it. Crossed-out work won't be graded.
- Always show your work, even when you are using a graphing calculator. Show all the steps that you took to reach your solution on questions involving calculations. You may not receive credit for answers without supporting work.
- Clearly label any tables, graphs, functions, or anything else that is needed.
- Unless otherwise specified, answers (numeric or algebraic) need not be simplified. If you use decimal approximations in calculations, your work will be scored on accuracy. Unless otherwise specified, your final answers should be accurate to 3 places after the decimal.
- Often a question has several parts. Credit for each part is awarded independently, so you should attempt to solve each part. For example, if the answer for part (b) depends on

the answer to part (a), you may still be able to receive full credit for part (b) even if the answer for part (a) is wrong.

- Read the question carefully. Know what information is being given and what is being asked.
- After answering the question, go back and read it again to confirm that you answered the question that was being asked.
- As with solving multiple-choice questions, trust your instincts. Your first approach to solving a problem is usually the correct one.

### How the Free-Response Questions Are Graded

The free-response questions (FRQ) section is graded by an expert group of high school teachers that are currently teaching an AP Precalculus course and college/university teachers and professors that are teaching a comparable AP course. This group of graders is referred to as "readers". Do your best to write legibly so your answer can easily be read by the reader.

### Scoring Guidelines

To help the exam readers be consistent when grading tens of thousands of exams, a scoring rubric is used. This rubric dictates how many points are awarded for each part of the response. Each part is broken down into its most important components and each of these is assigned a point value. The total of all these components from all parts make up a question's final score.

### Using a Graphing Calculator

- The use of a graphing calculator is required for answering questions in Section I— Part B multiple-choice and Section II—Part A free-response.
- You should specifically practice using technology to do the following:
  - Perform calculations (e.g., exponents, roots, trigonometric values, logarithms)
  - Graph functions and analyze graphs
  - Generate a table of values for a function
  - Find real zeros of a function
  - Find points of intersection of graphs and functions
  - Find minima/maxima of functions
  - Find numerical solutions to equations in one variable
  - Find regression equations to model data
- Set your calculator to radian mode and change to degree mode only if necessary.
- When decimal numbers are involved, do not round until the final answer. Unless otherwise stated, your final answer should be accurate to 3 decimal places.
- You may bring up to two calculators to the exam.
- You are not allowed to share calculators with another test taker.
- Replace old batteries with new ones and make sure that the calculator is functioning properly before the exam.

## Taking the Exam

### What Do I Need to Bring to the Exam?
- Several number 2 pencils.
- A good eraser and pencil sharpener.
- A black or blue pen.

- One or two approved calculators with fresh batteries.
- A watch to keep track of time.
- Photo ID if your school or test site requires it.
- Quick snack to eat between taking Section I multiple-choice and Section II free-response if your school or test site permits.

STEP 4

# Review the Knowledge You Need to Score High

Important Note: We have included a "Unit 0" in this book to help you brush up on Algebra and Geometry concepts before diving into the AP Precalculus content. Also, while Unit 4 (Functions Involving Parameters, Vectors, and Matrices) may be covered in your class, this unit will not yet be tested on the AP exam, so will not be included in this review.

# CHAPTER 5

# Unit 0: Review of Algebra and Geometry

**IN THIS CHAPTER**

**Summary:** Many questions on the AP Precalculus Exam will require the application of algebraic and geometric concepts. In this unit, you will be guided through a summary of those concepts. It is important that you review this unit thoroughly. Your ability to solve the problems here is a prerequisite for performing well on the AP Precalculus Exam.

**Key Ideas**

○ Manipulating linear equations and expressions
○ Solving linear equations and inequalities
○ Adding and multiplying polynomials
○ Factoring quadratic trinomials
○ Using the quadratic formula
○ Solving quadratic equations and inequalities
○ Solving systems of equations in two and three variables
○ Familiarity with piecewise-defined functions
○ Familiarity with exponential functions and rules for exponents
○ Familiarity with radicals (e.g., square roots, cube roots)
○ Familiarity with complex numbers
○ Solving right triangle problems involving trigonometry

## Linear Functions

A linear function is a function that graphs as a straight line, which means there are at most two variables and no exponents. It can be defined as $y = mx + b$, or when using function notation $f(x) = mx + b$. The independent variable is $x$ and the dependent variable is $y$.

### Slope of a Line

The slope of a line is the measure of its steepness. It can be found by calculating the ratio of the "rise" (change in $y$-coordinates) to the "run" (change in $x$-coordinates). Given two points $(x_1, y_1)$ and $(x_2, y_2)$, the slope of the line passing through the two points is defined as

$$m = \frac{rise}{run} = \frac{\Delta y}{\Delta x} = \frac{y_2 - y_1}{x_2 - x_1}, \text{ where } x_2 - x_1 \neq 0.$$

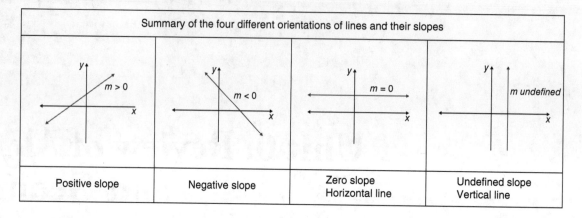

| Summary of the four different orientations of lines and their slopes | | | |
|---|---|---|---|
| $m > 0$ | $m < 0$ | $m = 0$ | $m$ undefined |
| Positive slope | Negative slope | Zero slope Horizontal line | Undefined slope Vertical line |

**Example 1**

Find the slope of the line passing through the points $(2, -5)$ and $(-3, 9)$.

Solution: $m = \dfrac{y_2 - y_1}{x_2 - x_1} = \dfrac{9 - (-5)}{-3 - 2} = \dfrac{14}{-5} = -\dfrac{14}{5}$

**Example 2**

Find the slope of the line passing through the points $(3, 1)$ and $(3, 8)$.

Solution: $m = \dfrac{y_2 - y_1}{x_2 - x_1} = \dfrac{8 - 1}{3 - 3} = \dfrac{7}{0}$

The points $(3, 1)$ and $(3, 8)$ are on a vertical line. Vertical lines have slopes that are undefined.

# Equation of a Line

There are three common forms for writing an equation of a line.

| FORM | EQUATION | NOTES |
|---|---|---|
| Slope-Intercept Form | $y = mx + b$ | $m$ is the slope, $b$ is the $y$-intercept |
| Point-Slope Form | $y - y_0 = m(x - x_0)$ | $m$ is the slope, $(x_0, y_0)$ is a point on the line |
| Standard Form | $Ax + By = C$ where $A$, $B$, and $C$ are integers with $A$ and $B$ not equal to 0, and $A > 0$. | $\dfrac{-A}{B}$ is the slope, $\dfrac{C}{B}$ is the $y$-intercept |

**Example 1**

Write an equation of the line with slope $-4$ and $y$-intercept 8 in standard form.

Solution: The slope and $y$-intercept are given, so slope-intercept form can be used. Substituting the values in for $m$ and $b$ gives the equation $y = -4x + 8$. Adding $4x$ to both sides of the equation gives the equation in standard form, which is $4x + y = 8$.

**Example 2**

Write an equation of the line through the points $(4, -6)$ and $(12, -2)$.

Solution: The slope of the line is $m = \dfrac{y_2 - y_1}{x_2 - x_1} = \dfrac{-2 - (-6)}{12 - 4} = \dfrac{4}{8} = \dfrac{1}{2}$. Using the point-slope form of the line and the point $(4, -6)$ (either point can be used),

$$y - y_0 = m(x - x_0)$$

$$y - (-6) = \frac{1}{2}(x - 4)$$

$$y + 6 = \frac{1}{2}(x - 4)$$

$$y + 6 = \frac{1}{2}x - 2.$$

The equation of the line in slope-intercept form is $y = \dfrac{1}{2}x - 8$.
In standard form it would be written $x - 2y = 16$.

**Example 3**

If an equation of a line is $5x - 4y = 9$, find the $x$-intercept, $y$-intercept, and slope.

Solution: The $x$-intercept can be found by setting $y = 0$ and solving for $x$. This gives us the equation $5x = 9$, which is equivalent to $x = \dfrac{9}{5}$. Therefore, the $x$-intercept is $\left(\dfrac{9}{5}, 0\right)$.

The $y$-intercept can be found by setting $x = 0$ and solving for $y$. This gives us the equation $-4y = 9$, which is equivalent to $y = \dfrac{-9}{4}$. The $y$-intercept is $\left(0, -\dfrac{9}{4}\right)$.

The slope can be found by changing the equation into slope-intercept form.

$$5x - 4y = 9$$

$$-4y = -5x + 9$$

$$y = \frac{5}{4}x - \frac{9}{4}.$$ Therefore, the slope is $\dfrac{5}{4}$ (and the $y$-intercept as found before is $-\dfrac{9}{4}$)

As an alternative, because the equation is in standard form, the slope is $\dfrac{-A}{B} = \dfrac{-5}{-4} = \dfrac{5}{4}$.

## Solving Linear Equations and Inequalities

To solve a linear equation means to find the value of the variable that makes the equation true. The value is called the solution. This means you will need to isolate the variable on one side of the equal sign. A linear inequality is like a linear equation, but instead of having an equal sign, it has an inequality sign. Solving a linear inequality means finding all values of the variable that make the inequality true.

**Example 1**

Solve for $x$: $5x + 2 = -13$

Solution: Isolate the $x$ on one side of the equation by first subtracting 2 from both sides of the equation, which yields $5x = -15$. Then divide both sides of the equation by 5 to get $x = -3$.

    The solution to the equation $5x + 2 = -13$ is $x = -3$.

**Example 2**

Solve for $x$: $26 - 12x \geq 89$

Solution: Isolate $x$ on one side of the inequality by subtracting 26 from both sides.
    $-12x \geq 63$. Then divide both sides by $-12$ to get $x \leq -5.25$.
    The solution $x \leq -5.25$.

---

*Remember, whenever you multiply or divide an inequality by a negative number, you must reverse the direction of the inequality sign.*

---

# Polynomials

A polynomial is a type of algebraic expression in which the exponents of each variable should be a positive integer. An example would be $4x^3 - 5x^2 + x + 8$, but not $3x^3 - 4x^{-2} + 6x^{1/2}$, due to the negative and fractional exponents. The general form of a polynomial in a single variable is $a_n x^n + a_{n-1} x^{n-1} + a_{n-2} x^{n-2} + \ldots + a_1 x + a_0$, where $a_0, a_1, \ldots, a_n$ are constants (with $a_n$ not equal to 0) that are called the coefficients of the polynomial. The degree of the polynomial is $n$, where $n$ is the largest exponent. The constant of the polynomial is $a_0$, which is the term without a variable and is the $y$-intercept of the graph of the polynomial. In most cases the polynomial is written with the exponents in decreasing order (largest to smallest), meaning $4x^3 - 5x^2 + x + 8$ would be written instead of $x - 5x^2 + 4x^3 + 8$, although they are equivalent polynomials with degree 3 and constant 8.

## Addition/Subtraction

Polynomials can be added or subtracted by combining like terms. Like terms means that each term has the same variables along with their exponents. $5x^2$ and $-4x^2$ are like terms, but $5x^2$ and $-4x^3$ are not because the exponents on $x$ are different when comparing the two terms.

**Example 1**

Find the sum: $(4x^3 - 5x^2 + x + 8) + (7x^3 + 3x^2 + 4x - 9)$.

Solution: Rearrange the expression by combining like terms.

$(4x^3 + 7x^3) + (-5x^2 + 3x^2) + (x + 4x) + (8 + -9) = 11x^3 - 2x^2 + 5x - 1$.

**Example 2**

Find the sum: $(5x^3 - 3x^2 + 9x - 1) + (12x^3 + 4x^2 + 2x + 8) - (6x^3 + x^2 + 5)$.

Solution: Rearrange the expression by combining like terms. Notice that every polynomial may not have the same terms, so be careful. Also remember to distribute a negative sign when outside a polynomial.

$$(5x^3 + 12x^3 - 6x^3) + (-3x^2 + 4x^2 - x^2) + (9x + 2x) + (-1 + 8 - 5) = 11x^3 + 11x + 2.$$

## Multiplication

Polynomials can be multiplied by using the distributive property repeatedly for each term in one of the polynomials to the other, then combining like terms.

### Example
Find the product $(4x^2 + 2x + 3) \times (4x^3 - 5x^2 + x + 8)$

Solution: Distribute each term in the first polynomial to the second polynomial.

$$4x^2(4x^3 - 5x^2 + x + 8) + 2x(4x^3 - 5x^2 + x + 8) + 3(4x^3 - 5x^2 + x + 8)$$

$$= (16x^5 - 20x^4 + 4x^3 + 32x^2) + (8x^4 - 10x^3 + 2x^2 + 16x) + (12x^3 - 15x^2 + 3x + 24)$$

$$= 16x^5 - 12x^4 + 6x^3 + 19x^2 + 19x + 24$$

An alternative would be to distribute the second polynomial to the first polynomial.

$$4x^3(4x^2 + 2x + 3) - 5x^2(4x^2 + 2x + 3) + x(4x^2 + 2x + 3) + 8(4x^2 + 2x + 3)$$

$$= (16x^5 + 8x^4 + 12x^3) + (-20x^4 - 10x^3 - 15x^2) + (4x^3 + 2x^2 + 3x) + (32x^2 + 16x + 24)$$

$$= 16x^5 - 12x^4 + 6x^3 + 19x^2 + 19x + 24$$

# Quadratics

A quadratic is a polynomial of one variable whose degree is two. The standard form of a quadratic expression is $ax^2 + bx + c$, where $a \neq 0$ and $a$, $b$, and $c$ are real numbers.

## Factoring

Factoring is a method of expressing a polynomial as a product of its factors. It's like breaking down a number into a product of its prime factors, e.g., $70 = 2 \times 5 \times 7$.

Factoring allows us to simplify quadratic expressions, find their roots, and solve equations. This means that we want to rewrite $ax^2 + bx + c = 0$ as $(a_1 x + c_1) \times (a_2 x + c_2) = 0$, where $a_1 \cdot a_2 = a$, $c_1 \cdot c_2 = c$, and $a_1 c_2 + a_2 c_1 = b$. The roots of the equation are $-\frac{c_1}{a_1}$ and $-\frac{c_2}{a_2}$. The roots of an equation are where the graph of the equation crosses the $x$-axis.

A quadratic can have either 0, 1, or 2 distinct real roots.

The most successful way that I've found with my classes to teach factoring is to use the "diamond method." But once you are comfortable with factoring, the diamond shape visual tool isn't needed. Here is how it works:

1. Draw an "X" shape, which is referred to as the diamond. Put the value of the product $(a \cdot c)$ in the top and the value of $(b)$ in the bottom.

2. Write down all the pairs of factors of the top value ($a \cdot c$) somewhere off to the side.
3. Once you have all the factors, look for the one pair that adds up to the bottom value ($b$).
4. Place those factors in the right and left sides of the diamond. It doesn't matter which one is on the left and which one is on the right.
5. If the value of $a = 1$, then you are finished. The factors of the quadratic are ($x - left$) and ($x - right$).
6. If the value of $a \neq 1$, then you have at least two more steps.

   a. Write the left and right values as $\dfrac{left}{a}$ and $\dfrac{right}{a}$. Reduce the fractions if possible.

   b. If a fraction reduces to a whole number, then the factor is ($x - that\ value$). If the value is still a fraction $\left(\dfrac{numerator}{denominator}\right)$, then the factor is ($denominator\ x - numerator$).

7. If the value of $a \neq 1$ and the description in step 6 didn't make any sense, then you can factor by grouping.

   a. Rewrite the middle term in the original equation as the sum of the two terms formed using the left and right sides of the diamond: ($ax^2 + left\ x + right\ x + c$).
   b. Group the first two terms together and the last two terms together: ($ax^2 + left\ x$) + ($right\ x + c$)
   c. Factor out the common factors of each group.
   d. Factor out the common binomial factor. This gives you the factorization of the quadratic.

**Example 1**
Factor $2x^2 + 22x + 56$.

Solution: First, you always want to see if there is a common factor of each term of the quadratic. In this case, we can factor out 2. This leaves $2(x^2 + 11x + 28)$.

Step 1: Draw the diamond and place 28 ($a \cdot c$) in the top, 11 ($b$) in the bottom. Don't use the original equation once you factored out the common factor of 2.

Step 2: Write down all the factors of 28: 1(28), 2(14), 4(7).
Step 3: The pair that adds to 11 (the value in the bottom of the diamond) is 4 and 7.
Step 4: Place those factors in the left and right sides of the diamond.

Step 5: Because $a = 1$ (in the part we are factoring), we are finished factoring.

$$2x^2 + 22x + 56 = 2(x^2 + 11x + 28) = 2(x - 7)(x - 4)$$

**Example 2**
Factor $3x^2 - 14x - 5$.

Solution: There is no common factor, so we proceed to the diamond.
Step 1: Draw the diamond and place −15 ($a \cdot c$) in the top, and −14, the value of $b$, in the bottom.

Step 2: Write down all the factors of −15: 1(−15), −1(15), 3(−5), −3(5)

Step 3: The pair that adds to −14 is 1 and −15.

Step 4: Place those factors in the left and right sides of the diamond.

Step 6: Because $a \neq 1$, we skip step 5 and need to do more steps. Divide $-15$ and 1 by 3 (the value of $a$).

$\dfrac{-15}{3}$ reduces to $-5$, which means one factor is $(x - 5)$,

but $\dfrac{1}{3}$ does not reduce, which means the other factor is $(3x + 1)$.

Therefore, $3x^2 - 14x - 5 = (3x + 1)(x - 5)$.

Step 7: Alternate method: Factoring by grouping means rewriting the original expression but replacing the middle term $(bx)$ with the values of the left and right numbers in the diamond. This gives $3x^2 - 15x + x - 5$.

Group the first two terms and last two terms: $(3x^2 - 15x) + (x - 5)$
Factor out a common factor from each group: $3x(x - 5) + 1(x - 5)$
Factor out the common binomial factors: $(x - 5)(3x + 1)$
Therefore, $3x^2 - 14x - 5 = (3x + 1)(x - 5)$.

**Example 3**
Find the solutions to the equation $8x^2 - 10x = 3$.

Solution: The quadratic needs to be set equal to 0 and then factored; this gives us $8x^2 - 10x - 3 = 0$. Using the diamond method to factor:

divide left and right by the value of $a$      then simplify the fractions.
The equation $8x^2 - 10x - 3 = 0$ can be rewritten as $(2x - 3)(4x + 1) = 0$. Applying the zero-product property, we set each factor equal to 0 and solve for $x$.

$$2x - 3 = 0, \; x = \frac{3}{2} \text{ and } 4x + 1 = 0, \; x = -\frac{1}{4}$$

The solution to the equation $8x^2 - 10x = 3$ is $x = \dfrac{3}{2}$ or $x = -\dfrac{1}{4}$.

# Solving Quadratic Equations

Not all quadratics can be factored. When that is the case, we need to use the quadratic formula.

$$x = \frac{-b \pm \sqrt{b^2 - 4ac}}{2a}$$

The quadratic formula can be used even if the equation is able to be factored, but factoring is typically faster when you know how to factor.

**Example 1**
Find the solution to the equation $2x^2 + 8x + 3 = 0$.

Solution: Substituting the values of $a = 2$, $b = 8$, and $c = 3$ into the quadratic formula

$$x = \frac{-8 \pm \sqrt{8^2 - 4(2)(3)}}{2(2)} = \frac{-8 \pm \sqrt{40}}{4} = \frac{-8}{4} \pm \frac{2\sqrt{10}}{4} = -2 \pm \frac{\sqrt{10}}{2},$$

the solution to the equation $2x^2 + 8x + 3 = 0$ is $x = -2 + \frac{\sqrt{10}}{2}$ or $x = -2 - \frac{\sqrt{10}}{2}$.

**Example 2**
Find the solution to the equation $3x^2 - 6x + 5 = 0$.

Solution: Substituting the values of $a = 3$, $b = -6$, and $c = 5$ into the quadratic formula

$$x = \frac{6 \pm \sqrt{(-6)^2 - 4(3)(5)}}{2(3)} = \frac{6 \pm \sqrt{-24}}{6} = \frac{6 \pm \sqrt{4}\sqrt{6}\sqrt{-1}}{6} = \frac{6 \pm 2i\sqrt{6}}{6} = 1 \pm \frac{i\sqrt{6}}{3},$$

the solution to the equation $3x^2 - 6x + 5 = 0$ is $x = 1 \pm \frac{\sqrt{6}}{3i}$.

# Solving Quadratic Inequalities

Solving a quadratic inequality involves the same steps as solving a quadratic equation, but with a few more steps.

**Example 1**
Find the solution to the inequality $x^2 + 9x + 14 \leq 0$.

Solution:

Step 1: Determine the critical numbers (roots of the graph/solutions to the equation) by setting the corresponding equation equal to 0 and solving (factoring or using quadratic formula).

$x^2 + 9x + 14 = 0$

$(x + 2)(x + 7) = 0$

$x + 2 = 0$ or $x + 7 = 0$

$x = -2$ or $x = -7$

The critical numbers are −2 and −7.

Rewrite the inequality as a product of its factors: $(x + 2)(x + 7) \leq 0$. Using the zero-product property with inequalities, the only time that an even number of factors multiply to give a negative value is if one factor is positive and one factor is negative.

Step 2: The critical numbers represent where the equation equals zero, so those numbers will serve as partitions. Draw a number line that includes the critical numbers; choose a number in each of the intervals as a test value. The intervals that contain test values that make the original inequality true are part of the solution to the inequality.

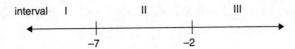

Let's test a value that is in interval I, such as −10, and see if that value makes the inequality true.

$$x^2 + 9x + 14 \leq 0 \qquad \text{or you could use the factored form: } (x+2)(x+7) \leq 0$$

$$(-10)^2 + 9(-10) + 14 \leq ? \ 0 \qquad (-10+2)(-10+7) \leq ? \ 0$$

$$24 \leq ? \ 0 \text{ is not true} \qquad (\text{neg number})(\text{neg number}) \leq ? \ 0 \text{ not true}$$

Therefore, no values in the interval $(-\infty, -7)$ are part of the solution to the inequality.

Let's test a value that is in interval II, such as −5, and see if that value makes the original inequality true.

$$x^2 + 9x + 14 \leq 0 \qquad \text{or } (x+2)(x+7) \leq 0$$

$$(-5)^2 + 9(-5) + 14 \leq ? \ 0 \qquad (-5+2)(-5+7) \leq ? \ 0$$

$$-6 \leq ? \ 0 \text{ is true} \qquad (\text{neg number})(\text{pos number}) \leq ? \ 0 \text{ is true}$$

Therefore, all values in the interval $(-7, -2)$ are solutions to the inequality.

Let's test a value that is in interval III, such as 0, and see if that value makes the original inequality true.

$$x^2 + 9x + 14 \leq 0 \qquad \text{or } (x+2)(x+7) \leq 0$$

$$(0)^2 + 9(0) + 14 \leq ? \ 0 \qquad (0+2)(0+7) \leq ? \ 0$$

$$14 \leq ? \ 0 \text{ is not true} \qquad (\text{pos number})(\text{pos number}) \leq ? \ 0 \text{ not true}$$

Therefore, no values in the interval $(-2, \infty)$ are part of the solution to the inequality.

The solution to the inequality $x^2 + 9x + 14 \leq 0$ is the interval $[-7, -2]$.

**Example 2**

Find the solution to the inequality $6x^2 - 3 > -7x$.

Solution: Rewrite the inequality so it is in standard form, with 0 on one side of the inequality.

$$6x^2 + 7x - 3 > 0$$

Step 1: Determine the critical numbers (roots of the graph/solutions to the equation) by setting the corresponding equation equal to 0 and solving (factoring or quadratic formula).

$$(2x + 3)(3x - 1) = 0$$

$$2x + 3 = 0 \quad \text{or} \quad 3x - 1 = 0$$

$$x = -\frac{3}{2} \quad \text{or} \quad x = \frac{1}{3}$$

The critical numbers are $-\frac{3}{2}$ and $\frac{1}{3}$.

Rewrite the inequality as a product of its factors. $(2x + 3)(3x - 1) > 0$. Using the zero-product property with inequalities, the only time that an even number of factors multiply to give a positive value is if both factors are positive or both factors are negative.

Step 2:

Let's test a value that is in interval I, such as −5, and see if that value makes the factored inequality true.

$$(2x + 3)(3x - 1) > 0$$

$(-7)(-16) > 0$ is true, therefore, all values in the interval $\left(-\infty, -\dfrac{3}{2}\right)$ are solutions to the inequality.

Let's test a value that is in interval II, such as 0, and see if that value makes the original inequality true.

$$(2x + 3)(3x - 1) > 0$$

$(3)(-1) > 0$ is not true, therefore, no values in the interval $\left(-\dfrac{3}{2}, \dfrac{1}{3}\right)$ are part of the solution to the inequality.

Let's test a value that is in interval III, such as 2, and see if that value makes the original inequality true.

$$(2x + 3)(3x - 1) > 0$$

$(7)(5) > 0$ is true, therefore, all values in the interval $\left(\dfrac{1}{3}, \infty\right)$ are solutions to the inequality.

The solutions to the inequality $6x^2 - 3 > -7x$ is $\left(-\infty, -\dfrac{3}{2}\right) \cup \left(\dfrac{1}{3}, \infty\right)$ because the inequality is strictly greater than and *not* equal to.

## Complex Numbers

A complex number is a combination of a real number and an imaginary number and is written in the form $a + bi$, where $a$ and $b$ are real numbers. The real part is represented by $a$ and the imaginary part is represented by $bi$. The "unit" imaginary number is $i$, which is defined as $\sqrt{-1}$.

Complex numbers can be added, subtracted, multiplied, and divided, similar to how polynomials are added, subtracted, multiplied, and divided. The following are common rules that allow you to operate on complex numbers.

| OPERATION | RULE | EXAMPLES |
|---|---|---|
| Addition | $(a + bi) + (c + di) = (a + c)$ $+ (b + d)i$ | $(3 - 9i) + (4 + 2i) = (3 + 4) + (-9 + 2)i$ $= 7 - 7i$ |
| Subtraction | $(a + bi) - (c + di) = (a - c)$ $+ (b - d)i$ | $(4 + 2i) - (3 - i) = (4 - 3) + (2 - (-1))i$ $= 1 + 3i$ |
| Multiplication | $(a + bi)(c + di) = (ac - bd)$ $+ (ad + bc)i$ | $(7 + 5i)(2 + 3i) = 14 + 21i + 10i + 15i^2$    FOIL $= 14 + 21i + 10i - 15$    $(i^2 = -1)$ $= -1 + 31i$ |
| Division | $\dfrac{a + bi}{c + di} = \dfrac{ac + bd}{c^2 + d^2} + \dfrac{bc - ad}{c^2 + d^2}i$ | $\dfrac{8 + 2i}{4 - 5i} = \dfrac{8 + 2i}{4 - 5i} \cdot \dfrac{4 + 5i}{4 + 5i}$ multiply numerator and denominator by the complex conjugate $= \dfrac{(8 + 2i)(4 + 5i)}{(4 - 5i)(4 + 5i)} = \dfrac{32 + 40i + 8i + 10i^2}{16 + 20i - 20i - 25i^2}$ $= \dfrac{32 + 40i + 8i - 10}{16 + 20i - 20i + 25} = \dfrac{22 + 48i}{41} = \dfrac{22}{41} + \dfrac{48}{41}i$ |

# Solving Systems of Equations in Two and Three Variables

A system of linear equations with two variables is a system that can be written as

$$ax + by = c$$

$$dx + ey = f$$

When we find the solution to the system, we are finding the values of $x$ and $y$ that when substituted into the equations make *both* equations true. Graphically it is where the two lines intersect. There are two common methods to solving a system: substitution method and linear combination (elimination) method. A third method is solving by graphing, but this is only precise when the solutions are integers values for $x$ and $y$.

## Substitution Method

The substitution method involves substituting one equation into the other equation, then solving for the variable.

Step 1: Rewrite one of the equations in terms of one of the variables (either $x$ or $y$).

Step 2: Substitute that equation into the other equation.

Step 3: Solve the new equation.

Step 4: Find the value of the other variable by substitution into either one of the equations and solving.

### Example

Solve the system $2x + 4y = -10$

$$5x + y = 2$$

Solution: Step 1: We can choose either equation, but it looks like the second equation would be easiest to solve for $y$. Rewriting we get $y = -5x + 2$.

Step 2: Substitute $y = -5x + 2$ into the first equation for $y$.

$$2x + 4(-5x + 2) = -10$$

Step 3: Solve that equation for $x$.

$$2x - 20x + 8 = -10$$

$$-18x = -18$$

$$x = 1$$

Step 4: Now that we know one of the values of the variables, in this case $x$, we can substitute that into either the first equation or the second equation. I'll choose the first equation.

$$2(1) + 4y = -10$$

$$2 + 4y = -10$$

$$4y = -12$$

$$y = -3$$

The solution to the system is $(1, -3)$.

### Linear Combination (Elimination) Method

Linear combination involves eliminating one of the variables from both equations.

Step 1: Make sure both equations are written in standard form $ax + by = c$. Choose a variable to eliminate from both equations.

Step 2: Multiply all the terms of one equation by a constant, and then multiply all the terms of the other equation by a constant so that when the two equations are added together, one of the variables will be eliminated from both equations because the coefficients have the same magnitude but opposite signs.

Step 3: Add the two equations together and solve for the remaining variable.

Step 4: Substitute the value of that variable into one of the two equations, and solve for the other variable.

**Example**

Solve the system $2x + 7y = -2$

$$3x + 4y = 10$$

Solution:

Step 1: Both equations are in standard form. Let's eliminate $x$ from both equations.

Step 2: Multiply both sides of the first equation by $-3$ and the second equation by 2.

$$-3(2x + 7y) = -3(-2) \quad \rightarrow \quad -6x - 21y = 6$$
$$2(3x + 4y) = 2(10) \quad \rightarrow \quad 6x + 8y = 20$$

Step 3: Adding the two equations: $(-6x + 6x) + (-21y + 8y) = (6 + 20)$

$\quad\quad -13y = 26$ (notice the $x$ terms were eliminated)

$\quad\quad y = -2$

Step 4: Substitute $y = -2$ into either equation to solve for $x$. Let's choose the first equation.

$$2x + 7(-2) = -2$$
$$2x - 14 = -2$$
$$2x = 12$$
$$x = 6$$

The solution to the system is $(6, -2)$.

# Piecewise-Defined Functions

A piecewise function is a function that is defined in "pieces" or different nonoverlapping intervals.

**Example 1**

Graph the function $y = \begin{cases} 3x & x < -1 \\ -2x + 5 & x \geq -1 \end{cases}$

Solution: The first equation has slope 3 and $y$-intercept 0, but it is only defined when $x < -1$. The second equation has slope $-2$ and $y$-intercept 5, but is only defined when $x \geq -1$.

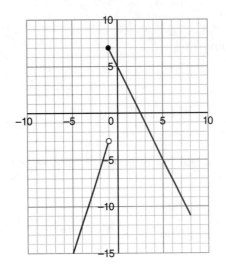

# Exponential Functions and Rules for Exponents

The following are common rules for exponents that allow you to rewrite exponential expressions in equivalent forms.

| LAW | DEFINITION | EXAMPLE |
|---|---|---|
| Law of Zero Exponent | $a^0 = 1$, where $a \neq 0$ | $5^0 = 1$ |
| Law of Product | $a^m \cdot a^n = a^{m+n}$ | $4^3 \cdot 4^2 = 4^{3+2} = 4^5$ |
| Law of Quotient | $\dfrac{a^m}{a^n} = a^{m-n}$ | $\dfrac{7^6}{7^2} = 7^{6-2} = 7^4$ |
| Law of Power of a Power | $(a^m)^n = a^{mn}$ | $(3^4)^2 = 3^{4 \cdot 2} = 3^8$ |
| Law of Power of a Product | $(ab)^m = a^m b^m$ | $(2x)^3 = 2^3 x^3 = 8x^3$ |
| Law of Power of a Quotient | $\left(\dfrac{a}{b}\right)^m = \dfrac{a^m}{b^m}$ | $\left(\dfrac{6}{7}\right)^2 = \dfrac{6^2}{7^2} = \dfrac{36}{49}$ |
| Law of Negative Exponent | $a^{-m} = \dfrac{1}{a^m}$ | $8^{-2} = \dfrac{1}{8^2} = \dfrac{1}{64}$ |

An exponential function has the form $f(x) = a(b)^x$, where $a > 0$ and $b \neq 1$. When the value of $b$ is $> 1$, it is known as exponential growth. When $0 < b < 1$, it is known as exponential decay.

**Example 1**

Simplify the expression $\dfrac{\left(5x^2 y^7\right)^3}{\left(2x^{-1}y^2\right)^3}$ completely.

Solution: First, use the law of power of a product property to simplify the numerator and denominator.

$$\frac{\left(5x^2 y^7\right)^3}{\left(2x^{-1}y^2\right)^3} = \frac{\left(5\right)^3\left(x^2\right)^3\left(y^7\right)^3}{\left(2\right)^3\left(x^{-1}\right)^3\left(y^2\right)^3}$$

Next, use the law of power of a power property: $\dfrac{\left(5\right)^3\left(x^2\right)^3\left(y^7\right)^3}{\left(2\right)^3\left(x^{-1}\right)^3\left(y^2\right)^3} = \dfrac{125x^{2\cdot3}\,y^{7\cdot3}}{8x^{-1\cdot3}\,y^{2\cdot3}} = \dfrac{125x^6\,y^{21}}{8x^{-3}\,y^6}$

Next, use the law of quotient property: $\dfrac{125x^6\,y^{21}}{8x^{-3}\,y^6} = \dfrac{125}{8}x^{6-(-3)}\,y^{21-6} = \dfrac{125x^9\,y^{15}}{8}$

**Example 2**

Graph the function $f(x) = 3(2)^x$ and find the $x$-intercept, $y$-intercept, domain, range, and asymptotes of the graph.

Solution: The graph has no $x$-intercept. The $y$-intercept is $(0, 3)$. The domain is all real numbers. The range is $y > 0$. There is a horizontal asymptote at $y = 0$. There are no vertical asymptotes.

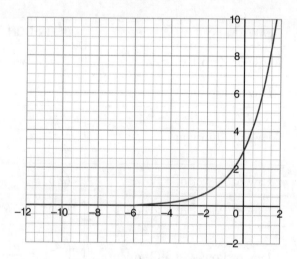

# Radicals

The inverse operator of an exponent is a radical, which is represented by the symbol $\sqrt{\ }$. For example, the inverse of a square is a square root $\sqrt{\ }$, and the inverse of a cube is a cube root $\sqrt[3]{\ }$. If the number under the radical is positive, then the result will be positive. If the number under the radical is negative and the root is even (such as a square root), then the result will not be a real number.

| PROPERTY | DEFINITION | EXAMPLES |
|---|---|---|
| Product Property | $\sqrt{pq} = \sqrt{p}\sqrt{q},$ $p > 0, q > 0$ | $\sqrt{300} = \sqrt{100}\sqrt{3}$ $= 10\sqrt{3}$ $\sqrt[3]{54x^4y^7} = \sqrt[3]{27}\sqrt[3]{2}\ \sqrt[3]{x^3}\sqrt[3]{x}\ \sqrt[3]{y^6}\sqrt[3]{y}$ $= 3xy^2\sqrt[3]{2xy}$ |
| Quotient Property | $\sqrt{\dfrac{p}{q}} = \dfrac{\sqrt{p}}{\sqrt{q}},$ $p > 0, q > 0$ | $\sqrt{\dfrac{75}{2}} = \dfrac{\sqrt{75}}{\sqrt{2}} = \dfrac{\sqrt{25}\sqrt{3}}{\sqrt{2}} = \dfrac{5\sqrt{3}}{\sqrt{2}} \cdot \dfrac{\sqrt{2}}{\sqrt{2}} = \dfrac{5\sqrt{6}}{2}$ |

**Example**

Simplify completely. $\dfrac{\sqrt[3]{250x^7}}{\sqrt[3]{108x^3}}$

Solution: Use the product property to write the expression as a product of radicals.

$$\frac{\sqrt[3]{250x^7}}{\sqrt[3]{108x^3}} = \frac{\sqrt[3]{250}\ \sqrt[3]{x^7}}{\sqrt[3]{108}\ \sqrt[3]{x^3}} = \frac{\sqrt[3]{125}\sqrt[3]{2}\ \sqrt[3]{x^6}\sqrt[3]{x}}{\sqrt[3]{27}\sqrt[3]{4}\ \sqrt[3]{x^3}} = \frac{5\sqrt[3]{2}\ x^2\sqrt[3]{x}}{3\sqrt[3]{4}\ x} = \frac{5x\sqrt[3]{2x}}{3\sqrt[3]{4}} = \frac{5x\sqrt[3]{x}}{3\sqrt[3]{2}}$$

# Solving Right Triangle Problems Involving Trigonometry

Right triangle trigonometry problems are all about understanding the relationship between side lengths, angle measurements, and trigonometric ratios in right triangles.

For the right triangle ABC with angle $\theta$ shown,

$\sin\theta = \dfrac{opposite\ leg}{hypotenuse} = \dfrac{AC}{AB}$

$\cos\theta = \dfrac{adjacent\ leg}{hypotenuse} = \dfrac{BC}{AB}$

$\tan\theta = \dfrac{opposite\ leg}{adjacent\ leg} = \dfrac{AC}{BC}$

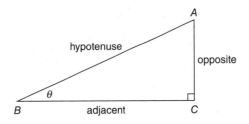

A helpful mnemonic device for remembering the three trig ratios is "SOH CAH TOA". This stands for "Sine equals Opposite over Hypotenuse, Cosine equals Adjacent over Hypotenuse, Tangent equals Opposite over Adjacent."

**Example 1**

Given $\triangle ABC$, find the value of $x$.

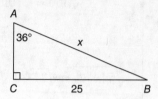

Solution: $\sin 36° = \dfrac{opposite\ leg}{hypotenuse} = \dfrac{25}{x}$

$$x = \dfrac{25}{\sin 36°} = 42.533$$

Note: This is one of the few times your calculator should be in degree mode. For the AP Precalculus course it should be in radian mode.

Also note that the final answer should be rounded to three decimal places. Do not round any answers until the end.

**Example 2**

Given $\triangle ABC$, find the value of $\angle B$.

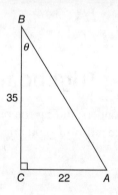

Solution: $\tan B = \dfrac{opposite\ leg}{adjacent\ leg} = \dfrac{22}{35}$

$$B = \tan^{-1}\dfrac{22}{35} = 32.152°$$

# › Review Questions

**1.** Find the slope of the line passing through the points $(-5, 8)$ and $(2, 8)$.

**2.** If the slope of the line passing through the points $(9, k)$ and $(k, 12)$ has slope $-\dfrac{8}{5}$, find $k$.

**3.** What is the equation of the line shown?

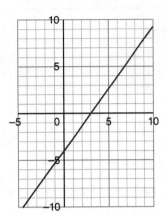

**4.** Solve for $y$: $16 - 5y > 9$

**5.** Find the sum: $(4x^2 + 8x^3 - 2x + 5) + (6x^2 - 3x^3 + 2x)$

**6.** Find the product: $(3x^2 - 5)(4x^2 + x + 9)$

**7.** Factor completely: $10x^3 + 38x^2 - 8x$

**8.** Find the solution to $y^2 + 3y \geq 40$.

**9.** Simplify and write as a complex number in the form $a + bi$: $(7 + 2i) - (5 + 6i)$

**10.** Simplify and write as a complex number in the form $a + bi$: $\dfrac{7 + 2i}{5 + 6i}$

**11.** Solve the system: $5x - 3y = -7$
$\qquad\qquad\qquad\quad 6x + 5y = -17$

**12.** Solve the system: $4x + 7y = 32$
$\qquad\qquad\qquad\quad x - 3y = -11$

**13.** Graph the function $f(x) = \begin{cases} 2x + 9 & x \leq -1 \\ x^2 & x > -1 \end{cases}$

**14.** Solve for $x$:

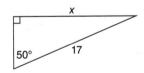

**15.** Solve for $\theta$:

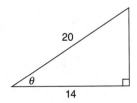

# ❯ Answers and Explanations

**1.** • $m = \dfrac{y_2 - y_1}{x_2 - x_1} = \dfrac{8 - (8)}{2 - (-5)} = \dfrac{0}{7} = 0$

**2.** • $m = \dfrac{y_2 - y_1}{x_2 - x_1}$; so $-\dfrac{8}{5} = \dfrac{12 - k}{k - 9}$

• Cross multiply: $-8(k - 9) = 5(12 - k) \rightarrow$
$-8k + 72 = 60 - 5k$

• Isolate $k$ and solve: $-3k = -12 \rightarrow k = 4$

**3.** • The slope of the graph can be found by examining some points.

• The $y$-intercept is $(0, -4)$ and the $x$-intercept, $(3, 0)$.

• Using those two points we can calculate the slope: $m = \dfrac{y_2 - y_1}{x_2 - x_1} = \dfrac{0 - (-4)}{3 - 0} = \dfrac{4}{3}$

• The equation of the line in slope-intercept form is $y = mx + b \rightarrow y = \dfrac{4}{3}x - 4$.

**4.** • Isolate the variable: $-5y > -7$

• Divide both sides by $-5$, remembering to switch the inequality sign because there was a division by a negative number. $-5y > -7 \rightarrow y < \dfrac{7}{5}$

**5.** • To find the sum, like terms must be combined.

• $(4x^2 + 6x^2) + (8x^3 - 3x^3) + (-2x + 2x) + 5 =$
$10x^2 + 5x^3 + 5$

• Rewriting with descending exponents:
$5x^3 + 10x^2 + 5$

**6.** • Use the distributive property:
$(3x^2 - 5)(4x^2 + x + 9)$
$= 3x^2(4x^2 + x + 9) - 5(4x^2 + x + 9)$
$= (12x^4 + 3x^3 + 27x^2) + (-20x^2 - 5x - 45)$
$= 12x^4 + 3x^3 + 7x^2 - 5x - 45$

**7.** • Factor out the greatest common factor,
$2x$: $2x(5x^2 + 19x - 4)$

• Find factors of $-20$ ($ac$), that add to 19 ($b$). They are 20 and $-1$.

• Rewrite $5x^2 + 19x - 4$ as $5x^2 + 20x - x - 4$.

• Group the first two terms and last two terms:
$(5x^2 + 20x) + (-x - 4)$.

• Factor out any common factors from each grouping: $5x(x + 4) - 1(x + 4)$.

• Factor out the common factor: $(x + 4)(5x - 1)$.

• Therefore, $10x^3 + 38x^2 - 8x = 2x(x + 4)(5x - 1)$.

**8.** • The first step is to move all terms to one side of the inequality: $y^2 + 3y - 40 \geq 0$

• Next, try factoring the quadratic by finding factors of $-40$ ($ac$) that add to 3 ($b$). They are 8 and $-5$.

• $y^2 + 3y - 40 \geq 0 \rightarrow (y + 8)(y - 5) \geq 0$

• Setting each factor equal to 0 and solving gives the critical numbers $-8$ and 5.

• Interval I: Choose a value less than $-8$, such as $-10$ and see if the inequality is true. $(-2)(-15)$ ?$\geq 0$
It is true; therefore, all values in the interval $(-\infty, -8)$ are solutions to the inequality.

• Interval II: Choose a value between $-8$ and 5 for $y$, such as 0 and see if the inequality is true. $(8)(-5)$ ?$\geq 0$
It is not true; therefore, no values in the interval $(-8, 5)$ are part of the solution to the inequality.

• Interval III: Choose a value greater than 5, such as 10, and see if the inequality is true. $(18)(5)$ ?$\geq 0$
It is true; therefore, all values in the interval $(5, \infty)$ are solutions to the inequality.

• The solution to $y^2 + 3y \geq 40$ is $(-\infty, -8) \cup (5, \infty)$.

**9.** • First, distribute the negative: $(7 + 2i) - (5 + 6i)$
$= (7 + 2i) + (-5 - 6i)$.

• Combine the real part and the imaginary part:
$(7 - 5) + (2i - 6i)$.

• Simplify: $2 - 4i$.

**10.** • Multiply the numerator and denominator by the complex conjugate of the denominator.

• $\dfrac{7 + 2i}{5 + 6i} \cdot \dfrac{5 - 6i}{5 - 6i} = \dfrac{35 - 42i + 10i - 12i^2}{25 - 30i + 30i - 36i^2}$

• Substitute $i^2 = (-1)$:

$\dfrac{35 - 42i + 10i - 12(-1)}{25 - 30i + 30i - 36(-1)} = \dfrac{35 - 42i + 10i + 12}{25 - 30i + 30i + 36}$

• Combine like terms and rewrite in $a + bi$ form:

$\dfrac{47 - 32i}{61} = \dfrac{47}{61} - \dfrac{32}{61}i$

**11.** • Use the linear combination method: Multiply the top equation by $-6$ and the bottom equation by 5:
$-6(5x - 3y) = -6(-7) \rightarrow -30x + 18y = 42$

$5(6x + 5y) = 5(-17) \rightarrow 30x + 25y = -85$

- Add the two equations to eliminate $x$: $43y = -43$, thus $y = -1$
- Substitute $y = -1$ into one of the equations: $5x - 3(-1) = -7 \rightarrow 5x + 3 = -7 \rightarrow$ $5x = -10 \rightarrow x = -2$
- The solution to the system is $(-2, -1)$.

**12.**
- Using the substitution method, rewrite the bottom equation to isolate $x$: $x = 3y - 11$.
- Substitute that equation into the top equation for $x$: $4(3y - 11) + 7y = 32$
- $12y - 44 + 7y = 32 \rightarrow 19y - 44 = 32 \rightarrow$ $19y = 76 \rightarrow y = 4$
- Substitute $y = 4$ into one of the equations: $x - 3(4) = -11 \rightarrow x - 12 = -11 \rightarrow x = 1$.
- The solution to the system is $(1, 4)$.

**13.** •

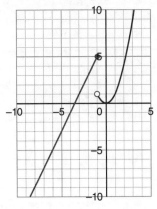

**14.** • $\sin 50° = \dfrac{x}{17} \rightarrow x = 17 \sin 50° \rightarrow x = 13.023$

**15.** • $\cos\theta = \dfrac{14}{20} \rightarrow \theta = \cos^{-1}\dfrac{14}{20} \rightarrow \theta = 45.573°$

# CHAPTER 6

# Unit 1: Polynomial and Rational Functions

**IN THIS CHAPTER**

**Summary:** This chapter reviews functions and properties of their graphs as well as introduces new topics that are important when graphing functions. Polynomial and rational functions are also introduced, along with the properties of their graphs. Modeling aspects of contextual scenarios and data sets through transformations are also discussed. Rate of change and functions are the themes of the course and will be seen in all units.

**Key Ideas**

✪ Learning change in tandem
✪ Finding average rates of change
✪ Identifying increasing and decreasing intervals of a function
✪ Identifying concavity, points of inflection of a graph
✪ Finding local (relative) and global (absolute) maximum(s) and minimum(s) of a graph
✪ Finding zeros of a function and their multiplicities
✪ Determining if a polynomial is even, odd, or neither
✪ Describing the end behaviors of polynomial functions
✪ Describing the end behaviors of rational functions
✪ Determining vertical asymptotes of graphs and rational functions
✪ Determining holes in graphs of rational functions
✪ Rewriting polynomial and rational expressions in equivalent forms
✪ Using long division to determine the quotient and remainder of two polynomial functions
✪ Using the binomial theorem to expand $(x + y)^n$
✪ Constructing a function that is an additive and/or multiplicative transformation of another function
✪ Identifying an appropriate function type to construct a function model for a given scenario

# Functions and Their Graphs

A *function* is a mathematical relation that maps a set of input values to a set of output values such that each input value is mapped to exactly one output value. The set of input values is called the *domain* of the function, and the set of output values is called the *range* of the function. The variable representing input values is called the *independent variable*, and the variable representing the output values is called the *dependent variable*. The input and output values of a function vary in *tandem* according to the function rule, which can be expressed graphically, numerically, analytically, or verbally.

A function is most often denoted by letters such as *f*, *g*, and *h*, and the value of a function *f* at an element *x* of its domain is denoted by $f(x)$. For example, the value of *f* at $x = 3$ is denoted by $f(3)$.

### Example

Find the domain and range of the function $f(x) = \dfrac{1}{\sqrt{x+7}}$.

Solution: The fraction $\dfrac{1}{\sqrt{x+7}}$ is not defined when the denominator equals zero. This occurs when $x = -7$. Also, $\sqrt{x+7}$ is not a real number when $x + 7 < 0$ or when $x < -7$.

Therefore, the domain of *f* in set builder notation is $\{x \mid x > -7\}$ and the range is $\{y \mid y > 0\}$, which can be written in interval notation as $(-7, \infty)$ and $(0, \infty)$.

## Rate of Change

The *average rate of change* of a function over an interval of the function's domain is the value of the slope between the two points. A positive rate of change indicates that as one quantity increases or decreases, the other quantity does the same. Whereas a negative rate of change indicates that as one quantity increases, the other decreases.

$$\text{Average rate of change} = \frac{\Delta y}{\Delta x} = \frac{f(x_2) - f(x_1)}{x_2 - x_1}.$$

For a linear function, the average rate of change over any length input-value is constant. For a quadratic function, the average rates of change over consecutive equal-length input-value intervals can be given by a linear function. The average rate of change over the closed interval $[a, b]$ is the slope of the secant line from the point $(a, f(a))$ to $(b, f(b))$.

### Example

Find the average rate of change of the function $f(x) = 4x^2 + 3x + 2$ over the interval $[-1, 3]$.

Solution: $f(3) = 4(3)^2 + 3(3) + 2 = 47$.

$\qquad f(-1) = 4(-1)^2 + 3(-1) + 2 = 3$.

The slope of the secant line from $(-1, 3)$ to $(3, 47)$ is $\dfrac{f(3) - f(-1)}{3 - (-1)} = \dfrac{47 - 3}{3 - (-1)} = \dfrac{44}{4} = 11$.

## Increasing and Decreasing

A function $f(x)$ is *increasing* over an interval of its domain if as the $x$ values increase, the $y$ values also increase. That is, for all $a$ and $b$ in the interval if $a < b$, then $f(a) < f(b)$. Likewise, a function $f(x)$ is *decreasing* over an interval of its domain if as the $x$ values increase, the $y$ values decrease. That is, for all $a$ and $b$ in the interval if $a < b$, then $f(a) > f(b)$.

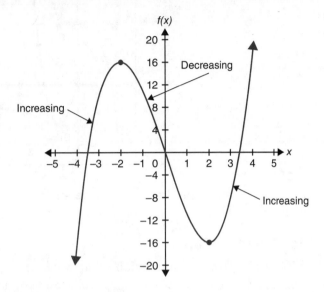

## Minima and Maxima

The point at which a function changes from increasing to decreasing is known as a *local*, or *relative*, *maximum*. Likewise, the point at which a function changes from decreasing to increasing is known as a *local*, or *relative*, *minimum*. The *maxima* and *minima* of a function are the largest and smallest values of a function either within a specific range or the entire domain. They are the "peaks" and "valleys" in the curve of a function. Some functions have one maximum value, and other functions have several maximum values, or maxima. Of all the local maxima, the greatest is called the *global*, or *absolute*, *maximum*. Likewise, the least of all local minima is called the *global*, or *absolute*, *minimum*.

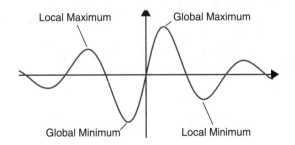

## Concavity

The graph of a function is *concave up* on intervals in which the rate of change is increasing and *concave down* on intervals in which the rate of change is decreasing.

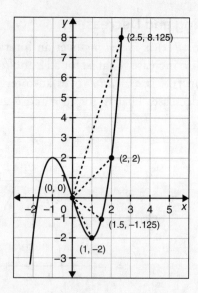

Example: In the graph shown, as $x$ increases from 0, the slopes of the secant line segments increase, so the function is concave up for $x > 0$.

### Point of Inflection

A *point of inflection* of a function occurs when the rate of change of the function changes from decreasing to increasing or from increasing to decreasing. It is also the point at which the polynomial function changes from concave up to concave down or from concave down to concave up.

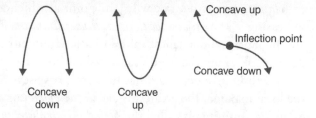

### Intercepts and Zeros

Graphically, the *zeros* of a function are the point(s) on the $x$-axis where the graph crosses the $x$-axis, also known as *x-intercepts*. The point(s) at which the graph crosses the $y$-axis is known as the *y-intercept(s)*.

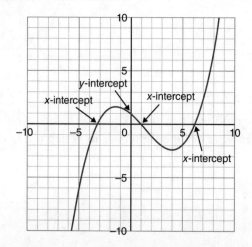

**Example 1**

The graph $f$ is shown in the following figure. Use the graph to approximate each of the following: interval(s) where the graph of $f$ is increasing, interval(s) where the graph is decreasing, interval(s) where the graph is concave up, interval(s) where the graph is concave down, point(s) of inflection, $x$-intercept(s), and $y$-intercept.

Solution:

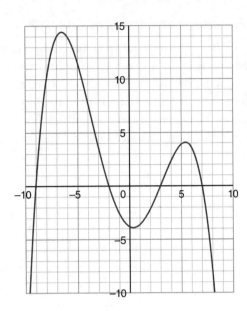

Increasing: $(-\infty, -6.5)$, $(0.5, 5.5)$     Decreasing: $(-6.5, 0.5)$, $(5.5, \infty)$
Concave up: $(-4, 3.5)$     Concave down: $(-\infty, -4)$, $(3.5, \infty)$
Point of inflection: $x = -4$ and $x = 3.5$
$x$-intercept(s): $(-9, 0)$, $(-2, 0)$, $(3, 0)$ $(7, 0)$     $y$-intercept: $(0, -3.8)$

**Example 2**

Using your graphing calculator, identify the maximum and minimum values for the function $f(x) = x^3 - 6x^2 + 2x + 3$. Identify the intervals that are increasing and the intervals that are decreasing.

Solution:

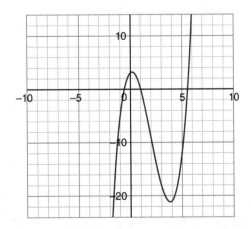

Relative maximum: $(0.174, 3.172)$     Relative minimum: $(3.826, -21.171)$.
Increasing: $(-\infty, 0.174)$ and $(3.826, \infty)$.     Decreasing: $(0.174, 3.826)$

# Polynomial Function

A nonconstant *polynomial function* of $x$ is any function of the form $p(x) = a_n x^n + a_{n-1} x^{n-1} + a_{n-2} x^{n-2} + \ldots + a_2 x^2 + a_1 x + a_0$, where $n$ is a positive integer, $a_i$ is a real number for each $i$ from 1 to $n$, and $a_n$ is nonzero. The *degree* of the polynomial is $n$, the largest exponent. The *leading term* is $a_n x^n$, and the *leading coefficient* is $a_n$.

## Polynomial Functions and Rates of Change

Linear functions have a constant rate of change, which we refer to as slope. But the rate of change for quadratic functions is not as straightforward, because the graph is a curve and does not have constant rate of change between two separate points. The number of differences needed between equal length intervals of the input values until a constant difference is calculated indicates the degree of the polynomial. For example, to show that a set of points models a quadratic function, you need to find the "second differences."

### Example

Show that the table of values models a quadratic function.

| x | y |
|---|---|
| −2 | 21 |
| −1 | 13 |
| 0 | 7 |
| 1 | 3 |
| 2 | 1 |
| 3 | 1 |
| 4 | 3 |

Solution: Because the $x$ values increase at a constant rate, in this case by 1, we can calculate the first differences and the second differences of the $y$ values between each $x$ interval of length 1.

| x | y | FIRST DIFFERENCE | SECOND DIFFERENCE |
|---|---|---|---|
| −2 | 21 | | |
| −1 | 13 | 21 − 13 = 8 | |
| 0 | 7 | 13 − 7 = 6 | 8 − 6 = 2 |
| 1 | 3 | 7 − 3 = 4 | 6 − 4 = 2 |
| 2 | 1 | 3 − 1 = 2 | 4 − 2 = 2 |
| 3 | 1 | 1 − 1 = 0 | 2 − 0 = 2 |
| 4 | 3 | 1 − 3 = −2 | 0 − (−2) = 2 |

Because the second difference for the $y$ values is constant (they all equal 2), the table models a quadratic function.

## Polynomial Functions and Complex Zeros

The fundamental theorem of algebra states that every polynomial of degree $n \geq 1$ with real or nonreal complex coefficients has at least one complex zero. If $a + bi$ is a nonreal zero of a polynomial with real coefficients, then its conjugate $a - bi$ is also a zero.

Sometimes a particular zero of a polynomial can occur more than once. This is known as *multiplicity*. If a linear factor $(x - a)$ is repeated $n$ times, the corresponding zero of the polynomial function has multiplicity $n$. This means that a polynomial of degree $n$ has exactly $n$ complex zeros when counting multiplicities. Zeros of multiplicity 1 are called *simple zeros*. If a real zero has even multiplicity, then the graph will be tangent to the $x$-axis at that zero.

### Example 1
Find all zeros and their corresponding multiplicities for the polynomial $p(x) = x^5 - 2x^3 + x$, then graph the polynomial.

Solution: We can factor the polynomial: $p(x) = x(x^4 - 2x^2 + 1)$
$$= x(x^2 - 1)^2$$
$$= x(x - 1)^2(x + 1)^2.$$

Setting each factor equal to 0 and solving gives $x = 0$ (multiplicity 1), $x = 1$ (multiplicity 2), $x = -1$ (multiplicity 2). The zeros of 1 and −1 have even multiplicity, which means the graph is tangent to the $x$-axis at those points, as opposed to the zero at 0, which has odd multiplicity and the graph crosses through that point as shown in the graph.

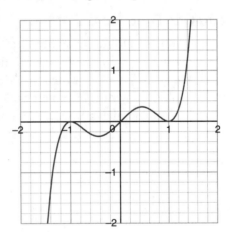

### Example 2
Given $p(x) = x^4 + 2x^3 - 9x^2 - 20x + 44$, use the fact that 2 is a zero of $p(x)$ with multiplicity 2 to find all zeros and their multiplicities.

Solution: Because 2 is a zero with multiplicity 2, that means $(x - 2)^2$ is a factor of the polynomial. We need to divide the polynomial by $(x - 2)^2$ (actually divide by its equivalent of $x^2 - 4x + 4$).

$$
\begin{array}{r}
x^2 + 6x + 11 \\
x^2 - 4x + 4 \enclose{longdiv}{x^4 + 2x^3 - 9x^2 - 20x + 44} \\
\underline{-(x^4 - 4x^3 + 4x^2)} \\
6x^3 - 13x^2 - 20x + 44 \\
\underline{-(6x^3 - 24x^2 + 24x)} \\
11x^2 - 44x + 44 \\
\underline{-(11x^2 - 44x + 44)} \\
0
\end{array}
$$

The result of the division is $x^2 + 6x + 11$. Because the result is not factorable (there is no pair of numbers that multiplies to 11 and adds to 6), we need to use the quadratic formula to solve for the remaining zeros.

$$x = \frac{-b \pm \sqrt{b^2 - 4ac}}{2a} = \frac{-6 \pm \sqrt{6^2 - 4(1)(11)}}{2(1)} = \frac{-6 \pm \sqrt{-8}}{2} = \frac{-6 \pm 2\sqrt{2}i}{2} = \frac{-6}{2} \pm \frac{2\sqrt{2}i}{2} = -3 \pm \sqrt{2}i.$$

The zeros are 2 (multiplicity 2), $-3 + \sqrt{2}i$ (multiplicity 1) and $-3 - \sqrt{2}i$ (multiplicity 1). It should be noted that the zero 2 has even multiplicity, so the graph is tangent at that point. The other two zeros are complex, which won't be seen on a graph with real axes. In other words, the graph crosses or touches the $x$-axis at the real roots and not the complex roots.

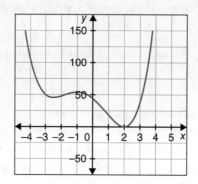

## Even and Odd Functions

An *even* function is graphically symmetric over the vertical line $x = 0$ and analytically has the property $f(-x) = f(x)$. A polynomial is an even function if it is of the form $p(x) = a_n x^n + a_{n-2} x^{n-2} + \cdots$ where each exponent of the polynomial is even. An *odd* function is graphically symmetric about the origin $(0, 0)$ and analytically has the property $f(-x) = -f(x)$. A polynomial is an odd function if it is of the form $p(x) = a_n x^n + a_{n-2} x^{n-2} + \cdots$, where each exponent of the polynomial is odd.

### Example 1

Determine if the polynomial $p(x) = 3x^4 - 8x^2 + 3$ is even, odd, or neither.

Solution: The exponents of the polynomial are 4, 2, and 0, which are all even numbers; therefore the polynomial is even. Analytically, it can be shown that $p(-x) = 3(-x)^4 - 8(-x)^2 + 3 = 3x^4 - 8x^2 + 3$, which proves the polynomial is even. Graphically, it can be seen that the graph is symmetric over the line $x = 0$.

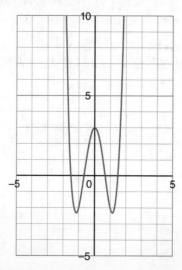

**Example 2**

Determine if the polynomial $p(x) = 2x^5 + 6x^3 + 5x$ is even, odd, or neither.

Solution: The exponents of the polynomial are 5, 3, and 1, which are all odd numbers; therefore the polynomial is odd. Analytically, it can be shown that $p(-x) = 2(-x)^5 + 6(-x)^3 + 5(-x) = -2x^5 - 6x^3 - 5x = -p(x)$, which proves the polynomial is odd. Graphically, it can be seen that the graph is symmetric over the point $(0, 0)$.

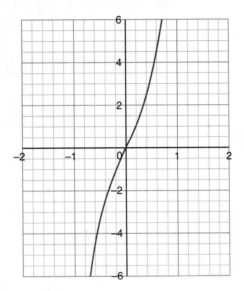

## Polynomial Functions and End Behavior

The end behavior of a function $p(x)$ is a description of what happens to the values $p(x)$ of the function as $x$ grows larger and larger in magnitude, meaning as $x \to \infty$ and as $x \to -\infty$. As the input values increase or decrease without bound, the values of the leading term dominate the values of all lower-degree terms. The sign of the leading term of a polynomial also determines the end behavior of the polynomial function.

| LEADING TERM | EXAMPLE $p(x) =$ | $\lim\limits_{x \to -\infty} p(x) =$ | $\lim\limits_{x \to \infty} p(x) =$ |
|---|---|---|---|
| Positive sign, even degree | $7x^4$ | $\infty$ | $\infty$ |
| Negative sign, even degree | $-7x^4$ | $-\infty$ | $-\infty$ |
| Positive sign, odd degree | $7x^5$ | $-\infty$ | $\infty$ |
| Negative sign, odd degree | $-7x^5$ | $\infty$ | $-\infty$ |

**Example 1**

Describe the end behavior of $p(x) = 7x^5 + x^4 - 8x^2 - 5x + 3$.

Solution: The leading term, $7x^5$, has a positive sign and an odd degree (5). Therefore $\lim\limits_{x \to -\infty} p(x) = -\infty$ and $\lim\limits_{x \to \infty} p(x) = \infty$. A graph is shown below.

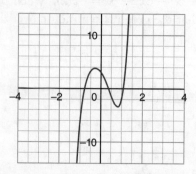

**Example 2**

Describe the end behavior of $p(x) = -x^4 + 6x^3 - 8x^2 - 4x + 8$.

Solution: The leading term, $-x^4$, has a negative sign and has an even degree (4). Therefore, $\lim\limits_{x \to -\infty} p(x) = -\infty$ and $\lim\limits_{x \to \infty} p(x) = -\infty$. A graph is shown as follows:

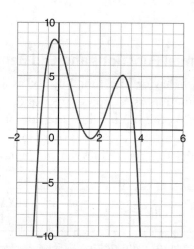

# Rational Functions

A rational function is represented as a quotient of two polynomial functions. It can be represented as $f(x) = \dfrac{p(x)}{q(x)}$, where $p(x)$ and $q(x)$ are polynomials and $q(x) \neq 0$.

## Rational Functions and End Behavior

The end behavior of a rational function will be affected by the numerator and denominator polynomials with greatest degree, as its values will dominate the values of the rational function for input values of large magnitude. For input values of large magnitude, a polynomial is dominated by its leading term. Therefore, the end behavior of a rational function can be understood by examining the quotient of leading terms.

| LEADING TERM DEGREE | ASYMPTOTE | $\lim_{x \to -\infty} f(x) =$ | $\lim_{x \to \infty} f(x) =$ |
|---|---|---|---|
| Numerator < Denominator | Horizontal asymptote $y = 0$ | 0 | 0 |
| Numerator = Denominator | Horizontal asymptote $y = \dfrac{a}{b}$, where $a$ is the leading coefficient of the numerator, and $b$ is the leading coefficient of the denominator | $\dfrac{a}{b}$ | $\dfrac{a}{b}$ |
| Numerator > Denominator | End behavior is similar to the quotient of the two polynomials without the remainder | | |

**Example 1**
Describe the end behavior of $f(x) = \dfrac{3x^3 - 8x^2 - 4x + 2}{2x^3 - 2x^2 + 5x - 1}$.

Solution: The leading term of the numerator is $3x^3$ and the leading term of the denominator is $2x^3$. Because the degrees of the leading term of the numerator and denominator are equal, there is a horizontal asymptote at $y = \dfrac{3}{2}$. A graph is shown as follows:

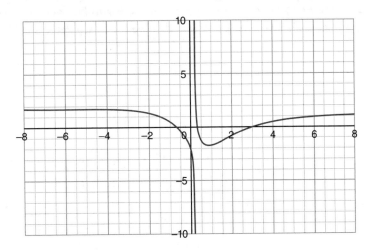

The end behavior can be described as $\lim_{x \to -\infty} f(x) = \dfrac{3}{2}$ and $\lim_{x \to \infty} f(x) = \dfrac{3}{2}$.

**Example 2**
Describe the end behavior of $f(x) = \dfrac{2x^2 + 8x + 9}{x^3 + x + 4}$.

Solution: The leading term of the numerator is $2x^2$ and the leading term of the denominator is $x^3$. Because the degree of the leading term of the numerator is less than the degree of the leading term of the denominator, there is a horizontal asymptote at $y = 0$. A graph is shown as follows:

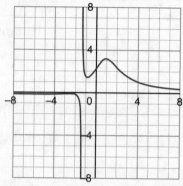

The end behavior can be described as $\lim_{x \to -\infty} f(x) = 0$ and $\lim_{x \to \infty} f(x) = 0$.

## Rational Functions and Zeros

The real zeros of a rational function correspond to the real zeros of the numerator for such values in its domain.

### Example

Find the zeros of $f(x) = \dfrac{x^2 - 2x - 15}{x^2 - 5x - 14}$.

Solution: We need to find the zeros of the numerator, $x^2 - 2x - 15$. Because $p(x)$ is a quadratic, we can factor or use the quadratic formula. Factoring we get $p(x) = (x + 3)(x - 5)$. If we set each factor equal to 0 and solve for $x$, we get $x = -3$ and $x = 5$.

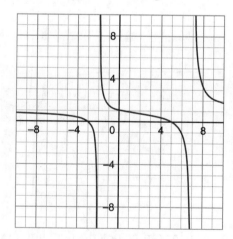

Because both of these values are in the domain of $f(x)$, the zeros of $f(x) = \dfrac{x^2 - 2x - 15}{x^2 - 5x - 14}$ are $x = -3$ or $x = 5$. The domain of the function is all real numbers except for input values that make the denominator zero. In this case, $x = 7$ and $x = -2$ are the values that make the denominator zero. Therefore, the domain is all real numbers except 7 and $-2$.

Also notice that there is a horizontal asymptote at $y = 1$ because the degree of the numerator equals the degree of the denominator, and the coefficients of the leading terms are $\frac{1}{1}$.

## Rational Functions and Vertical Asymptotes

A rational function will have a *vertical asymptote* when the denominator is equal to zero, provided that the numerator is not equal to zero at the same time. If the value of $a$ is a real zero of the polynomial in the denominator and is also not a real zero of the polynomial in the numerator, then the graph of the rational function has a vertical asymptote at $x = a$. If the rational function has zeros in both the numerator and the denominator, the graph will have a vertical asymptote if the multiplicity of the zero of the denominator is > the multiplicity of the zeros in the numerator.

Near the vertical asymptote, $x = a$, of a rational function, the values of the polynomial in the denominator are arbitrarily close to zero, so the values of the rational function $r$ increase or decrease without bound. Using math notation, we say $\lim_{x \to a^+} r(x) = \infty$ or $\lim_{x \to a^+} r(x) = -\infty$ for input values near $a$ and greater than $a$, and $\lim_{x \to a^-} r(x) = \infty$ or $\lim_{x \to a^-} r(x) = -\infty$ for input values near $a$ and less than $a$.

To find the equations of vertical asymptotes:

1. Simplify the rational function to the lowest terms by factoring the numerator and denominator if possible.
2. Divide out (my high school calculus teacher hated using the term "cancel") all common factors.
3. Set the denominator of the simplified fraction equal to zero and solve. If $x = a$ is a real zero of the denominator, then $x = a$ is the equation of the vertical asymptote.

### Example

What are the equations of all vertical asymptotes of the function $f(x) = \dfrac{2x^2 - 4x - 30}{x^2 + 4x + 3}$?

Solution: We need to factor both the numerator and the denominator.

$$f(x) = \frac{2x^2 - 4x - 30}{x^2 + 4x + 3} = \frac{2(x+3)(x-5)}{(x+3)(x+1)} = \frac{2(x-5)}{x+1}$$

Setting the denominator $x + 1 = 0$ gives a vertical asymptote of $x = -1$. A graph is shown as follows:

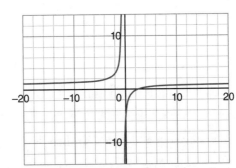

The vertical asymptotes can be written as $\lim_{x \to -1^-} f(x) = \infty$ and $\lim_{x \to -1^+} f(x) = -\infty$.

The horizontal asymptotes/end behavior can be written as $\lim_{x \to -\infty} f(x) = 2$ and $\lim_{x \to \infty} f(x) = 2$.

## Rational Functions and Holes

A rational function will have a *hole* when the multiplicity of a real zero in the numerator is greater than or equal to its multiplicity in the denominator. If the graph of a rational function has a hole at $x = c$, then the location of the hole can be determined by examining the output values corresponding to input values sufficiently close to $c$. If input values sufficiently close to $c$ correspond to output values arbitrarily close to $L$, then the hole is located at the point with coordinates $(c, L)$. The corresponding math notation is $\lim_{x \to c} f(x) = L$.

**Example**

Where is the location of the hole of the function $f(x) = \dfrac{3x^2 - 24x + 48}{2x^2 - 18x + 40}$?

Solution: We need to factor both the numerator and the denominator and then divide out common factors.

$$f(x) = \frac{3x^2 - 24x + 48}{2x^2 - 18x + 40} = \frac{3(x^2 - 8x + 16)}{2(x^2 - 9x + 20)} = \frac{3(x-4)^2}{2(x-4)(x-5)} = \frac{3(x-4)}{2(x-5)}$$

Because $(x - 4)$ is a factor with equal to or higher degree in the numerator than the denominator, setting $x - 4 = 0$ gives us a hole at $x = 4$. Substituting $x = 4$ into the simplified equation gives a $y$-coordinate of the hole of 0, which means the hole is located at (4, 0). In mathematical notation, $\lim_{x \to 4} f(x) = 0$.

It should be noted that graphing technology typically does not show holes in graphs. When showing a graph with a hole, an open circle should be placed at the hole.

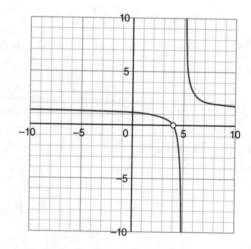

As a review, setting the denominator $2(x - 5)$ gives $x = 5$ as the vertical asymptote. The leading term of the numerator is $3x^2$ and the leading term of the denominator is $2x^2$, which means they have equal degrees, so there is a horizontal asymptote at $y = \dfrac{3}{2}$. The domain of $f$ is $\{x : x \neq 4, \text{ or } x \neq 5\}$. The range is $\{y : y \neq 0, y \neq \dfrac{3}{2}\}$

The vertical asymptotes can be written as $\lim\limits_{x \to 5^-} f(x) = -\infty$ and $\lim\limits_{x \to 5^+} f(x) = \infty$.

The horizontal asymptotes/end behavior can be written as $\lim\limits_{x \to -\infty} f(x) = \dfrac{3}{2}$ and $\lim\limits_{x \to \infty} f(x) = \dfrac{3}{2}$.

| TYPE | WHEN | EXAMPLE | GRAPH |
|---|---|---|---|
| Vertical Asymptote | Multiplicity of real zero in numerator < multiplicity of real zero in denominator | $f(x) = \dfrac{x+1}{(x+1)^2}$ |  |
| Hole | Multiplicity of real zero in numerator ≥ multiplicity of real zero in denominator | $f(x) = \dfrac{(x+1)^2}{x+1}$ | |

**KEY IDEA**

The factored form of a polynomial or rational function provides information about zeros, $x$-intercepts, asymptotes, holes, domain, and range.

The standard form of a polynomial or rational function provides information about the end behaviors of the function.

## Polynomial Division

*Polynomial long division* is an algebraic process similar to numerical long division involving quotient and remainder. If the polynomial $f$ is divided by the polynomial $g$, then $f$ can be written as $f(x) = g(x)q(x) + r(x)$, where $q$ is the quotient, $r$ is the remainder, and the degree of $r$ is less than the degree of $g$. The result of polynomial long division is helpful in finding equations of slant asymptotes for graphs of rational functions. A *slant asymptote* is a linear, nonhorizontal asymptote and occurs when the degree of the numerator is one more than the degree of the denominator.

### Example

What is the equation of the slant asymptote of $f(x) = \dfrac{8x^3 + 10x^2 + 7x + 4}{4x^2 + 3x - 1}$?

**STRATEGY**

Solution: Use long division

$$4x^2 + 3x - 1 \overline{\smash{)}\, 8x^3 + 10x^2 + 7x + 4}$$

Step 1: Divide the leading terms of each polynomial. In this case $\dfrac{8x^3}{4x^2} = 2x$. This is the first term in the quotient.

Step 2: Multiply the result by each term in the divisor. In this case, multiply $2x\,(4x^2 + 3x - 1) = 8x^3 + 6x^2 - 2x$

$$
\begin{array}{r}
2x \phantom{{}+10x^2+7x+4} \\
4x^2 + 3x - 1 \overline{\smash{\big)}\; 8x^3 + 10x^2 + 7x + 4} \\
8x^3 + 6x^2 - 2x \phantom{{}+7x+4}
\end{array}
$$

Step 3: Subtract that result from the dividend, then bring down the remaining term(s). This leaves $4x^2 + 9x + 4$.

$$
\begin{array}{r}
2x \phantom{{}+10x^2+7x+4} \\
4x^2 + 3x - 1 \overline{\smash{\big)}\; 8x^3 + 10x^2 + 7x + 4} \\
-(8x^3 + 6x^2 - 2x) \phantom{{}+4} \\
\hline
4x^2 + 9x + 4
\end{array}
$$

Step 4: Continue the process until the degree of the remainder is less than the degree of the divisor.

$\dfrac{4x^2}{4x^2} = 1$. This will be the second term in the quotient.

$$
\begin{array}{r}
2x + 1 \phantom{{}+7x+4} \\
4x^2 + 3x - 1 \overline{\smash{\big)}\; 8x^3 + 10x^2 + 7x + 4} \\
-(8x^3 + 6x^2 - 2x) \phantom{{}+4} \\
\hline
4x^2 + 9x + 4 \\
-(4x^2 + 3x - 1) \\
\hline
6x + 5
\end{array}
$$

The equation of the slant asymptote is $y = 2x + 1$. A graph is shown as follows:

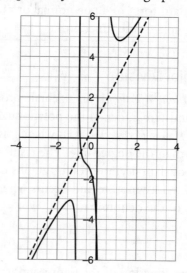

## Binomial Theorem

Suppose we have a binomial expression such as $(2x - y)^4$ that needs to be expanded. Hopefully, you won't be writing out $(2x - y)$ four times and then multiplying each pair until the binomial is expanded. Luckily, there is an easier way. The binomial theorem uses the values in a row of Pascal's Triangle to help expand the binomial expression.

## Pascal's Triangle

Pascal's Triangle is a triangular array that is constructed by starting and ending with the number 1. The interior elements are found by adding adjacent elements in preceding rows. The first four rows are shown as follows:

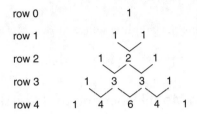

### Example

Write $(2x - y)^4$ in expanded form.

Solution: The entries of row 4 are the coefficients in the expansion. Each of these coefficients is multiplied by each term raised to a power according to the following algorithm: The sum of the exponents in each term will be 4. The powers of $(2x)$ begin at 4 and decrease to 0. The powers of $(-y)$ begin at 0 and increase to 4.

$$(2x - y)^4 = 1(2x)^4 (-y)^0 + 4(2x)^3 (-y)^1 + 6(2x)^2 (-y)^2 + 4(2x)^1 (-y)^3 + 1(2x)^0 (-y)^4$$

$$= 1(16x^4) (1) + 4(8x^3) (-y) + 6(4x^2) (y^2) + 4(2x) (-y^3) + 1(1) (y^4)$$

$$= 16x^4 - 32x^3y + 24x^2y^2 - 8xy^3 + y^4$$

**Fun Fact:** Blaise Pascal was a French mathematician, physicist, and philosopher who laid the foundation for the modern theory of probabilities and formulated what is known as Pascal's principle of pressure.

# Transformation of Functions

A function transformation is when we take a function and either move it to another location on the grid (translation) or stretch or squeeze the shape of the graph (dilation).

| TRANSFORMATION | $g(X) =$ | CHANGE | NOTE |
|---|---|---|---|
| Vertical translation | $f(x) + k$ | A vertical translation of $k$ units | |
| Horizontal translation | $f(x + h)$ | A horizontal translation of $-h$ units | |
| Vertical dilation | $a f(x)$, $a \neq 0$ | A vertical dilation of $|a|$ | If $a < 0$, reflection over $x$-axis |
| Horizontal dilation | $f(bx)$, $b \neq 0$ | A horizontal dilation of $|1/b|$ | If $b < 0$, reflection over $y$-axis |
| Reflection | $-g(x)$ | Reflection across the $x$-axis | |
| Reflection | $g(-x)$ | Reflection across the $y$-axis | |
| Reflection | $-g(-x)$ | Rotation of 180° about origin | |

**Example**

Explain how the graph of $g(x) = (-2x + 7)^2 + 4$ is related to the graph of $f(x) = x^2$.

Solution: The order of transformation is a dilation and then a translation. Therefore, the equation needs to be rewritten as $a(f(b(x+c))) + d$. In this case it would be $\left(-2\left(x - \dfrac{7}{2}\right)\right)^2 + 4$.

This means the graph is reflected over the $y$-axis and dilated horizontally by a factor of $\dfrac{1}{2}$. Then the graph is a translation right by $\dfrac{7}{2}$ units and up 4 units.

## Function Model Selection and Construction

Identifying an appropriate function type to construct a function model for a given scenario is important. Linear functions model data sets that demonstrate roughly constant rates of change. Quadratic functions model data sets that demonstrate roughly linear rates of change, or data sets that are roughly symmetric with a unique maximum or minimum value. The term "roughly" is used because it is rare to find real-world scenarios that will match a model perfectly.

Quadratic functions can also model geometric contexts involving area, or two dimensions. Cubic functions can be used to model geometric contexts involving volume, or three dimensions. Polynomial functions model data sets with multiple real zeros or multiple maxima or minima. A polynomial function of degree $n$ models data sets that demonstrate roughly constant nonzero $n$th differences. Rational functions model data sets involving quantities that are inversely proportional.

And sometimes there isn't just one function that models a scenario, due to different characteristics over different intervals. You might have to use a piecewise-defined function over nonoverlapping domain intervals to model your scenario.

## Assumptions and Restrictions Related to Building a Function Model

A model may have underlying assumptions about what is consistent in the model and about how quantities change together. A model may require domain restrictions and range restrictions based on mathematical clues, contextual clues, or extreme values in the data set.

**Example**

The game Monopoly is played on a square board with 40 spaces that have names. Players roll the dice and travel around the board the number of spaces equal to the number rolled. Twenty-eight of these spaces are properties that the first player to land on can purchase. The table shows the number of spaces a property is from the starting point and the cost of the property. Calculate a model to estimate the rate of change of the cost of the property as the number of spaces from the starting point changes. Be sure to state any restrictions necessary.

| PROPERTY | SPACES FROM GO | COST |
|---|---|---|
| Mediterranean Avenue | 1 | 60 |
| Baltic Avenue | 3 | 60 |
| Reading Railroad | 5 | 200 |
| Oriental Avenue | 6 | 100 |
| Vermont Avenue | 8 | 100 |
| Connecticut Avenue | 9 | 120 |
| St. Charles Place | 11 | 140 |
| Electric Company | 12 | 150 |
| States Avenue | 13 | 140 |
| Virginia Avenue | 14 | 160 |
| Penn Railroad | 15 | 200 |
| St. James Place | 16 | 180 |
| Tennessee Avenue | 18 | 180 |
| New York Avenue | 19 | 200 |
| Kentucky Avenue | 21 | 220 |
| Indiana Avenue | 23 | 220 |
| Illinois Avenue | 24 | 240 |
| B & O Railroad | 25 | 200 |
| Atlantic Avenue | 26 | 260 |
| Ventnor Avenue | 27 | 260 |
| Water Works | 28 | 150 |
| Marvin Gardens | 29 | 280 |
| Pacific Avenue | 31 | 300 |
| North Carolina Avenue | 32 | 300 |
| Pennsylvania Avenue | 34 | 320 |
| Short Line Railroad | 35 | 200 |
| Park Place | 37 | 350 |
| Boardwalk | 39 | 400 |

Solution: The graph of the data set and least-squares regression model is shown as follows. The domain is the set of integers in the interval $0 < x < 40$. The equation is predicted cost $\approx 67.28 + 6.78d$, where $d$ represents distance from the starting point. Therefore, for every space further from GO a player moves, the predicted cost of the property increases by approximately $6.78.

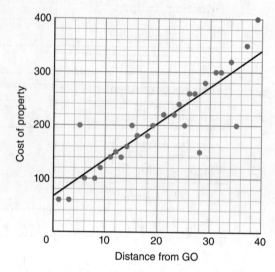

To determine if a model is appropriate, you should check that there is not an obvious pattern in the residuals. A residual is the difference between the observed value and the predicted value and is often referred to as the error of the model. In this case, the railroads and utility properties do not fit the model, so a linear model may not be appropriate.

# ❭ Rapid Review

## Function

- A function is a mathematical relation that maps a set of input values to a set of output values such that each input value is mapped to exactly one output value.
- The set of input values is called the domain of the function, and the set of output values is called the range of the function.
- The variable representing input values is called the independent variable, and the variable representing the output values is called the dependent variable.
- The average rate of change of a function over an interval of the function's domain is the value of the slope between the two points.
- A function is increasing over an interval of its domain if as the $x$ values increase, the $y$ values also increase.
- A function is decreasing over an interval of its domain if as the $x$ values increase, the $y$ values decrease.
- The point at which a function changes from increasing to decreasing is known as its maximum.
- The point at which a function changes from decreasing to increasing is known as its minimum.
- The graph of a function is concave up on intervals in which the rate of change is increasing and concave down on intervals in which the rate of change is decreasing.

- A point of inflection of a polynomial function occurs when the rate of change of the function changes from decreasing to increasing or from increasing to decreasing. It is also the point at which the polynomial function changes from concave up to concave down or from concave down to concave up.
- The zeros of a function are the points on the $x$-axis where the graph crosses the $x$-axis, also known as $x$-intercepts. The point(s) at which the graph crosses the $y$-axis is known as the $y$-intercept(s).

## Polynomial Function

- A nonconstant polynomial function of $x$ is any function of the form $p(x) = a_n x^n + a_{n-1}x^{n-1} + a_{n-2}x^{n-2} + \cdots + a_2 x^2 + a_1 x + a_0$, where $n$ is a positive integer, $a_i$ is a real number for each $i$ from 1 to $n$, and $a_n$ is nonzero.
- The degree of the polynomial is $n$, the largest exponent. The leading term is $a_n x^n$, and the leading coefficient is $a_n$.
- If a linear factor $(x - a)$ is repeated $n$ times, the corresponding zero of the polynomial function has multiplicity $n$.
- An even function is graphically symmetric over the line $x = 0$ and analytically has the property $f(-x) = f(x)$. A polynomial is an even function if it is of the form $p(x) = a_n x^n$, where each exponent of the polynomial is even.
- An odd function is graphically symmetric about the origin $(0, 0)$ and analytically has the property $f(-x) = -f(x)$. A polynomial is an odd function if it is of the form $p(x) = a_n x^n$, where each exponent of the polynomial is odd.
- The end behavior of a function $p$ is a description of what happens to the values $p(x)$ of the function as $x$ grows larger and larger in magnitude, meaning as $x \to \infty$ and as $x \to -\infty$.
- The sign of the leading term of a polynomial determines the end behavior of the polynomial function.

## Rational Functions

- A rational function is represented as a quotient of two polynomial functions. It can be represented as $f(x) = \dfrac{p(x)}{q(x)}$, where $p(x)$ and $q(x)$ are polynomials and $q(x) \neq 0$.
- The end behavior of a rational function can be understood by examining the quotient of leading terms.
- A horizontal asymptote at $y = 0$ occurs when the leading term degree of the numerator is smaller than the leading term degree of the denominator.
- A horizontal asymptote at $y = \dfrac{a}{b}$ occurs when the leading term degree of the numerator is equal to the leading term degree of the denominator. $a$ and $b$ represent the leading coefficient of the numerator and denominator respectively.
- When the leading term degree of the numerator is larger than the leading term degree of the denominator, the end behavior is similar to the end behavior of the quotient of the leading terms.
- The real zeros of a rational function correspond to the real zeros of the numerator for such values in its domain.
- A vertical asymptote occurs when the denominator of a rational function approaches zero.
- A hole occurs when the multiplicity of a real zero in the numerator is greater than or equal to its multiplicity in the denominator.

### Models

- Identifying an appropriate function type to construct a function model for a given scenario is important.
- A model may have underlying assumptions about what is consistent in the model and about how quantities change together.

### Miscellaneous

- Binomial theorem is used to expand $(x + y)^n$.

## > Review Questions

### Basic Level

1. Given the function $f(x) = 2x^2 + 6x - 1$, what is the domain and range of $f$? If the function $g(x) = f(3x) - 4$, what is the domain and range of the transformed graph of $g$?
2. Use limit notation to describe the end behavior of the graph of the polynomial $p(x)$ shown.

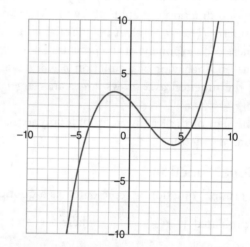

3. Given the following table of values for a polynomial function $f(x)$, what is the average rate of change of $f(x)$ in the interval $[3, 5]$?

| $x$ | 1 | 2 | 3 | 4 | 5 | 6 |
|---|---|---|---|---|---|---|
| $f(x)$ | 5 | 12 | 27 | 56 | 105 | 180 |

4. On what interval is the function $f(x) = 2x^3 - 6x^2 + 2x - 5$ increasing?
5. Is the function $f(x) = 6x^3 - 2x^2$ even, odd, or neither? Explain.
6. Given the following table of values for a polynomial function $f(x)$, for which interval of length 1 is the average rate of change the smallest number or smallest magnitude?

| $x$ | 0 | 1 | 2 | 3 | 4 | 5 |
|---|---|---|---|---|---|---|
| $f(x)$ | 8 | 12 | 20 | 21 | 17 | 10 |

7. If $f(x) = -3x^3 + 2x^2 - 4x + 8$, what is the average rate of change from $x = 2$ to $x = 5$?

**8.** How many distict real roots does the function $r(x) = \dfrac{(x+5)^2(x-1)}{(x-3)(x+5)}$ have?

**9.** Find the third term in the expansion of $(5x - 2y)^6$.

## Advanced Level

**10.** Where is the location of the hole(s) in the function $f(x) = \dfrac{(x-5)^3(x-7)(x+1)^2}{(x-5)(x-7)^2}$?

**11.** Approximate the point(s) of inflection in the graph shown.

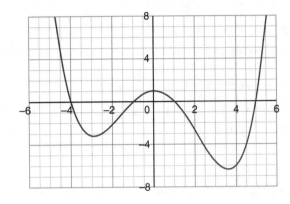

**12.** If $p(x) = x^4 - 31x^2 - 30x$ has a real zero at $x = -5$, find the other zeros.

**13.** Find all horizontal and vertical asymptotes of the function $f(x) = \dfrac{x^3 + x^2 - 12x}{4x^3 - 16x^2 + 12x}$.

**14.** Using limit notation, describe the end behavior of $r(x) = \dfrac{5x^3 + x^2 - 30x + 1}{x^2 - 3x + 2}$.

**15.** Given the table of values shown for the polynomial $p(x)$, what is the value of $p(5)$?

| $x$ | −2 | −1 | 0 | 1 | 2 | 3 |
|---|---|---|---|---|---|---|
| $p(x)$ | −49 | −15 | −5 | −7 | −9 | 1 |

**16.** Using limit notation, describe the end behavior of $r(x) = \dfrac{3x^2 - 7x - 2}{2x^2 - 7x + 6}$.

**17.** If a polynomial of even degree has zeros at 4 (multiplicity 2), 1 (multiplicity 3), −3 (multiplicity 1), and −5 (multiplicity 2), sketch a possible graph.

**18.** Expand $(3x - y)^5$.

**19.** A graph of a function $f$ passes through the point (6, 5). If $g$ is a translation of $f$ and passes through the point (10, 3), what is the transformation that maps $f$ to $g$?

**20.** The height (in meters) $t$ seconds after an object is thrown vertically up is given by the formula $h(t) = -4.9t^2 + 25t + 1$. When does the object reach its maximum height?

**21.** Find all horizontal and vertical asymptotes of $r(x) = \dfrac{x^2 - 2x - 8}{x^2 - x - 6}$.

**22.** For what values is $p(x) = x^3 - 3x^2 - 10x + 24$ positive? For what values is $p(x)$ decreasing?

# ❯ Answers and Explanations

1. • The domain of $f(x) = 2x^2 + 6x - 1$ is all real numbers.

   • The $x$-coordinate of the vertex of a parabola is $-\dfrac{b}{2a}$, where the parabola is defined as $ax^2 + bx + c$.

   • The $x$-coordinate is $x = -\dfrac{b}{2a} = -\dfrac{6}{2(2)} = -\dfrac{3}{2} = -1.5$.

   • The $y$-coordinate is $f(-1.5) = 2(-1.5)^2 + 6(-1.5) - 1 = -5.5$.
   • Or you can use the calculate minimum feature of a graphing calculator to determine that the minimum point is $(-1.5, -5.5)$.
   • The range is $y \geq -5.5$ or $[-5.5, \infty)$.

   • The transformed function $g(x) = f(3x) - 4$ has a vertical translation of $-4$ units and a horizontal dilation of $\dfrac{1}{3}$.
   • The domain of $g(x)$ is all real numbers.
   • The minimum point is translated 4 units down, which is $(-0.500, -9.500)$.
   • The range is $y \geq -9.5$ or $[-9.5, \infty)$.

2. • As $x$ increases, the graph increases. This is written $\lim\limits_{x \to \infty} f(x) = \infty$.

   • As $x$ decreases, the graph decreases. This is written $\lim\limits_{x \to -\infty} f(x) = -\infty$.

3. • The average rate of change is defined as $\dfrac{f(x_2) - f(x_1)}{x_2 - x_1}$.

   • Using the points $(3, 27)$ and $(5, 105)$ gives us $\dfrac{105 - 27}{5 - 3} = \dfrac{78}{2} = 39$.

4. • The graph of $f(x) = 2x^3 - 6x^2 + 2x - 5$ is shown as follows:

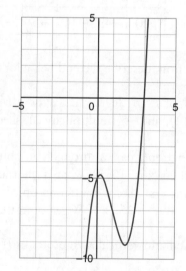

   • Using the calculate maximum feature of a graphing calculator, the local maximum point is $(0.184, -4.823)$.
   • Using the calculate minimum feature of a graphing calculator, the local minimum point is $(1.816, -9.177)$.
   • The graph is increasing $(-\infty, 0.184)$ and $(1.816, \infty)$.
   • The graph is decreasing $(0.184, 1.816)$.

**5.** • To prove it is odd, we need to show $f(-x) = -f(x)$.
  • $f(-x) = 6(-x)^3 - 2(-x)^2 = -6x^3 - 2x^2 \neq -f(x)$, so it is not odd.
  • To prove it is even, we need to show $f(-x) = f(x)$.
  • $f(-x) = 6(-x)^3 - 2(-x)^2 = -6x^3 - 2x^2 \neq f(x)$, so it is not even.
  • The function $f(x) = 6x^3 - 2x^2$ is neither odd nor even.

**6.** • In the interval [0, 1] the rate of change is $\dfrac{12-8}{1-0} = 4$.

  • In the interval [1, 2] the rate of change is $\dfrac{20-12}{2-1} = 8$.

  • In the interval [2, 3] the rate of change is $\dfrac{21-20}{3-2} = 1$.

  • In the interval [3, 4] the rate of change is $\dfrac{17-21}{4-3} = -4$.

  • In the interval [4, 5] the rate of change is $\dfrac{10-17}{5-4} = -7$.

  • The interval [4, 5] has the smallest rate of change.

**7.** • The rate of change is $\dfrac{f(5)-f(2)}{5-2} = \dfrac{-337-(-16)}{5-2} = \dfrac{-321}{3} = -107$.

**8.** • The function $r(x) = \dfrac{(x+5)^2(x-1)}{(x-3)(x+5)}$ can be simplified to $r(x) = \dfrac{(x+5)(x-1)}{(x-3)}$.

  • The zero(s) can be found by setting the numerator = 0 and solving for $x$.

  • In this case $x - 1 = 0$, so $x = 1$ is a real zero. The function has a hole at $x = -5$, so $x = -5$ is not a zero.

**9.** • Row 6 of Pascal's Triangle is 1   6   15   20   15   6   1.
  • The third term would be $15(5x)^4(-2y)^2 = 15(625x^4)(4y^2) = 37500x^4y^2$.

**10.** • The function $f(x) = \dfrac{(x-5)^3(x-7)(x+1)^2}{(x-5)(x-7)^2}$ can be simplified to $f(x) = \dfrac{(x-5)^2(x+1)^2}{(x-7)}$.

  • Because the multiplicity of $(x - 5)$ in the numerator is 3, which is larger than the multiplicity in the denominator of 1, there will be a hole at $x - 5 = 0$, or $x = 5$.
  • Substituting $x = 5$ into the simplified equation gives a $y$-coordinate of the hole of 0, which means the hole is located at (5, 0).
  • In mathematical notation, $\lim\limits_{x \to 5} f(x) = 0$.

  • Because the multiplicity of $(x - 7)$ is 1 in the numerator and 2 in the denominator, a vertical asymptote occurs at $x = 7$.

**11.** • A point of inflection occurs when the polynomial function changes concavity.
  • The graph changes from concave up to concave down approximately at the point (−1.5, −1.016) and changes from concave down to concave up approximately at the point (2, −2.7).

**12.** • If $x = -5$ is a zero of $p(x)$, the other zeros can be found by dividing $p(x) = x^4 - 31x^2 - 30x$ by $(x + 5)$.
  • Using division results in the quotient $q(x) = x^3 - 5x^2 - 6x$.
  • Factoring $q(x) = x^3 - 5x^2 - 6x$ gives us $q(x) = x(x - 6)(x + 1)$.
  • Setting $q(x) = 0$ and setting each factor = 0 gives us the other zeros of $x = 0$, $x = 6$, or $x = -1$.

**13.** • A vertical asymptote occurs when the denominator is equal to zero and has a higher multiplicity of zeros than the numerator.

• Factoring $f(x) = \dfrac{x^3 + x^2 - 12x}{4x^3 - 16x^2 + 12x}$ gives us $\dfrac{x(x+4)(x-3)}{4x(x-1)(x-3)} = \dfrac{(x+4)}{4(x-1)}$.

• Setting the denominator = 0 and solving gives us $x = 1$. So $x = 1$ is a vertical asymptote.

• The degree of both numerator and denominator are 3, so there will be a horizontal asymptote.

• The equation of the horizontal asymptote is $y = \dfrac{a}{b}$, where $a$ = leading coefficient of the numerator and $b$ = leading coefficient of the denominator. Therefore, the horizontal asymptote is $y = \dfrac{1}{4}$.

**14.** • The end behavior of a rational function can be found by first looking at the leading term of the numerator and denominator.

• The leading term of the numerator is $5x^3$ and the leading term of the denominator is $x^2$. When the degree of the numerator > degree of the denominator, the end behavior is similar to the quotient of the two polynomials (without the remainder).

• Dividing $r(x) = \dfrac{5x^3 + x^2 - 30x + 1}{x^2 - 3x + 2}$ gives a quotient of $5x + 16$.

• $\lim\limits_{x \to -\infty} r(x) = 5x + 16$ and $\lim\limits_{x \to \infty} r(x) = 5x + 16$

**15.** • In order to find the degree of the polynomial, we need to find the differences until the differences in $y$ values are constant.

| $x$ | $y$ | First difference | Second difference | Third difference |
|-----|-----|------------------|-------------------|------------------|
| −2 | −49 | | | |
| −1 | −15 | −15 − (−49) = 34 | | |
| 0 | −5 | −5 − (−15) = 10 | 10 − 34 = −24 | |
| 1 | −7 | −7 − (−5) = −2 | −2 − 10 = −12 | −12 − (−24) = 12 |
| 2 | −9 | −9 − (−7) = −2 | −2 − (−2) = 0 | 0 − (−12) = 12 |
| 3 | 1 | 1 − (−9) = 10 | 10 − (−2) = 12 | 12 − 0 = 12 |

• Because the third differences are all the same, the table models a cubic function.
• After entering the values from the table into a graphing calculator and using the cubic regression feature, the cubic equation is $p(x) = 2x^3 - 6x^2 + 2x - 5$.
• So $p(5) = 2(5)^3 - 6(5)^2 + 2(5) - 5 = 105$.

**16.** • The degree of the leading term of the numerator and denominator are equal, so there will be a horizontal asymptote at $y = \dfrac{a}{b}$ where $a$ is the leading coefficient of the numerator and $b$ is the leading coefficient of the denominator.

• The horizontal asymptote is a $y = \dfrac{3}{2}$.

• $\lim\limits_{x \to -\infty} r(x) = \dfrac{3}{2}$ and $\lim\limits_{x \to \infty} r(x) = \dfrac{3}{2}$.

**17.** • A polynomial of even degree has end behavior (as $x$ gets larger and as $x$ gets smaller) that approaches $\infty$ (or $-\infty$ if the leading term is negative).
   • An even multiplicity means the graph will be tangent (won't cross) to the $x$-axis at that point.
   • An odd multiplicity means the graph will cross the $x$-axis at that point.
   • Two possible graphs are shown.

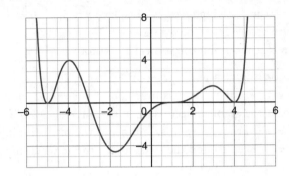

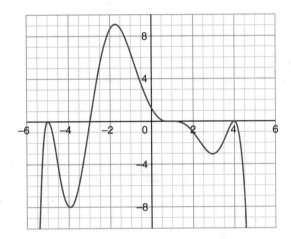

**18.** • The entries of row 5 of Pascal's Triangle are the coefficients in the expansion. The sum of the exponents in each term will be 5. The powers of $(3x)$ begin at 5 and decrease to 0. The powers of $(-y)$ begin at 0 and increase to 5.

   • $(3x - y)^5 = 1(3x)^5 (-y)^0 + 5(3x)^4 (-y)^1 + 10(3x)^3 (-y)^2 + 10(3x)^2 (-y)^3 + 5(3x)^1 (-y)^4 + 1(3x)^0 (-y)^5$

   $\qquad = 1(243x^5)(1) + 5(81x^4)(-y) + 10(27x^3)(y^2) + 10(9x^2)(-y^3) + 5(3x)(y^4) + 1(1)(-y^5)$

   $\qquad = 243x^5 - 405x^4y + 270x^3y^2 - 90x^2y^3 + 15xy^4 - y^5$

**19.** • $f$ contains the point $(6, 5)$ and $g$ contains the point $(10, 3)$. This means that $x$ has a horizontal translation of $10 - 6 = 4$ units and a vertical translation of $3 - 5 = -2$ units.
   • This gives us $g(x) = f(x - 4) - 2$.

**20.** • Using the graphing calculator to graph $h(t) = -4.9t^2 + 25t + 1$ shows that the quadratic has a maximum value.

   • The $x$-coordinate of the vertex of a parabola is $-\dfrac{b}{2a}$, where the parabola is defined as $ax^2 + bx + c$.

   • The $t$-coordinate is $t = -\dfrac{b}{2a} = -\dfrac{25}{2(-4.9)} = -\dfrac{25}{-9.8} = 2.551$.

   • The $y$-coordinate is $h(2.551) = -4.9(2.551)^2 + 25(2.551) + 1 = 32.888$.
   • Or using the trace feature of the calculator shows a maximum value of $(2.551, 32.888)$.
   • The object reaches its maximum height of $32.888$ meters at $2.551$ seconds.

**21.** • The rational function $r(x) = \dfrac{x^2 - 2x - 8}{x^2 - x - 6}$ factors as $r(x) = \dfrac{(x-4)(x+2)}{(x-3)(x+2)} = \dfrac{x-4}{x-3}$.

• Because the degree of the numerator = degree of the denominator, the horizontal asymptote is at the coefficient of the leading coefficients, or $y = \dfrac{1}{1} = 1$.

• Setting the denominator = 0 and solving gives $x - 3 = 0$, or $x = 3$.

• There is a hole in the graph at $x + 2 = 0$, or $x = -2$.

• The horizontal asymptote is at $y = 1$ and the vertical asymptote at $x = 3$.

**22.** • Use the graphing calculator to graph $p(x) = x^3 - 3x^2 - 10x + 24$.

• Using the calculate feature we see that the maximum point is $(-1.082, 30.041)$ and the minimum point is $(3.082, -6.041)$. This means the graph is decreasing in the interval $(-1.082, 3.082)$.

• The graph is decreasing between the relative maximum and the relative minimum.

• Using the calculate feature we need to find the zeros to determine when the graph is positive.

• The zeros occur at $(-3, 0)$, $(2, 0)$, and $(4, 0)$.

• The graph is above the $x$-axis on the intervals $(-3, 2)$ and $(4, \infty)$.

• The maximum occurs between $x = -3$ and $x = 2$ and the maximum is at $x = -1.082$ with a $y$-value of 30.041; therefore, the graph is above the $y$-axis between $x = -3$ and $x = 2$.

• None of the zeros have an even multiplicity, so the graph crosses the $x$-axis at each of the zeros.

• Therefore, the graph is positive in the interval $(-3, 2)$ and $(4, \infty)$.

• A graph follows.

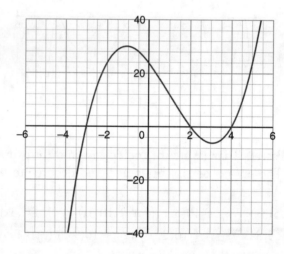

# CHAPTER 7

# Unit 2: Exponential and Logarithmic Functions

**IN THIS CHAPTER**

**Summary:** This chapter introduces arithmetic and geometric sequences and shows their relationship with linear and exponential functions. It also introduces the composition of functions and the inverse of a function. Using inverses, the logarithmic function is introduced, along with properties and graphs of exponential and logarithmic functions. Modeling aspects of contextual scenarios are also examined.

**Key Ideas**
- ✪ A sequence is an ordered list of numbers.
- ✪ Arithmetic sequences are sequences that have a common difference between terms.
- ✪ Geometric sequences are sequences that have a common ratio between terms.
- ✪ Arithmetic and geometric sequences are similar to linear and exponential functions.
- ✪ Functions can be combined using composition.
- ✪ Inverse functions are essential to solving equations and inequalities.
- ✪ Properties of exponential functions and their inverse function logarithms can be used to solve equations and inequalities.
- ✪ Exponential and logarithmic functions can be used to model many phenomena.

# Sequences

A *sequence* is an ordered list of numbers that often follow a specific pattern or function. Each number in a sequence is called a *term*. Each term has a whole number position such as first, second, or third.

### Example
The first 10 terms of a sequence are 1, 1, 2, 3, 5, 8, 13, 21, 34, 55. Find the next 3 terms.

Solution: The terms of the sequence are found by adding together the two preceding numbers in the sequence: $1 + 1 = 2$, $1 + 2 = 3$, $2 + 3 = 5$, and so on.

Term 11 = term 9 + term 10 = 34 + 55 = 89

Term 12 = term 10 + term 11 = 55 + 89 = 144

Term 13 = term 11 + term 12 = 89 + 144 = 233

 **Fun Fact:** The preceding sequence is known as the Fibonacci Sequence, named after Leonardo of Pisa, later known as Fibonacci. Many real-world illustrations of the Fibonacci Sequence are found in nature. If you count the seed spirals of a sunflower in one direction, you will get the numbers in the Fibonacci Sequence.

## Arithmetic Sequences

An *arithmetic sequence* is a sequence that has successive terms that have a constant rate of change or a common difference.

The general term of an arithmetic sequence is $a_n = a_0 + dn$, where $a_0$ is the initial value and $d$ is the common difference. An alternate form is $a_n = a_k + d(n - k)$, where $a_k$ is the $k$th term of the sequence.

### Example
Write a formula for the sequence 6, 10, 14, 18, 22, . . . , then use that formula to find the 100th term of the sequence.

Solution: We first need to determine if the sequence is arithmetic by finding the difference between successive terms. The difference between term 2 and term 1 is $10 - 6 = 4$. The difference between term 3 and term 2 is $14 - 10 = 4$. The difference between term 4 and term 3 is $18 - 14 = 4$. The difference between term 5 and term 4 is $22 - 18 = 4$. Because the differences are the same, it is an arithmetic sequence.

Next, substitute values into the formula $a_n = a_0 + dn$. The initial value $a_0$ is found by subtracting the difference $d$ from the first term in the sequence: $a_0 = a_1 - d = 6 - 4 = 2$.

Therefore, the formula is $a_n = 2 + 4n$. Term 100, or $a_{100} = 2 + 4(100) = 402$.

## Geometric Sequences

A *geometric sequence* is a sequence that has successive terms that have a constant proportional change or a common ratio.

> The general term of a geometric sequence is $g_n = g_0 r^n$, where $g_0$ is the initial value and $r$ is the common ratio. An alternate form is $g_n = g_k r^{(n-k)}$, where $g_k$ is the $k$th term of the sequence.

### Example

Write a formula for the sequence 2, –6, 18, –54, 162, . . . . Use that formula to find the 12th term of the sequence.

Solution: We first need to determine if the sequence is geometric by finding the ratio between successive terms. The ratio between term 2 and term 1 is $\frac{-6}{2} = -3$. The ratio between term 3 and term 2 is $\frac{18}{-6} = -3$. The ratio between term 4 and term 3 is $\frac{-54}{18} = -3$. The ratio between term 5 and term 4 is $\frac{162}{-54} = -3$. Because the ratios are all the same, it is a geometric sequence.

Next, substitute values into the formula $g_n = g_0 r^n$. The initial value $g_0$ is found by dividing the ratio $r$ by the first term in the sequence: $g_n = \frac{g_1}{r} = \frac{2}{-3} = -\frac{2}{3}$. Therefore, the formula is $g_n = -\frac{2}{3}(-3)^n$. The 12th term is $g_{12} = -\frac{2}{3}(-3)^{12} = -\frac{2}{3}(531,441) = 354,294$.

> Arithmetic sequences are based on addition, while geometric sequences are based on multiplication.

## Change in Linear and Exponential Functions

Linear functions of the form $f(x) = b + mx$ are similar to arithmetic sequences of the form $a_n = a_0 + dn$, because both can be expressed as an initial value ($b$ or $a_0$) plus repeated addition of a constant rate of change, the slope ($m$ or $d$). Similar to arithmetic sequences of the form $a_n = a_k + d(n - k)$, which are based on a known difference, $d$, and a $k$th term, linear functions can be expressed in the form $f(x) = y_i + m(x - x_i)$ based on a known slope, $m$, and a point $(x_i, y_i)$.

Exponential functions of the form $f(x) = ab^x$ are similar to geometric sequences of the form $g_n = g_0 r^n$, as both can be expressed as an initial value ($a$ or $g_0$) times repeated multiplication by a constant proportion ($b$ or $r$). Similar to geometric sequences of the form $g_n = g_k r^{(n-k)}$, which are based on a known ratio, $r$, and a $k$th term, exponential functions can be expressed in the form $f(x) = y_i r^{(x - x_i)}$ based on a known ratio, $r$, and a point, $(x_i, y_i)$. It should be noted that sequences and their corresponding functions may have different domains. Specifically, linear and exponential function domains are all real numbers, but sequences have domains of whole numbers.

Over equal-length input-value intervals, if the output values of a function change at a constant rate, then the function is linear; if the output values change proportionally, then the function is exponential. Also of note is that arithmetic sequences, linear functions, geometric sequences, and exponential functions all have the same property that they can be determined by two distinct sequence or function values.

### Example 1

If the 6th term of an arithmetic sequence is 28 and the 15th term is 73, find the 30th term of the sequence.

Solution: Substituting $n = 6$ and $a_6 = 28$ into the formula $a_n = a_0 + dn$, we get the equation $28 = a_0 + 6d$ and substituting $n = 15$ and $a_{15} = 73$ into the same formula, we get the equation $73 = a_0 + 15d$. We can subtract the two equations to eliminate $a_0$.

$$73 = a_0 + 15d$$
$$\underline{- 28 = -(a_0 + 6d)}$$
$$45 = 9d \qquad \text{so, } d = 5$$

We can take the first (or second) equation and substitute $d = 5$ to find $a_0$:
$28 = a_0 + 6(5)$, so $a_0 = -2$. The formula for the arithmetic sequence is $a_n = -2 + 5n$.
Therefore, the 30th term is $a_{30} = -2 + 5(30) = 148$.

### Example 2

If the 5th term of a geometric sequence is 4 and the 10th term is $\frac{1}{8}$, find the 20th term of the sequence.

Solution: Substituting $n = 5$ and $g_5 = 4$ into the formula $g_n = g_0 r^n$ we get the equation $4 = g_0 r^5$, and substituting $n = 10$ and $g_{10} = \frac{1}{8}$ into the formula we get the equation $\frac{1}{8} = g_0 r^{10}$.

We can divide the two equations to eliminate $g_0$. $\dfrac{\frac{1}{8}}{4} = \dfrac{g_0 r^{10}}{g_0 r^5} \rightarrow \dfrac{1}{32} = r^5 \rightarrow r = \sqrt[5]{\dfrac{1}{32}} \rightarrow r = \dfrac{1}{2}$.

We can take the first (or second) equation and substitute $r = \dfrac{1}{2}$ to find $g_0$.
$4 = g_0 \left(\dfrac{1}{2}\right)^5 \rightarrow 4 = g_0 \left(\dfrac{1}{32}\right) \rightarrow g_0 = 128$.
The formula for the geometric sequence is $g_n = 128\left(\dfrac{1}{2}\right)^n$.

Therefore, the 20th term is $g_{20} = 128\left(\dfrac{1}{2}\right)^{20}$.

Rewritten as powers of 2 results in $g_{20} = (2)^7 (2^{-1})^{20} = (2)^7 (2^{-20}) = 2^{-13} = \dfrac{1}{8{,}192}$.

# Exponential Functions

Exponential functions were introduced along with geometric sequences in the previous section. Let's take a closer look at them now.

> The general form of an *exponential function* is $f(x) = ab^x$, with initial value $a$, where $a \neq 0$, and base $b$, where $b > 0$ and $b \neq 1$. When $a > 0$ and $b > 1$, the exponential function is known as *exponential growth*. When $a > 0$ and $0 < b < 1$, the exponential function is known as *exponential decay*.

## Graphs of Exponential Functions

Let's look at a graph of the exponential function $f(x) = 2(7)^x$ and identify some of the key characteristics.

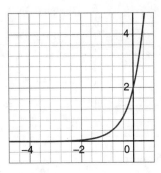

| CHARACTERISTIC | VALUE |
|---|---|
| Domain | All reals |
| Range | Positive reals |
| Intercept(s) | (0, 2) |
| Increasing/Decreasing | Always increasing |
| Concavity | Always concave up |
| Extrema | None |
| Point of Inflection | None |
| Asymptote | Horizontal at $y = 0$ |
| End Behavior | $\lim\limits_{x \to -\infty} f(x) = 0$ and $\lim\limits_{x \to \infty} f(x) = \infty$ |

For an exponential function in general form, as the input values increase or decrease without bound, the output values will increase or decrease without bound or will get arbitrarily close to zero. That is, for an exponential function in general form, $\lim\limits_{x \to \pm\infty} ab^x = \infty$, $\lim\limits_{x \to \pm\infty} ab^x = -\infty$, or $\lim\limits_{x \to \pm\infty} ab^x = 0$.

### Example

When Brody entered kindergarten, his grandparents gave him a certificate of deposit (CD) for $5,000 to help him pay for college. If the bank pays an annual rate of 3.5% compounded yearly, how much will Brody have when he starts college 13 years later?

Solution: Substituting the value 5,000 for $a$, 1.035 for $b$ (3.5% must be converted to a decimal, which is 0.035. Then 1 must be added because each period of time we have an increase of the initial amount), and 13 for $x$ results in the equation $y = 5,000(1.035)^{13}$.

Therefore, Brody will have $7,819.78 when he starts college.

## Properties of Exponential Functions

Exponential expressions can be rewritten using the properties of exponents.

| PROPERTY | DEFINITION | EXAMPLE |
|---|---|---|
| Product Property | $b^m \cdot b^n = b^{m+n}$ | $7^4 \cdot 7^5 = 7^{4+5} = 7^9$ |
| Quotient Property | $\dfrac{b^m}{b^n} = b^{m-n}$ | $\dfrac{4^8}{4^3} = 4^{8-3} = 4^5$ |
| Power Property | $(b^m)^n = b^{mn}$ | $(5^2)^3 = 5^{2 \cdot 3} = 5^6$ |
| Negative Exponent Property | $b^{-n} = \dfrac{1}{b^n}$ | $8^{-3} = \dfrac{1}{8^3}$ |
| Root Property | $b^{1/k} = \sqrt[k]{b}$, $k$ is a natural number | $3^{1/4} = \sqrt[4]{3}$ |
| Zero Power Property | $b^0 = 1,\ b \neq 0$ | $2^0 = 1$ |

**Example**

Sketch the graphs of $f(x) = 10^x$ and $g(x) = \dfrac{1}{10^x}$ on the same axis. Analyze the graphs.

Solution: The graph of $g(x)$ is a reflection image of the graph of $f(x)$ over the $y$-axis because $g(x) = \dfrac{1}{10^x}$ can be rewritten as $g(x) = 10^{-x}$.

Domain: All real. Range: All positive real numbers.

Increasing/Decreasing: $f$ is increasing over its entire domain, whereas $g$ is decreasing over its entire domain.

Maxima/minima: None.

End behavior: $\lim\limits_{x \to -\infty} f(x) = 0$, $\lim\limits_{x \to \infty} f(x) = \infty$, $\lim\limits_{x \to -\infty} g(x) = \infty$, $\lim\limits_{x \to \infty} g(x) = 0$.

Model: $f(x)$ is exponential growth, whereas $g(x)$ is exponential decay.

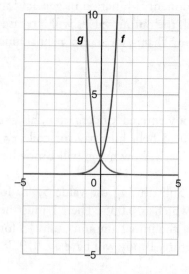

Like $\pi$ for circles, an important exponential base that occurs naturally in higher order problems is base $e$, known as the natural number. The value of $e$ is approximately 2.71828. The following is a graph of $e^x$.

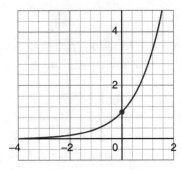

# Composition of Functions

The *composition of functions* $f(x)$ and $g(x)$ is the process of combining the two functions into a single function. If $g(x)$ is the first function and $f(x)$ is the second function, then it is represented as $f(g(x))$ or $(f \circ g)(x)$. The output values of $g$ are used as input values of $f$. For this reason, the domain of the composite function is restricted to those input values of $g$ for which the corresponding output value is in the domain of $f$.

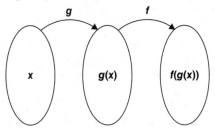

**Example 1**
If $f(x) = \sqrt{x}$ and $g(x) = 2x - 1$, find $(f \circ g)(x)$ and $(g \circ f)(x)$. State the domain of each composition.

Solution: $f(g(x)) = f(2x - 1) = \sqrt{2x - 1}$. We need to restrict the domain to only nonnegative numbers under the radical, or $2x - 1 \geq 0$. This is equivalent to $\{x : x \geq \frac{1}{2}\}$.
$g(f(x)) = g(\sqrt{x}) = 2\sqrt{x} - 1$. The domain is $\{x : x \geq 0\}$.
Notice that the composition of functions is generally not commutative, meaning $(f \circ g)(x) \neq (g \circ f)(x)$.

**Example 2**
Find $g(f(-2))$ using the following tables.

| $x$ | $f(x)$ |
| --- | --- |
| $-1$ | $-2$ |
| $-2$ | $0$ |
| $-3$ | $2$ |
| $-4$ | $4$ |

| $x$ | $g(x)$ |
| --- | --- |
| $0$ | $5$ |
| $1$ | $8$ |
| $2$ | $11$ |
| $3$ | $14$ |

Solution: From the table of $f(x)$, $f(-2) = 0$. So $g(f(-2)) = g(0)$. From the table of $g(x)$, $g(0) = 5$.
Therefore, $g(f(-2)) = 5$.

### Example 3

For the given two functions $f(x) = kx - 4$ and $g(x) = kx + 6$, if the two composite functions $f(g(x))$ and $g(f(x))$ are equal, find $k$.

Solution: First let's find $f(g(x))$ and $g(f(x))$.
$f(g(x)) = f(kx + 6) = k(kx + 6) - 4 = k^2x + 6k - 4$
$g(f(x)) = g(kx - 4) = k(kx - 4) + 6 = k^2x - 4k + 6$
Because $f(g(x)) = g(f(x))$, then $k^2x + 6k - 4 = k^2x - 4k + 6$,
$$6k - 4 = -4k + 6,$$
$$10k = 10, \text{ which makes } k = 1.$$

## Inverse Functions

An *inverse function* can be thought of as a reverse mapping of the function. An inverse function, $f^{-1}$, maps the output values of a function, $f$, on its invertible domain to their corresponding input values; that is, if $f(a) = b$, then $f^{-1}(b) = a$. Alternately, on its invertible domain, if a function consists of input-output pairs $(a, b)$, then the inverse function consists of input-output pairs $(b, a)$. The domain may need to be restricted in order to make the function invertible.

> The composition of a function $f$, and its inverse function, $f^{-1}$, is the identity function; that is, $f(f^{-1}(x)) = f^{-1}(f(x)) = x$.

On a function's invertible domain, the function's domain and range are the inverse function's range and domain. The inverse of the table of values of $y = f(x)$ can be found by reversing the input-output pairs; that is, $(a, b)$ corresponds to $(b, a)$.

The inverse of the graph of the function $y = f(x)$ can be found by reversing the roles of the $x$- and $y$-axes; that is, by reflecting the graph of the function over the graph of the identity function $h(x) = x$.

The inverse of the function can be found by determining the inverse operations to reverse the mapping. One method for finding the inverse of the function $f$ is reversing the roles of $x$ and $y$ in the equation $y = f(x)$, then solving for $y = f^{-1}(x)$.

### Example 1

If $f(x) = 7x + 1$, find $f^{-1}(x)$.

Solution:

Step 1: Rewrite the equation as $y = 7x + 1$.

Step 2: Reverse the roles of $x$ and $y$. This results in $x = 7y + 1$.

Step 3: Solve for $y$. This results in $x - 1 = 7y$, so $y = \dfrac{x-1}{7}$.

Therefore, $f^{-1}(x) = \dfrac{x-1}{7}$.

**Example 2**

Show that $f(x) = 2x^2 + 1$ and $g(x) = \sqrt{\dfrac{x-1}{2}}$ are inverses.

Solution:

Step 1: Find $f(g(x)) = f\left(\sqrt{\dfrac{x-1}{2}}\right) = 2\left(\sqrt{\dfrac{x-1}{2}}\right)^2 + 1 = 2\left(\dfrac{x-1}{2}\right) + 1 = x - 1 + 1 = x$,

for $x \geq 1$ because of the domain of $g(x)$.

Step 2: Because $f(x)$ is not one-to-one, that is, $f(x)$ has multiple values of $y$ from different values of $x$, the domain must be restricted in order to find the inverse. In this case, restricting the domain of $f(x)$ to $x \geq 0$ means we can find the inverse.

Find $g(f(x)) = g(2x^2 + 1) = \sqrt{\dfrac{(2x^2 + 1) - 1}{2}} = \sqrt{\dfrac{2x^2}{2}} = \sqrt{x^2} = x$.

Because $f(g(x)) = g(f(x)) = x$, $f$ and $g$ are inverses on the appropriately restricted domains.

# Logarithmic Expressions

Addition and subtraction are inverse operations. Multiplication and division are inverse operations. Exponentials and logarithms are inverse operations. The *logarithmic expression log$_b$c* is equal to the value that the base $b$ must be exponentially raised to in order to obtain the value $c$.

$$\log_b c = a \text{ if and only if } b^a = c, \text{ where } a \text{ and } c \text{ are constants, } b > 0, \text{ and } b \neq 1.$$

When the base of a logarithmic expression is not specified, it is understood to be the common logarithm with base 10 and written $\log x$. When the base of a logarithm expression is $e$, it is referred to as natural logarithm and written $\ln x$.

On a logarithmic scale, each unit represents a multiplicative change of the base of the logarithm. For example, on a standard scale, the units might be 0, 1, 2, . . . , while on a logarithmic scale using logarithm base 10, the units might be 1, 10, 100, 1000, . . ., corresponding to $10^0$, $10^1$, $10^2$, . . ..

**Example 1**

Find the value of $\log_2 32$.

Solution: Rewrite the logarithm as an exponential expression. $\log_2 32 = x$ can be written as $2^x = 32$. Because $2^5 = 32$, this means $x = 5$. Therefore, $\log_2 32 = 5$.

**Example 2**

Find the value of $\log_5 256$.

Solution: Rewrite the logarithm as an exponential expression $\log_5 256 = x$ can be written as $5^x = 256$. Because $5^3 = 125$ and $5^4 = 625$, the value for $x$ must be between 3 and 4. Using a calculator, it can be approximated that $5^{3.445} \approx 256$. Therefore, $\log_5 256 \approx 3.445$.

## Properties of Logarithms

The following table has several properties of logarithms that can be applied to solve logarithmic problems.

| PROPERTY NAME | PROPERTY | GRAPHIC PROPERTY |
|---|---|---|
| Product Property | $\log_b(x \cdot y) = \log_b x + \log_b y$ | Every horizontal dilation of a logarithmic function $f(x) = \log_b(kx)$, is equivalent to a vertical translation, $f(x) = \log_b(kx) = \log_b k + \log_b x = a + \log_b x$, where $a = \log_b k$. |
| Quotient Property | $\log_b \dfrac{x}{y} = \log_b x - \log_b y$ | |
| Power Property | $\log_b x^n = n\log_b x$ | Raising the input of a logarithmic function to a power, $f(x) = \log_b x^k$ results in a vertical dilation, $f(x) = \log_b x^k = k\log_b x$. |
| Change of Base Property | $\log_b x = \dfrac{\log_a x}{\log_a b}$, where $a > 0$ and $a \neq 1$ | All logarithmic functions are vertical dilations of each other. |

**Example 1**

Solve $15^x = 30$.

Solution: Let's rewrite the exponential equation as a logarithmic equation. $15^x = 30 \rightarrow \log_{15} 30 = x$. We can use the change of base property to rewrite $\log_{15} 30 = \dfrac{\log 30}{\log 15}$. Using a calculator $\dfrac{\log 30}{\log 15} = 1.256$. Therefore, $x = 1.256$. You can use a calculator to confirm $15^{1.256} \approx 30$.

**Example 2**

Use the properties to expand the expression $\log_b \dfrac{5x}{y^2}$.

Solution:

Step 1: Use the quotient property to rewrite: $\log_b \dfrac{5x}{y^2} = \log_b(5x) - \log_b y^2$

Step 2: Use the product and power properties: $= (\log_b 5 + \log_b x) - 2\log_b y$

$$\log_b \frac{5x}{y^2} = \log_b 5 + \log_b x - 2\log_b y$$

## Inverses of Exponential Functions

Because $f(x) = \log_b x$ and $g(x) = b^x$ are inverse functions, this means that when the functions are composed with one another the result is $x$. Meaning $f(g(x)) = g(f(x)) = x$. If $(s, t)$ is an ordered pair of the exponential function, then $(t, s)$ is an ordered pair of the logarithmic function. Graphically because the functions are inverses, the graph of the logarithmic function is a reflection of the graph of the exponential function over the graph of the identity function $h(x) = x$.

**Example**

Graph $f(x) = 3^x$ and its inverse.

Solution: The inverse, $f^{-1}(x) = \log_3 x$. Notice that the graphs are reflections across the line $y = x$. The $y$-intercept of $f(x) = 3^x$ is $(0, 1)$. The $x$-intercept of $f^{-1}(x) = \log_3 x$ is $(1, 0)$.

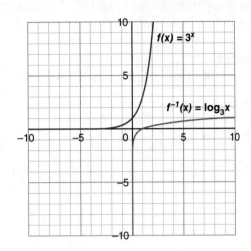

## Graphs of Logarithmic Functions

Let's look at a graph of the logarithmic function $f(x) = \log x$ and identify some of the key characteristics.

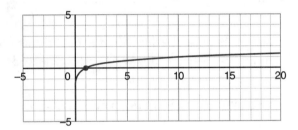

| CHARACTERISTIC | VALUE |
|---|---|
| Domain | All reals greater than 0 |
| Range | All reals |
| Intercept(s) | $(1, 0)$ |
| Increasing/Decreasing | Always increasing |
| Concavity | Always concave down |
| Extrema | None |
| Point of Inflection | None |
| Asymptote | Vertical at $x = 0$ |
| End Behavior | $\lim\limits_{x \to 0^+} f(x) = -\infty$ and $\lim\limits_{x \to \infty} f(x) = \infty$ |

# Exponential and Logarithmic Inequalities

Properties of exponents, properties of logarithms, and the inverse relationship between exponential and logarithmic functions can be used to solve equations and inequalities involving exponents and logarithms. When solving exponential and logarithmic equations found through analytical or graphical methods, the results should be examined for extraneous solutions precluded by the mathematical or contextual limitations.

**Example 1**

What are all values of $x$ for which $2\log(x+1)=\log(x+13)$?

Solution:

Step 1: Set the equation equal to 0. $\qquad\qquad\qquad\qquad 2\log(x+1)-\log(x+13)=0$

Step 2: Rewrite using the power and quotient properties. $\qquad \log\dfrac{(x+1)^2}{(x+13)}=0$

Step 3: Rewrite as an exponential equation. $\qquad\qquad\qquad\qquad 10^0=\dfrac{(x+1)^2}{(x+13)}$

Step 4: Rewrite $10^0$ as 1. $\qquad\qquad\qquad\qquad\qquad\qquad\qquad 1=\dfrac{(x+1)^2}{(x+13)}$

Step 5: Multiply both sides by $(x+13)$. $\qquad\qquad\qquad\quad x+13=(x+1)^2$

Step 6: Replace $(x+1)^2$ with $x^2+2x+1$ and set equal to 0. $\quad x^2+x-12=0$

Step 7: Factor and set each factor equal to 0 and solve. $\qquad (x+4)(x-3)=0$

$$x=-4 \text{ or } x=3$$

Step 8: Because the domain of a logarithmic function is all reals greater than 0, substituting $x=-4$ into $2\log(x+1)$ yields $2\log(-3)$, which is not defined; therefore $x=-4$ is an extraneous solution.

The value that solves the equation is $x=3$.

**Example 2**

What are all values of $x$ for which $2^x \geq 100$?

Solution:

Step 1: Rewrite the inequality as a logarithmic inequality. $\qquad\qquad \log_2 2^x \geq \log_2 100$

Step 2: Use the power property and change of base property to rewrite. $\quad x\log_2 2 \geq \dfrac{\log 100}{\log 2}$

Step 3: Use a calculator to evaluate the logarithms. $\qquad\qquad\qquad\qquad x \geq 6.644$

The solution is $x \geq 6.644$.

# Modeling

Two variables in a data set that demonstrate a slightly changing rate of change can be modeled by linear, quadratic, and exponential function models. Models can be compared based on contextual clues and applicability to determine which model is most appropriate. A model is justified as *appropriate* for a data set if the graph of the residuals of a regression, the residual plot, appear without pattern. The *error* in the model is the difference between the predicted and actual values. Depending on the data set and context, it may be more appropriate to have an underestimate or overestimate for any given interval.

## Exponential Function Context and Data Modeling

For an exponential model in general form $f(x) = ab^x$, the base of the exponent, $b$, can be understood as a growth factor in successive unit changes in the input values and is related to a percent change in context. An exponential function model can be constructed from an appropriate ratio and initial value or from two input-output pairs. The initial value and the base can be found by solving a system of equations resulting from the two input-output pairs.

Exponential function models can be constructed by applying transformations to $f(x) = ab^x$ based on characteristics of a contextual scenario or data set. They can be used to predict values for the dependent variable, depending on the contextual constraints on the domain. A constant may need to be added to the dependent variable values of a data set to reveal a proportional growth pattern.

### Example 1

A new car sells for $38,500. The value of the car decreases by 17% annually. What will be the value of the car in 5 years?

Solution: The growth factor is $1 - 0.17$, or $0.83$. Using the general form of the exponential model yields, $f(x) = 38,500(0.83)^5$. Therefore, the car will be worth $15,165.31 after 5 years.

### Example 2

The number of bacteria on the fourth day of an experiment was 58. On the tenth day, the number increased to 368. Write an exponential model to represent the number of bacteria present $d$ days after the experiment began.

Solution:

Step 1: Represent the model $f(d) = ab^d$ with the points $(4, 58)$ and $(10, 368)$. This results in $58 = ab^4$ and $368 = ab^{10}$.

Step 2: Divide the second equation by the first equation to eliminate $a$. $\dfrac{368}{58} = \dfrac{ab^{10}}{ab^4}$

$$6.345 = b^6$$

Step 3: Solve for $b$. $\qquad b = \sqrt[6]{6.345} \approx 1.361$

Step 4: Substitute $b$ into one of the equations to solve for $a$. $\qquad 58 = a(1.361)^4$

$$\frac{58}{1.361^4} = a$$

$$16.923 \approx a$$

Step 5: Because $a$ represents the starting amount of bacteria, it should be represented by the whole number 17.

Therefore, the exponential model is $f(d) = 17(1.361)^d$.

---

Values that are used when solving an equation should be stored in a graphing calculator so as not to have a round-off error.

---

**Example 3**

The half-life of carbon-14 is known to be 5,720 years. If 400 grams of carbon-14 are stored for 1,000 years, how many grams will remain?

Solution: Half-life is the time required for a quantity to reduce to half of its value. When solving half-life formulas, we use the formula $A = A_0 \left(\dfrac{1}{2}\right)^{t/H}$, where $A$ = the amount remaining, $A_0$ = initial amount, $t$ = time, $H$ = half-life. Substituting the known information into the formula results in

$A = 400 \left(\dfrac{1}{2}\right)^{1{,}000/5{,}720}$ · After 1,000 years 354.350 grams will remain.

### Logarithmic Function Context and Data Modeling

Logarithmic functions are inverses of exponential functions and can be used to model situations involving proportional growth, or repeated multiplication, where the input values change proportionally over equal-length output-value intervals. Alternately, if the output value is a whole number, it indicates how many times the initial value has been multiplied by the proportion.

**Example**

A concert starts at 7:00 p.m. and the doors to the concert venue open at 5:00 p.m. The number of patrons in the concert venue $t$ minutes after 5:00 p.m. is listed in the following table. Using technology, estimate the logarithmic function $N(t) = a + b\ln t$ that models the data.

| Minutes since 5:00 p.m. | 15 | 30 | 45 | 60 | 75 | 90 | 105 | 120 |
|---|---|---|---|---|---|---|---|---|
| Number of patrons in the venue | 270 | 340 | 380 | 410 | 430 | 450 | 465 | 480 |

Solution:

Step 1: Enter the value from the table into a graphing calculator.

Step 2: Use the calculator's calculate function to determine the logarithmic function.

The function that models how many patrons are in the venue at time $t$ minutes after 5:00 p.m. is $N(t) = -2.029 + 100.444(\ln t)$.

# Semi-Log Plots

In a *semi-log plot*, one of the axes is logarithmically scaled. When the $y$-axis of a semi-log plot is logarithmically scaled, data or functions that demonstrate exponential characteristics will appear linear. An advantage of semi-log plots is that a constant never needs to be added to the dependent variable values to reveal that an exponential model is appropriate. Techniques used to model linear functions can be applied to a semi-log graph. For an exponential model of the form $y = ab^x$, the corresponding linear model for the semi-log plot is $y = (\log_n b)x + \log_n a$, where $n > 0$ and $n \neq 1$. Specifically, the linear rate of change is $\log_n b$, and the initial value is $\log_n a$.

**Example**

Consider the following graphs of two data sets. Both appear to have models that would be increasing and concave up. Which data set, if any, can be modeled by an exponential function? A quick check to determine if the model is exponential is to change the $y$-axis to a logarithmic scale.

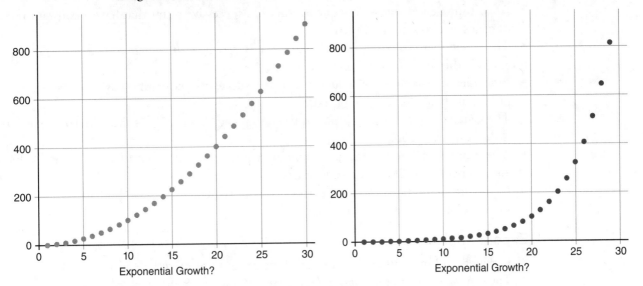

The same data graphed with a logarithmic scale for the $y$-axis are shown in the following graphs. As you can see, the $y$-axis now is scaled 1, 10, 100, 1,000. This is equivalent to $10^0$, $10^1$, $10^2$, and $10^3$, which is a proportional scale.

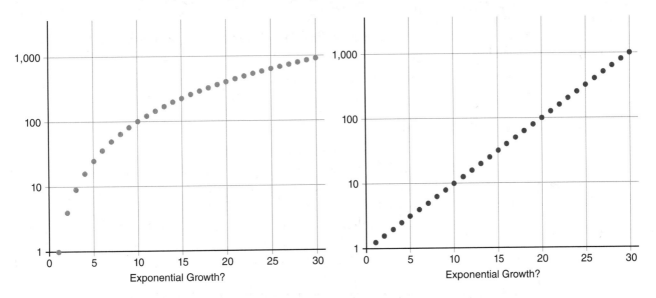

Recall, exponential functions model growth patterns where successive output values over equal-length input-value intervals are proportional. The graph on the right appears to be linear, while the graph on the left does not appear to be linear. Because the graph on the right is linear on the new proportional scale, the original data for the right graph is exponential; the graph on the left does not appear linear, so the original data for the left graph is not exponential. In fact, the left graph can be modeled by $f(x) = x^2$ while the graph on the right can be modeled by $g(x) = (1.26)^x$.

# ❯ Rapid Review

### Sequence

- A sequence is an ordered list of numbers that follow a specific pattern.
- An arithmetic sequence is a sequence that has successive terms that have a constant rate of change or common difference.
- The general term of an arithmetic sequence is $a_n = a_0 + dn$, where $a_0$ is the initial value and $d$ is the common difference.
- A geometric sequence is a sequence that has successive terms that have a constant proportional change or a common ratio.
- The general term of a geometric sequence is $g_n = g_0 r^n$, where $g_0$ is the initial value and $r$ is the common ratio.
- Linear functions are similar to arithmetic sequences because both have an initial value and a repeated addition of a constant.
- Exponential functions are similar to geometric sequences because both have an initial value and a repeated constant proportion.

### Exponential Function

- Exponential functions arise from situations of constant growth.
- The general form of an *exponential function* is $f(x) = ab^x$, with initial value $a$, where $a \neq 0$, and base $b$, where $b > 0$ and $b \neq 1$. When $a > 0$ and $b > 1$, the exponential function is known as *exponential growth*. When $a > 0$ and $0 < b < 1$, the exponential function is known as *exponential decay*.
- When the base of an exponential function $f$ is greater than 1, $f$ is increasing, $\lim_{x \to -\infty} f(x) = 0$, $\lim_{x \to \infty} f(x) = \infty$.
- When the base of an exponential function $f$ is less than 1, $f$ is decreasing, $\lim_{x \to -\infty} f(x) = \infty$, and $\lim_{x \to \infty} f(x) = 0$.
- When $a > 0$, the graph is concave up, and when $a < 0$, the graph is concave down.
- Exponential expressions can be rewritten using the properties of exponents.

### Logarithmic Function

- Logarithmic functions are inverses of exponential functions.
- $\log_b c = a$ if and only if $b^a = c$, where $a$ and $c$ are constants, $b > 0$, and $b \neq 1$.
- When the base of a logarithmic function $g$ is greater than 1, $g$ is increasing, $\lim_{x \to \infty} g(x) = \infty$. The graph is concave down.
- When the base of a logarithmic expression is not specified, it is understood to be the common logarithm with base 10 and written $\log x$.
- When the base of a logarithm expression is $e$, it is referred to as natural logarithm and written $\ln x$.
- Logarithm expressions can be rewritten using the properties of logarithms.

### Modeling

- Two variables in a data set that demonstrate a slightly changing rate of change can be modeled by linear, quadratic, and exponential function models.

- Logarithmic functions are inverses of exponential functions and can be used to model situations involving proportional growth, or repeated multiplication, where the input values change proportionally over equal-length output-value intervals.
- Models can be used to predict values for the dependent variable, depending on the contextual constraints on the domain.

## Miscellaneous

- Two functions $f$ and $g$ can be combined using the composition $(f \circ g)(x)$.
- An inverse function is a reverse mapping of a function, and is written $f^{-1}$
- If $(f \circ g)(x) = (g \circ f)(x) = x$, then the functions $f$ and $g$ are inverses.
- When solving exponential or logarithmic equations or inequalities, extraneous solutions might exist and should be excluded.
- For the AP exam, logarithmic scaling will only be applied to the $y$-axis to linearize exponential functions.

# › Review Questions

## Basic Level

1. Describe the graph of $y = 3\left(\dfrac{1}{5}\right)^x$ using limit notation.

2. Let $f(x) = 5^x$. If $g(x)$ is a transformation of $f(x)$ with a horizontal shift of 3 units right and a vertical shift of 4 units up, what is the equation of $g(x)$?

3. Using the following tables, what is the value of $f(g(2))$? What is the value of $g(f(-2))$?

| $x$ | −3 | −2 | −1 | 0 | 1 | 2 |
|------|-----|-----|-----|-----|-----|-----|
| $f(x)$ | 6 | 0 | 3 | 5 | 1 | −2 |

| $x$ | −4 | −2 | 0 | 2 | 4 | 6 |
|------|-----|-----|-----|-----|-----|-----|
| $g(x)$ | 3 | 1 | −1 | −3 | −5 | −7 |

4. Simplify completely using only positive exponents: $(2x^3y^2)^3(3x^7y^{-3})^2$.
5. If $f(x) = \log_3(x-1)$, find $f^{-1}(x)$.
6. If $f(x) = \log_4 x$, find $f^{-1}(2)$.
7. Solve for $x$: $\log_x 300 = 2$.

## Advanced Level

8. If the 2nd term of a geometric sequence is 36 and the 6th term is 2916, what is the 10th term?
9. An arithmetic sequence has the 7th term 41 and the 18th term 74. Find the formula for the $n$th term.
10. Simplify without using a calculator: $\log_4 \dfrac{1}{2}$.

11. Let $f(x) = 5x - 7$ and $g(x) = \dfrac{2x+1}{x-8}$. Find $(f \circ g)(x)$ and $(g \circ f)(x)$.

**12.** $f(x)$ is graphed as follows. If $g(x) = 4 f(x) - 10$, what is the value of $g(0)$?

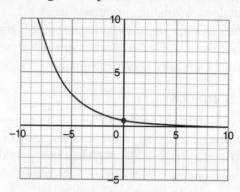

**13.** Rewrite $2\log x - \log(4y) + \log(3x^4)$ as a single logarithm.

**14.** If $f^{-1}(x) = \dfrac{2x-1}{x+5}$, find $f(x)$.

**15.** Simplify completely using all positive exponents: $\dfrac{(5x^2 y^4 z^{-2})^3}{(2xy^3 z^2)^{-2}}$

**16.** Solve for $x$: $\log(2x) + \log x^3 < 2$.

**17.** If Sam puts $10,000 into a retirement account at age 30 earning 2.6% compounded annually, how much will it grow to by retirement age 67 if no additional deposits or withdrawals are made?

**18.** Express $\log_b \sqrt[4]{nw^3}$ in terms of $\log_b n$ and $\log_b w$.

**19.** A wise old ruler wanted to reward his friend for an act of extraordinary bravery. The friend said, "I ask you for just one thing. Take the chessboard and place on the first square one grain of rice. On the first day I will take this grain home to feed my family. On the second day, place on the second square two grains for me to take home. On the third day cover the third square with four grains for me to take. Each day double the number of grains you give me until you have placed rice on every square of the chessboard, then my reward will be complete." The wise old ruler replied, "This sounds like a small price to pay for your act of incredible bravery, I will do as you ask immediately." If the friend's request was granted, how much rice would be given to them on day 64, the final square of the chessboard?

**20.** Using the information from question 19, what is the rate of change between the sixth and seventh days? What is the rate of change between the seventh and eighth days? What does this illustrate about an exponential curve $ab^x$ with $a > 0$?

## 〉 Answers and Explanations

**1.** • The following graph of $y = 3\left(\dfrac{1}{5}\right)^x$ is an exponential decay function (the base $b = 1/5$, is between 0 and 1 or $0 < 1/5 < 1$).

• When $a > 0$, exponential decay functions are always decreasing, always concave up, and have a horizontal asymptote at $y = 0$.

• $\lim\limits_{x \to -\infty} f(x) = \infty$ and $\lim\limits_{x \to \infty} f(x) = 0$

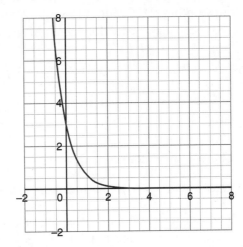

**2.** • A horizontal shift of 3 replaces $x$ with $x - 3$.

• A vertical shift of 4 adds 4 to the equation.

• $g(x) = 5^{x-3} + 4$

**3.** • To find $f(g(2))$, we first need to find $g(2)$. Using the bottom table, $g(2) = -3$.

• So $f(g(2)) = f(-3) = 6$.

• To find $g(f(-2))$, we first need to find $f(-2)$. Using the top table, $f(-2) = 0$.

• So $g(f(-2)) = g(0) = -1$.

**4.** • Let's simplify the first expression by using the power property: $(2x^3y^2)^3 = (2)^3(x^3)^3(y^2)^3 = 8x^9y^6$.

• Now the second: $(3x^7y^{-3})^2 = (3)^2(x^7)^2(y^{-3})^2 = 9x^{14}y^{-6}$.

• Now, apply the product property. $(8x^9y^6)(9x^{14}y^{-6}) = 72x^{23}y^0 = 72x^{23}$.

**5.** • Rewrite $f(x) = \log_3(x - 1)$ as $y = \log_3(x - 1)$.

• Interchange $x$ and $y$: $x = \log_3(y - 1)$.

• Rewrite as an exponential equation: $3^x = y - 1$.

• Solve for $y$: $y = 3^x + 1$.

• So $f^{-1}(x) = 3^x + 1$.

**6.** • The inverse can be found by rewriting the logarithmic equation as the corresponding exponential equation. $f^{-1}(x) = 4^x$.

• $f^{-1}(2) = 4^2 = 16$.

**7.** • Solving the equation $\log_x 300 = 2$ involves rewriting as the equivalent exponential equation.

• $\log_x 300 = 2$ can be rewritten as $x^2 = 300 \to x = \pm\sqrt{300} = \pm\sqrt{100}\sqrt{3} = \pm10\sqrt{3}$.

• Because the base of a logarithm must be positive, there is only one solution, $x = 10\sqrt{3}$.

**8.**
- Substituting $(2, 36)$ into the equation $g_n = g_0 r^n$ results in $36 = g_0 r^2$.
- Substituting $(6, 2916)$ into the equation results in $2916 = g_0 r^6$.
- Divide the two equations to eliminate $g_0$. $\dfrac{2916}{36} = \dfrac{g_0 r^6}{g_0 r^2} \rightarrow 81 = r^4 \rightarrow r = \pm\sqrt[4]{81} \rightarrow r = \pm 3$.
- Using the first equation and substituting the known values results in $36 = g_0(3)^2 \rightarrow 36 = 9g_0 \rightarrow g_0 = 4$. Note: Substituting $r = -3$ into the equation yields the same result.
- $g_{10} = 4(3)^{10} = 236{,}196$.

**9.**
- Substituting $(7, 41)$ into the equation $a_n = a_0 + dn$ results in $41 = a_0 + 7d$.
- Substituting $(18, 74)$ into the equation results in $74 = a_0 + 18d$.
- Subtract the two equations to eliminate $a_0$:

$$\begin{array}{r} 74 = a_0 + 18d \\ -41 = -(a_0 + 7d) \\ \hline 33 = 11d \\ d = 3. \end{array}$$

- Using the first equation and substituting the known values results in $41 = a_0 + 7(3) \rightarrow a_0 = 20$.
- The arithmetic formula is $a_n = 20 + 3n$.

**10.**
- Rewriting $\log_4 \dfrac{1}{2} = x$ as an exponential equation results in $4^x = \dfrac{1}{2}$.
- Rewriting both sides of the equation as a power of 2 results in $(2^2)^x = 2^{-1}$.
- Because the bases are equal, that means the exponents must be equal.
- $2x = -1$, so $\log_4 \dfrac{1}{2} = -\dfrac{1}{2}$.

**11.**
- $(f \circ g)(x) = f(g(x)) = f\left(\dfrac{2x+1}{x-8}\right) = 5\left(\dfrac{2x+1}{x-8}\right) - 7 = \dfrac{10x+5}{x-8} - \dfrac{7(x-8)}{x-8} = \dfrac{10x+5-7x+56}{x-8} = \dfrac{3x+61}{x-8}$
- $(g \circ f)(x) = g(f(x)) = g(5x-7) = \dfrac{2(5x-7)+1}{(5x-7)-8} = \dfrac{10x-14+1}{5x-15} = \dfrac{10x-13}{5x-15}$

**12.**
- From the graph it can been seen that $f(0) = \dfrac{1}{2}$.
- Because $g(x) = 4 f(x)$, the point $(0, \frac{1}{2})$ moves to $4[(0, \frac{1}{2})]$ or $(0, 2)$.
- Applying the vertical shift $-10$, the point $(0, 2)$ moves to $(0, -8)$.
- Therefore, $g(0) = -8$.

**13.**
- Applying the power property, $2\log x = \log x^2$.
- Applying the quotient and product properties gives $\log \dfrac{x^2(3x^4)}{4y} = \log \dfrac{3x^6}{4y}$.

**14.**
- Finding the function given its inverse is the same procedure as finding the inverse given a function.
- Rewrite the equation replacing $x$ with $y$ and $y$ with $x$. This results in $x = \dfrac{2y-1}{y+5}$.
- Solve for $y$. First cross-multiply: $x(y + 5) = 2y - 1$.
- Expand and isolate $y$: $xy + 5x = 2y - 1 \rightarrow xy - 2y = -5x - 1 \rightarrow y(x - 2) = -5x - 1$.
- $y = \dfrac{-5x-1}{x-2}$, so the function is $f(x) = \dfrac{-5x-1}{x-2}$.

**15.** • First, apply the power property (raise each term to the power) to the numerator and denominator: $\dfrac{(5x^2y^4z^{-2})^3}{(2xy^3z^2)^{-2}} = \dfrac{5^3(x^2)^3(y^4)^3(z^{-2})^3}{2^{-2}x^{-2}(y^3)^{-2}(z^2)^{-2}}$.

• Next, lets apply the power property (multiply the exponents) again to each individual term: $\dfrac{5^3(x^2)^3(y^4)^3(z^{-2})^3}{2^{-2}x^{-2}(y^3)^{-2}(z^2)^{-2}} = \dfrac{125x^{2\cdot3}y^{4\cdot3}z^{-2\cdot3}}{2^{-2}x^{-2}y^{3\cdot-2}z^{2\cdot-2}}$.

• Next, apply the quotient property (subtract exponents): $\dfrac{125x^6y^{12}z^{-6}}{2^{-2}x^{-2}y^{-6}z^{-4}} = \dfrac{125x^{6-(-2)}y^{12-(-6)}z^{-6-(-4)}}{2^{-2}}$.

• Simplify: $\dfrac{125x^{6-(-2)}y^{12-(-6)}z^{-6-(-4)}}{2^{-2}} = (125)(4)x^8y^{18}z^{-2}$.

• Finally, use the negative exponent property: $\dfrac{500x^8y^{18}}{z^2}$.

**16.** • Rewrite using a single logarithm: $\log(2x) + \log x^3 = \log(2x\cdot x^3) = \log(2x^4)$.
• Rewrite the inequality as an exponential inequality: $\log(2x^4) < 2 \to 10^2 < 2x^4$.
• Solve the inequality: $100 < 2x^4 \to 50 < x^4 \to \pm\sqrt[4]{50} < x$.
• Substituting $x = -\sqrt[4]{50}$ would lead to an extraneous solution because the logarithm of a negative number does not exist.

**17.** • Using the compound interest formula $A = B(1+r)^t$ where $B$ is the initial amount, $r$ is the interest rate, and $t$ is years, we have $A = 10,000(1.026)^{37} = 25,849.512$.
• Sam will have \$25,849.51 after 37 years.

**18.** • Using the product property, $\log_b\sqrt[4]{nw^3} = \log_b n^{\frac{1}{4}} + \log_b w^{\frac{3}{4}}$.

• Using the power property, $\log_b n^{\frac{1}{4}} + \log_b w^{\frac{3}{4}} = \frac{1}{4}\log_n n + \frac{3}{4}\log_b w$.

**19.** • The values in the sequence are 1, 2, 4, 8, 16, . . . .
• Using the formula $g_n = g_1 r^{(n-1)}$, we get $g_{64} = 1(2)^{64-1}$.
• On the 64th day the friend would receive $9.223 \times 10^{18}$ pieces of rice.

**20.** • Using the formula $g_n = g_1 r^{(n-1)}$, we get $g_6 = 1(2)^{6-1} = 32$, and $g_7 = 1(2)^{7-1} = 64$.
• The rate of change between the sixth and seventh day is $\dfrac{64-32}{7-6} = 32$ grains/day.
• Using the formula $g_n = g_1 r^{(n-1)}$, we get $g_8 = 1(2)^{8-1} = 128$.
• The rate of change between the seventh and eighth day is $\dfrac{128-64}{8-7} = 64$ grains/day.
• The graph of $f(x) = 1(2)^x$ is growing at a rate of $r = 2$.
• Because the rate of change is positive, exponential functions with $a > 0$ are concave up.

# CHAPTER 8

# Unit 3: Trigonometric and Polar Functions

**IN THIS CHAPTER**

**Summary:** This chapter reviews functions and properties of their graphs as well as introduces new topics that are important when graphing periodic functions. Trigonometric and polar functions are introduced, along with the properties of their graphs. Important identity equations are introduced, as well as how to create new identities from these known identities. Modeling aspects of contextual scenarios and data sets that are periodic is also discussed.

**Key Ideas**

✪ Periodic phenomena corresponding to horizontal translations
✪ The radian measure of an angle
✪ The sine, cosine, and tangent related to the coordinate $xy$-plane
✪ Identifying values of sine and cosine for common radian measures
✪ The relationship between the graphs of the sine and cosine functions
✪ Identifying the amplitude, midline, period, and frequency of sinusoidal functions
✪ Applying knowledge of transformations of functions to transformations of sinusoidal functions
✪ Identifying an appropriate sinusoidal function to construct a function model for a given scenario
✪ The relationship between the tangent function and the sine and cosine functions
✪ Identifying the asymptotes and period of tangent functions
✪ Applying knowledge of transformations of functions to transformations of tangent functions
✪ Determining the inverse of a trigonometric function
✪ Solving trigonometric equations and inequalities
✪ The secant, cosecant, and cotangent functions and their graphs

✪ Equivalent representations of trigonometric functions
✪ Polar coordinates
✪ Polar function graphs
✪ Rates of change of polar functions

# Periodic Phenomena

A periodic relationship can be identified between two aspects of a context if, as the input values increase, the output values demonstrate a repeating pattern over successive equal-length intervals. If you know the graph of a single cycle, you can construct the entire graph. The *period* of the function is the smallest positive value, $k$, for which $f(x + k) = f(x)$ for all $x$ in the domain. Like all functions, intervals of increasing, decreasing, and concavities can be estimated, and those characteristics found in one period will repeat in every period of the function.

### Example

In the following graph of the function, identify the period, the intervals where the function is increasing or decreasing, and where the graph of the function is concave up or concave down.

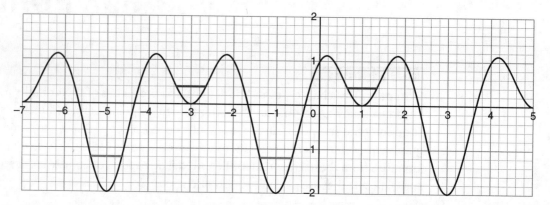

Solution: The period is 4. It appears that the graph has a global minimum at $x = -5$ and the again at $x = -1$ with an "M" shape pattern between that starts to repeat at $x = -1$. It appears the function is increasing on the interval $(-5, -3.9)$ and then the function is decreasing on the interval $(-3.9, -3)$. Then the function is increasing on the interval $(-3, -2.1)$ and decreasing on the interval $(-2.1, -1)$. After that, the graph of the function repeats the "M" pattern, so adding 4 to all the intervals listed previously will give corresponding increasing or decreasing intervals, such as increasing on $(-1, 0.1)$ can be found by adding 4 to the interval $(-5, -3.9)$. The graph is concave up from about $(-3.4, -2.6)$, $(0.6, 1.4)$, $(-5.5, -4.5)$, and $(-1.5, -0.5)$. All other concave-up intervals can be found by adding integer multiples of 4. In other words, $(0.6 + 4k, 1.4 + 4k)$ and $(-1.5 + 4k, -0.5 + 4k)$, where $k$ is an integer. It is concave down on all other intervals.

## Angles in the Coordinate Plane

In the coordinate plane, an angle is in *standard position* when the vertex coincides with the origin and one ray coincides with the positive $x$-axis. The other ray is called the *terminal ray*.

Positive and negative angle measures indicate rotations from the positive *x*-axis in the counterclockwise and clockwise directions, respectively. Angles in standard position that share a terminal ray differ by an integer number of revolutions. The radian measure of an angle in standard position is the ratio of the length of the arc of a circle centered at the origin subtended by the angle to the radius of that same circle. For a unit circle, which has radius 1, the radian measure is the same as the length of the subtended arc.

---

Important: Be sure you have your calculator in "radian" mode, as trigonometric functions in AP Precalculus are defined for input values that are radians and not degrees.

---

**Example**

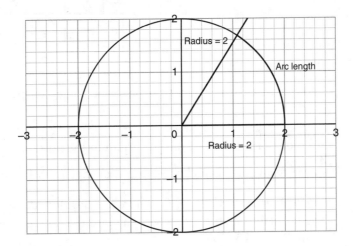

The graph above shows an acute angle that is 1 radian. The circle has a radius equal to 2, and the length of the arc subtended by the angle in standard position is also 2. Therefore, the acute angle measure is 1 radian.

## Sine, Cosine, and Tangent

Given an angle in standard position and a circle centered at the origin, there is a point, *P*, where the terminal ray intersects the circle. The *sine* of the angle is the ratio of the vertical displacement of *P* from the *x*-axis to the distance between the origin and point *P*. Therefore, for a unit circle, the sine of the angle is the *y*-coordinate of point *P*. The *cosine* of the angle is the ratio of the horizontal displacement of *P* from the *y*-axis to the distance between the origin and point *P*. Therefore, for a unit circle, the cosine of the angle is the *x*-coordinate of point *P*. The *tangent* of the angle is the slope, if it exists, of the terminal ray. The slope of the terminal ray is the ratio of the vertical displacement to the horizontal displacement. Therefore, the tangent of the angle is the ratio of the *y*-coordinate to the *x*-coordinate of the point at which the terminal ray intersects the unit circle.

---

This is equivalent to the ratio of the angle's sine to its cosine, so $\tan\theta = \dfrac{\sin\theta}{\cos\theta}$.

---

**Example 1**

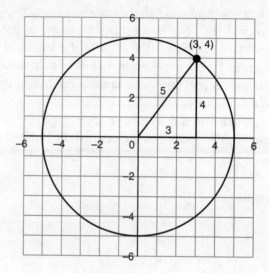

Find the sine, cosine, and tangent of the angle that passes through the point (3,4) on the circle $x^2 + y^2 = 25$.

Solution: The distance from the origin to the point is 5. Therefore, the sine of the angle is $\frac{4}{5}$, the cosine of the angle is $\frac{3}{5}$, and the tangent of the angle is $\frac{4}{3}$.

Given an angle of measure $\theta$ in standard position and a circle with radius $r$ centered at the origin, there is a point, $P$, where the terminal ray intersects the circle. The coordinates of point $P$ are $(r\cos\theta, r\sin\theta)$.

**Example 2**

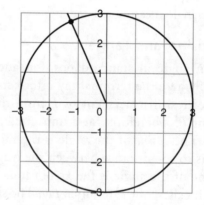

Find the point at which the ray with measure $\theta = 2$ intersects a circle centered at the origin with radius 3.

Solution: The point is located at $(3\cos(2), 3\sin(2))$, which is approximately $(-1.248, 2.728)$.

## Special Right Triangle Trigonometric Values

The radian angle measure and the degree angle measure can be found using the formula $\frac{radian}{degree} = \frac{2\pi}{360°}$, because the degree measure of the circle is 360°. Therefore, an angle with measure 45° can be converted to radians using the formula $\frac{radian}{45°} = \frac{2\pi}{360°}$. This means that an angle with measure 45° is equivalent to $\frac{\pi}{4}$. Notice that the degree symbols cancel each other out, so $\frac{\pi}{4}$ is a radian measure. Similarly, an angle with measure 30° is equivalent to $\frac{\pi}{6}$ and an angle with measure 60° is equivalent to $\frac{\pi}{3}$. This means that an isosceles right triangle and an equilateral triangle divided in half are useful for determining the exact value of the sine and cosine of angles that are multiples of $\frac{\pi}{4}$ and $\frac{\pi}{6}$.

> Recall that the *x*-coordinate and *y*-coordinate are related to the values of the sine and cosine of an angle, so it is important to pay attention to which quadrant the terminal side of the angle lies.

**Example**

Find $\sin\left(\frac{\pi}{4}\right)$ and $\cos\left(\frac{\pi}{3}\right)$.

Solution:
The figures above are special right triangles. Therefore,

$$\sin\left(\frac{\pi}{4}\right) = \frac{\sqrt{2}}{2} \text{ and } \cos\left(\frac{\pi}{3}\right) = \frac{1}{2}.$$

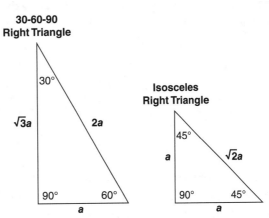

## Sine and Cosine Function Graphs

Given an angle of measure $\theta$ in standard position and a unit circle centered at the origin, there is a point, *P*, where the terminal ray intersects the circle. The sine function, $f(\theta) = \sin\theta$, gives the *y*-coordinate, or vertical displacement from the *x*-axis, of point *P*. The domain of the sine function is all real numbers. When these heights are graphed as a function, the input value is the angle $\theta$ and the output value is the sin$\theta$. As shown in the following pictures, when $\theta = 1$, $\theta = 2$, $\theta = 4$, and $\theta = 5$, the vertical displacement from the *x*-axis to the circle is shown.

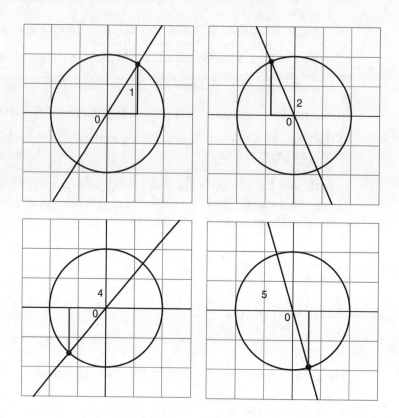

These values graphed with the independent axis as $\theta$ and the dependent axis is the vertical displacement from the *x*-axis to the following graph.

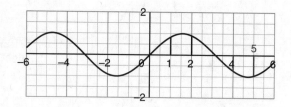

Note that the output values oscillate between −1 and 1 as the input values increase. Similarly, given an angle of measure $\theta$ in standard position and a unit circle centered at the origin, there is a point, *P*, where the terminal ray intersects the circle. The cosine function, $f(\theta) = \cos\theta$, gives the *x*-coordinate, or horizontal displacement from the *y*-axis, of point *P*. The domain of the cosine function is also all real numbers. On the unit circle, when the angle measure is 0, the horizontal displacement is 1, and as the angle increases to $\theta = \dfrac{\pi}{2}$, the horizontal distance decreases to 0. As the angles increases from $\theta = \dfrac{\pi}{2}$ to $\theta = \pi$, the distance continues to decrease until the displacement is −1. Once again, the output values oscillate between −1 and 1 as the input values increase.

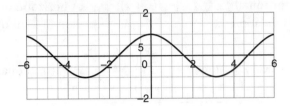

## Properties of Sine and Cosine Graphs

The sine and cosine functions are known as "sinusoidal" functions.

- The cosine function is a translation left $\dfrac{\pi}{2}$ units of the sine function. Therefore, it should be noted that $\cos\theta = \sin\left(\theta + \dfrac{\pi}{2}\right)$.

- Recall that the period is the distance along the independent axis until the graph repeats; therefore, the period of $f(\theta) = \sin\theta$ and $g(\theta) = \cos\theta$ is $2\pi$.

- The frequency is the number of cycles that occur in $2\pi$; therefore, the frequency of $f(\theta)$ and $g(\theta)$ is $\dfrac{1}{2\pi}$.

- The period and frequency of a sinusoidal function are reciprocals.

- The amplitude of a sinusoidal function is half the difference between its maximum and minimum values. The amplitude of $f(\theta) = \sin\theta$ and $g(\theta) = \cos\theta$ is 1.

- The midline of the graph of a sinusoidal function is determined by the average, or arithmetic mean, of the maximum and minimum values of the function. The midline of the graphs of $y = \sin\theta$ and $y = \cos\theta$ is $y = 0$.

- The phase shift of the graph is how many units left or right the graph is translated horizontally.

- As input values increase, the graphs of sinusoidal functions oscillate between concave down and concave up.

- The graph of $y = \sin\theta$ has rotational symmetry about the origin and is therefore an odd function.

- The graph of $y = \cos\theta$ has reflective symmetry over the $y$-axis and is therefore an even function.

## Transformations of Sinusoidal Functions

The transformations of sinusoidal functions are identical to the transformations discussed in earlier units. Recall:

| TRANSFORMATION | $g(x) =$ | CHANGE | NOTE |
|---|---|---|---|
| Vertical Translation | $f(x) + d$ | A vertical translation of $d$ units | |
| Horizontal Translation | $f(x + c)$ | A horizontal translation of $-c$ units | Referred to as the phase shift for sinusoidal functions. |
| Vertical Dilation | $a \cdot f(x)$, $a \neq 0$ | A vertical dilation of $\lvert a \rvert$ | If $a < 0$, the graph is a reflection over $x$-axis. |
| Horizontal Dilation | $f(b \cdot x)$, $b \neq 0$ | A horizontal dilation of $\left\lvert \dfrac{1}{b} \right\rvert$ | If $b < 0$, reflection over $y$-axis. |

If $f(\theta) = \sin\theta$ and $g(\theta) = a \cdot f(b(\theta + c)) + d$, then the graphs have the following characteristics.

| TRANSFORMATION | $f(\theta) = \sin\theta$ | $g(\theta) = a \cdot f(b(\theta + c)) + d$ |
|---|---|---|
| Amplitude, $a$ | 1 | $a$ |
| Period, $b$ | $2\pi$ | $\left\lvert \dfrac{2\pi}{b} \right\rvert$ |
| Phase Shift, $c$ | None | $-c$ units |
| Midline, $d$ | $y = 0$ | $y = d$ |
| Frequency, $b$ | 1 | $b$ |

Note: The same transformations of the cosine function yield the same results described earlier, because the cosine function is a phase shift of the sine function by $-\dfrac{\pi}{2}$ units.

**Example 1**
Identify the key characteristics of the graph of $y = 3\sin(2x + \pi) - 1$ and then graph the function.

Solution: To identify the values of $a$, $b$, $c$, and $d$, the equation should be rewritten as $y = 3\sin\left( 2\left( x + \dfrac{\pi}{2} \right) \right) - 1$. Therefore, $a = 3$, $b = 2$, $c = \dfrac{\pi}{2}$, and $d = -1$. This means that the midline of the graph is $y = -1$ and the amplitude is 3. The period of the graph is $\dfrac{2\pi}{\lvert 2 \rvert} = \pi$, meaning the frequency, or number of cycles in an $x$ interval of distance $2\pi$ is 2. Finally, the phase shift is $-\dfrac{\pi}{2}$. The graph of $y = \sin x$ starts at the origin, $(0,0)$. As you can see in the preceding graph, that point has moved left $\dfrac{\pi}{2}$ units and down 1 unit, consistent with the $c$ and $d$ identified earlier. Also, the maximum of the graph is 2 and the minimum is $-4$. The average of the maximum and minimum is $-1$, which is midline. The distance from the midline to the maximum or to the minimum is 3, consistent with $a$ identified earlier. Finally, the point $\left(-\dfrac{\pi}{2},-1\right)$ corresponds with $\left(\dfrac{\pi}{2},-1\right)$ before the sinusoidal pattern repeats, meaning the period is $\pi$, consistent with $b$ identified earlier.

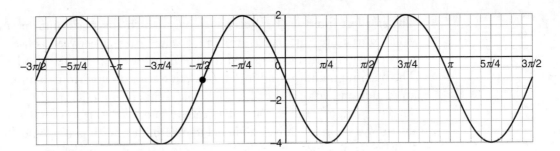

## Example 2

Identify the equation for the following graph.

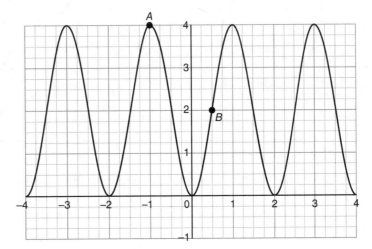

Solution: There are many possible answers to the question depending on your starting value. Two common answers using the points $A$ and $B$ are identified. The point $A$ would be used if the answer is in terms of the cosine function, and the point $B$ would be used if the answer is in terms of the sine function. The midline is $y = 2$, therefore $d = 2$. The vertical distance from the midline to the maximum or minimum is 2, therefore $a = 2$ or $a = -2$. Because the points $A$ and $B$ are identified, the graph is not a reflection about the midline, so $a = 2$. The horizontal distance between two consecutive maximums (or minimums) is 2, therefore $\dfrac{2\pi}{|b|} = 2$, or $|b| = \pi$. Because of the points $A$ and $B$ are identified, $b = \pi$. The cosine graph has a maximum at $(0,1)$, and the maximum identified by the point $A$ is at $(-1,4)$, the phase shift is left 1 unit. Similarly, the sine function intersects the origin, and the corresponding point identified by $B$ is at $\left(\dfrac{1}{2},2\right)$. This would indicate a phase shift of half a unit to the right. For the point $A$, a potential equation is $y = 2\cos(\pi(x+1))+2$. For the point $B$, a potential equation is $y = 2\sin\left(\pi\left(x-\dfrac{1}{2}\right)\right)+2$.

## Modeling Sinusoidal Functions

Sinusoidal functions that model a data set are frequently only useful over their contextual domain and can be used to predict values of the dependent variable from values of the independent variable.

- The smallest interval of input values over which the maximum or minimum output values start to repeat, that is, the input-value interval between consecutive maxima or consecutive minima, can be used to determine or estimate the period and frequency.
- The maximum and minimum output values can be used to determine or estimate the amplitude and vertical shift for a sinusoidal function model.
- An actual pair of input-output values can be compared to pairs of input-output values produced by a sinusoidal function model to determine or estimate a phase shift for the model.
- If more data points are available, sinusoidal function models can be constructed for a data set with technology by estimating key values or using sinusoidal regressions.

### Example

The following table shows the average number of daylight hours for the city Corona, California. Use technology to find an equation that models the data. The month is listed such that January is 1, February is 2, and so on.

| Month | 1 | 2 | 3 | 4 | 5 | 6 | 7 | 8 | 9 | 10 | 11 | 12 |
|---|---|---|---|---|---|---|---|---|---|---|---|---|
| Hours of Daylight | 10 | 11 | 12 | 13 | 14 | 14.5 | 14 | 13.5 | 12.5 | 11.5 | 10.5 | 10 |

Solution: Inputting the table into Desmos or a TI-84 calculator yields the following:

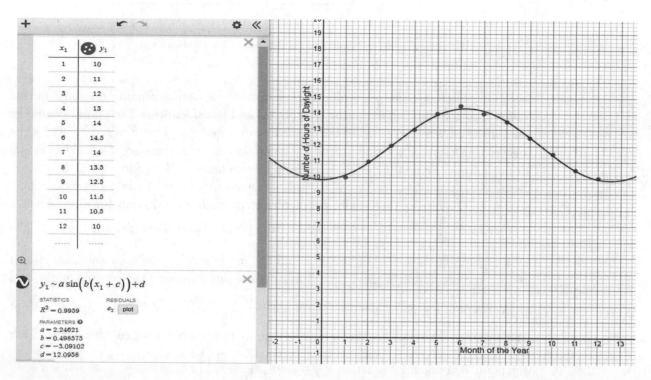

OR

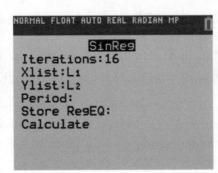 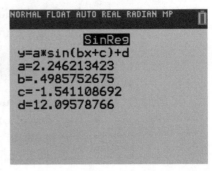

Note: The TI calculator does not write the answer as $y = a \cdot f(b(x+c)) + d$, but rather distributes the $b$ in the inner parenthesis. If you were to factor $b = 0.4985752675$, it would yield $c = -3.091025$ like the Desmos answer.

# The Tangent Function

Given an angle of measure $\theta$ in standard position and a unit circle centered at the origin, there is a point, $P$, where the terminal ray intersects the circle. The tangent function, $f(\theta) = \tan\theta$, gives the slope of the terminal ray. Because the slope of the terminal ray is the ratio of the change in the $y$-values to the change in the $x$-values between any two points on the ray, the tangent function is also the ratio of the sine function to the cosine function. Therefore,

$$\tan\theta = \frac{\sin\theta}{\cos\theta}, \text{ where } \cos\theta \neq 0.$$

**Example**

Calculate the following:

(a) $\tan\dfrac{\pi}{6}$  (b) $\tan\dfrac{2\pi}{3}$  (c) $\tan\dfrac{7\pi}{4}$  (d) $\tan\pi$  (e) $\tan\dfrac{\pi}{2}$

Solution:

(a) $\tan\dfrac{\pi}{6} = \dfrac{\sin\frac{\pi}{6}}{\cos\frac{\pi}{6}}$. This is equivalent to $\dfrac{\frac{1}{2}}{\frac{\sqrt{3}}{2}}$, or $\dfrac{1}{\sqrt{3}} = \dfrac{\sqrt{3}}{3}$.

(b) $\tan\dfrac{2\pi}{3} = \dfrac{\sin\frac{2\pi}{3}}{\cos\frac{2\pi}{3}}$. This is equivalent to $\dfrac{\frac{\sqrt{3}}{2}}{-\frac{1}{2}}$, or $\dfrac{\sqrt{3}}{-1} = -\sqrt{3}$.

(c) $\tan\dfrac{7\pi}{4} = \dfrac{\sin\frac{7\pi}{4}}{\cos\frac{7\pi}{4}}$. This is equivalent to $\dfrac{-\frac{\sqrt{2}}{2}}{\frac{\sqrt{2}}{2}}$, or $-1$.

(d) $\tan\pi = \dfrac{\sin\pi}{\cos\pi}$. This is equivalent to $\dfrac{0}{-1}$, or $0$.

(e) $\tan\dfrac{\pi}{2} = \dfrac{\sin\frac{\pi}{2}}{\cos\frac{\pi}{2}}$. This is equivalent to $\dfrac{1}{0}$, which is undefined.

### Characteristics and Graph of the Tangent Function

- Because the slope values of the terminal ray repeat every one-half revolution of the circle, the tangent function has a period of $\pi$.
- The tangent function demonstrates periodic asymptotic behavior at input values $\theta = \dfrac{\pi}{2} + k\pi$, for integer values of $k$, because $\cos\theta = 0$ at those values.
- The tangent function increases and its graph changes from concave down to concave up half-way between consecutive asymptotes. Therefore, the points of inflection are on the line $y = 0$.
- The graph of the tangent function is given as follows with the points in the previous example identified.

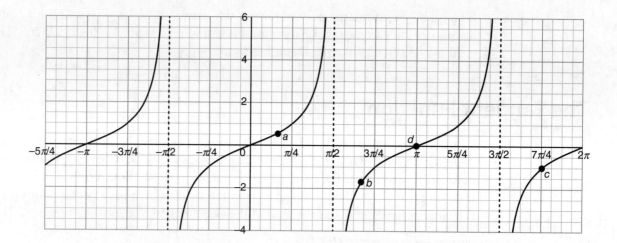

The domain of the tangent function is all real numbers except for $\theta = \dfrac{\pi}{2} + k\pi$.

## Transformations of the Tangent Function

The transformations of the tangent function are identical to the transformations discussed in earlier units. Recall:

| TRANSFORMATION | $g(\theta) =$ | CHANGE | NOTE |
|---|---|---|---|
| Vertical Translation | $f(\theta) + d$ | A vertical translation of $d$ units | The line containing the points of inflection is also translated $d$ units. |
| Horizontal Translation | $f(\theta + c)$ | A horizontal translation of $-c$ units | This is the phase shift. |
| Vertical Dilation | $a \cdot f(\theta),\ a \neq 0$ | A vertical dilation of $|a|$ | If $a < 0$, the graph is a reflection over $x$-axis. |
| Horizontal Dilation | $f(b \cdot \theta),\ b \neq 0$ | A horizontal dilation of $\left|\dfrac{1}{b}\right|$ | If $b < 0$, reflection over $y$-axis. Also, the period is $\left|\dfrac{1}{b}\right|\pi$. |

The combination of the transformations can all be applied to a given function.

**Example**

Identify the key characteristics of the graph of $y = \frac{1}{2}\tan\left(x + \frac{\pi}{4}\right) - 3$ and then graph the function.

Solution: The graph is shrunk vertically by a factor of $\frac{1}{2}$ because $a = \frac{1}{2}$. The line containing the points of inflection is $y = -3$ because $d = -3$. There is no horizontal dilation because $b = 1$, so the period is still $\pi$. The points of inflection are shifted $-\frac{\pi}{4}$ units, or $\frac{\pi}{4}$ units to the left, because $c = \frac{\pi}{4}$. The final graph is shown above with the point corresponding to $(0,0)$ on the graph of the tangent function identified on the graph at $\left(-\frac{\pi}{4}, -3\right)$.

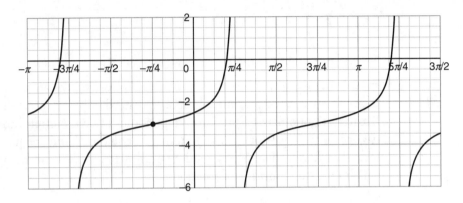

## Inverse Trigonometric Functions

For inverse trigonometric functions, the input and output values are switched from their corresponding trigonometric functions, so the output value of an inverse trigonometric function is often interpreted as an angle measure and the input is a value in the range of the corresponding trigonometric function. The inverse trigonometric functions are called *arcsine*, *arccosine*, and *arctangent* (also represented as $\sin^{-1}x$, $\cos^{-1}x$, and $\tan^{-1}x$). Because the corresponding trigonometric functions are periodic, they are only invertible if they have restricted domains. In order to define their respective inverse functions, the domain of the sine function is restricted to $\left[-\frac{\pi}{2}, \frac{\pi}{2}\right]$, the cosine function to $[0, \pi]$, and the tangent function to $\left(-\frac{\pi}{2}, \frac{\pi}{2}\right)$.

**Example**

Calculate the following:

(a) $\sin^{-1}\left(\frac{\sqrt{2}}{2}\right)$  (b) $\cos^{-1}\left(\frac{\sqrt{3}}{2}\right)$  (c) $\tan^{-1}(-1)$  (d) $\sin^{-1}(-1)$  (e) $\cos^{-1}\left(-\frac{1}{2}\right)$

Solution:

(a) Because the sine function is positive for angles in the interval $\left(0, \frac{\pi}{2}\right)$ and $\sin\frac{\pi}{4} = \frac{\sqrt{2}}{2}$, $\sin^{-1}\left(\frac{\sqrt{2}}{2}\right) = \frac{\pi}{4}$.

(b) Because the cosine function is positive for the angle in the interval $\left(0, \dfrac{\pi}{2}\right)$ and $\cos\dfrac{\pi}{6} = \dfrac{\sqrt{3}}{2}$, $\cos^{-1}\left(\dfrac{\sqrt{3}}{2}\right) = \dfrac{\pi}{6}$.

(c) Because the tangent function is negative for the angle in the interval $\left(-\dfrac{\pi}{2}, 0\right)$ and $\tan\left(-\dfrac{\pi}{4}\right) = -1$, $\tan^{-1}(-1) = -\dfrac{\pi}{4}$.

(d) Because the sine function is negative for the angle in the interval $\left(-\dfrac{\pi}{2}, 0\right)$ and $\sin\left(-\dfrac{\pi}{2}\right) = -1$, $\sin^{-1}(-1) = -\dfrac{\pi}{2}$.

(e) Because the cosine function is negative for the angle in the interval $\left(\dfrac{\pi}{2}, \pi\right)$ and $\cos\dfrac{2\pi}{3} = -\dfrac{1}{2}$, $\cos^{-1}\left(-\dfrac{1}{2}\right) = \dfrac{2\pi}{3}$.

## Trigonometric Equations and Inequalities

Inverse trigonometric functions are useful in solving equations and inequalities involving trigonometric functions, but solutions may need to be modified due to domain restrictions. Because trigonometric functions are periodic, there are often infinitely many solutions to trigonometric equations. In trigonometric equations and inequalities arising from a contextual scenario, there is often a domain restriction that can be implied from the context, which limits the number of solutions.

### Example 1
Find the solution to $\sin x = 1 - \sin x$.

Solution: Adding $\sin x$ to both sides of the equation yields $2\sin x = 1$. Dividing both sides of the equation by 2 yields $\sin x = \dfrac{1}{2}$. Performing the inverse sine function to both sides yields $x = \sin^{-1}\left(\dfrac{1}{2}\right)$, which is equivalent to $x = \dfrac{\pi}{6}$. Because the sine function has a restricted domain in order to have an inverse and there are no contextual restrictions to worry about, we must find all of the solutions. It should be noted that $\sin\dfrac{5\pi}{6}$ is also equal to $\dfrac{1}{2}$, as well as any angle that is coterminal with $\dfrac{\pi}{6}$ and $\dfrac{5\pi}{6}$. Therefore, the complete solution is $\dfrac{\pi}{6} + 2k\pi$ and $\dfrac{5\pi}{6} + 2k\pi$, with $k$ being any integer.

### Example 2
Solve $2\cos^2 x - 3\cos x + 1 = 0$.

Solution: Factoring the equation yields $(2\cos x - 1)(\cos x - 1) = 0$. Applying the zero-product property yields $2\cos x - 1 = 0$ or $\cos x - 1 = 0$. Rewriting these equations gives $\cos x = \dfrac{1}{2}$ or $\cos x = 1$. Using the inverse cosine functions yields $x = \arccos\left(\dfrac{1}{2}\right)$ or $x = \arccos(1)$, which is equivalent to $x = \dfrac{\pi}{3}$ or $x = 0$. Like the previous example, we must consider all solutions.

Recall that $\cos\left(\dfrac{5\pi}{3}\right)=\dfrac{1}{2}$; therefore, another solution is $x=\dfrac{5\pi}{3}$. Also, any angle that is coterminal to these angles is a solution as well. Therefore, the complete solution is given by $\dfrac{\pi}{3}+2k\pi$, $\dfrac{5\pi}{3}+2k\pi$, and $0+2k\pi$ (or just $2k\pi$), with $k$ being any integer.

**Example 3**
Solve $3\tan(2x)-\sqrt{3}=0$.

Solution: Adding $\sqrt{3}$ to both sides of this equation yields $3\tan(2x)=\sqrt{3}$. This can be rewritten as $\tan(2x)=\dfrac{\sqrt{3}}{3}$ by dividing both sides by 3. Applying the inverse tangent function yields $2x=\tan^{-1}\left(\dfrac{\sqrt{3}}{3}\right)$. The inverse tangent function is $\dfrac{\sqrt{3}}{3}$ when the angle is $\dfrac{\pi}{6}$. Because the tangent function has a period of $\pi$, the equation $2x=\tan^{-1}\left(\dfrac{\sqrt{3}}{3}\right)$ can be rewritten as $2x=\dfrac{\pi}{6}+k\pi$, where $k$ is any integer. Dividing both sides of this equation by 2 gives the final result $x=\dfrac{\pi}{12}+\dfrac{k\pi}{2}$.

## The Secant, Cosecant, and Cotangent Functions

There are a total of six trigonometric functions that are required for AP Precalculus. We have already discussed the sine, cosine, and tangent functions. The remaining three are related to those you already know!

| TRIGONOMETRIC FUNCTION (ABBREVIATED) | RELATIONSHIP TO KNOWN FUNCTION | FORMULA |
| --- | --- | --- |
| Secant (sec) | Reciprocal of the cosine function | $\sec\theta=\dfrac{1}{\cos\theta}$, where $\cos\theta\neq 0$ |
| Cosecant (csc) | Reciprocal of the sine function | $\csc\theta=\dfrac{1}{\sin\theta}$, where $\sin\theta\neq 0$ |
| Cotangent (cot) | Reciprocal of the tangent function | $\cot\theta=\dfrac{1}{\tan\theta}$, where $\sin\theta\neq 0$ |

Note: The cotangent function can also be written as $\cot\theta=\dfrac{\cos\theta}{\sin\theta}$.
Characteristics of these new functions:

| FUNCTION | VERTICAL ASYMPTOTES | RANGE |
| --- | --- | --- |
| Secant | When $\cos\theta=0$, which is $\dfrac{\pi}{2}+k\pi$, where $k$ is any integer | $(-\infty,-1]\cup[1,\infty)$ |
| Cosecant | When $\sin\theta=0$, which is $0+k\pi$, where $k$ is any integer | $(-\infty,-1]\cup[1,\infty)$ |
| Cotangent | When $\sin\theta=0$, which is $0+k\pi$, where $k$ is any integer | All real numbers |

Note: It is helpful to sketch the graph of the cosine, sine, or tangent function first and then find the reciprocal of the values to graph the secant, cosecant, and cotangent functions, respectively.

**Example 1**
Graph the secant function.

Solution: The graph of the cosine function is shown using a dotted curve and the vertical asymptotes are shown with dotted lines.

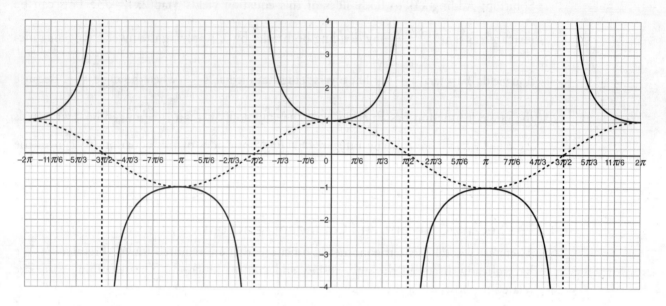

**Example 2**
Graph the cosecant function.

Solution: The graph of the sine function is shown using a dotted curve and the vertical asymptotes are shown with dotted lines.

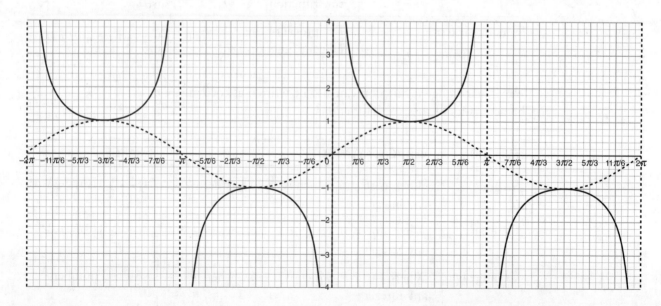

**Example 3**
Graph the cotangent function.

Solution: The graph of the tangent function is shown using a dotted curve and the vertical asymptotes are shown with dotted lines.

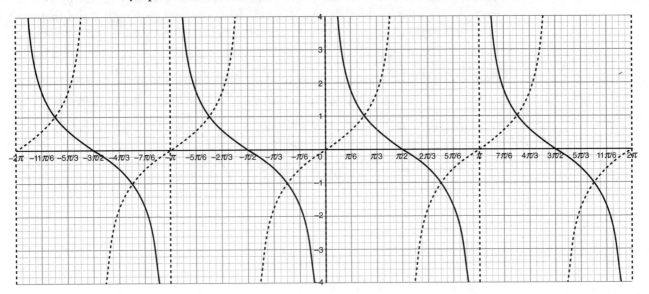

# Important Trigonometric Identities

Because trigonometric ratios are defined using the geometry of circles and right triangles, there are many commonly used trigonometric identities, or equivalent expressions to these identities, that can make information more accessible and are useful in solving trigonometric equations and inequalities.

1. Pythagorean Identity: $\sin^2\theta + \cos^2\theta = 1$. Recall, the coordinates of a point on the unit circle can be labeled $(\cos\theta, \sin\theta)$. As shown in the following figure, this means the terminal ray forms a right triangle with leg lengths $\cos\theta$ and $\sin\theta$ with a hypotenuse of length 1. Using the Pythagorean Theorem, $a^2 + b^2 = c^2$, it follows that $\sin^2\theta + \cos^2\theta = 1$.

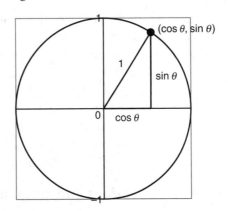

2. The sum identity for sine and cosine are $\sin(\alpha + \beta) = \sin\alpha\cos\beta + \cos\alpha\sin\beta$ and $\cos(\alpha + \beta) = \cos\alpha\cos\beta - \sin\alpha\sin\beta$, respectively.
3. Equivalent forms of the Pythagorean Identity are $\tan^2\theta + 1 = \sec^2\theta$ and $1 + \cot^2\theta = \csc^2\theta$. These follow by manipulating $\sin^2\theta + \cos^2\theta = 1$. Dividing both

sides of $\sin^2\theta + \cos^2\theta = 1$ by $\cos^2\theta$, yields $\dfrac{\sin^2\theta}{\cos^2\theta} + \dfrac{\cos^2\theta}{\cos^2\theta} = \dfrac{1}{\cos^2\theta}$. This is equivalent to $\tan^2\theta + 1 = \sec^2\theta$. The expression $1 + \cot^2\theta = \csc^2\theta$ can similarly be obtained by dividing $\sin^2\theta + \cos^2\theta = 1$ by $\sin^2\theta$.

4. Relationships between inverse trigonometric functions can also be established. For example, if $\sin\theta = x$, then the opposite side from the angle is length $x$ and the hypotenuse is length 1, as shown in the following figure. The Pythagorean Theorem can be used to find the length of the adjacent leg, which is $\sqrt{1-x^2}$. This means that $\cos\theta = \sqrt{1-x^2}$. Using the inverse function, $\sin\theta = x$ is equivalent to $\theta = \arcsin x$ and $\cos\theta = \sqrt{1-x^2}$ is equivalent to $\theta = \arccos\sqrt{1-x^2}$. Therefore, $\arcsin x = \arccos\left(\sqrt{1-x^2}\right)$.

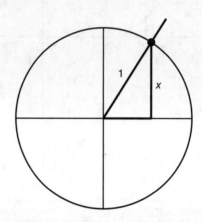

5. Equivalent forms of the sum identity for sine and cosine are $\sin(\alpha - \beta) = \sin\alpha\cos\beta - \cos\alpha\sin\beta$ and $\cos(\alpha - \beta) = \cos\alpha\cos\beta + \sin\alpha\sin\beta$, respectively. Recall that the sine function is odd and the cosine function is even. This means $\sin(-\theta) = -\sin\theta$ and $\cos(-\theta) = \cos\theta$. For the sum identity for sine, $\sin(\alpha + \beta) = \sin\alpha\cos\beta + \cos\alpha\sin\beta$, to find the difference $\sin(\alpha - \beta)$ is equivalent to $\sin(\alpha + (-\beta))$. Substituting $-\beta$ for $\beta$ in the formula sum identity for sine yields $\sin(\alpha + (-\beta)) = \sin\alpha\cos(-\beta) + \cos\alpha\sin(-\beta)$. By applying the even and odd function rules, this is equivalent to $\sin(\alpha - \beta) = \sin\alpha\cos\beta - \cos\alpha\sin\beta$. The expression $\cos(\alpha - \beta) = \cos\alpha\cos\beta + \sin\alpha\sin\beta$ can similarly be obtained by applying the rules to $\cos(\alpha + (-\beta))$.

6. Properties of trigonometric functions, known trigonometric identities, and other algebraic properties can be used to verify additional trigonometric identities, such as the double-angle identities. For example, it can be shown that $\sin(2\theta) = 2\sin\theta\cos\theta$ by substituting $\theta$ in for both $\alpha$ and $\beta$ in the formula $\sin(\alpha + \beta) = \sin\alpha\cos\beta + \cos\alpha\sin\beta$.

7. Similarly, $\cos(2\theta) = \cos^2\theta - \sin^2\theta$. Because the Pythagorean Identity is $\sin^2\theta + \cos^2\theta = 1$, the $\cos(2\theta)$ can also be written as $\cos(2\theta) = 2\cos^2\theta - 1$ or $\cos(2\theta) = 1 - 2\sin^2\theta$. For example, $\sin^2\theta + \cos^2\theta = 1$ means $\cos^2\theta = 1 - \sin^2\theta$. Substituting $1 - \sin^2\theta$ for $\cos^2\theta$ into $\cos(2\theta) = 1 - \sin^2\theta - \sin^2\theta$, which is equivalent to $\cos(2\theta) = 1 - 2\sin^2\theta$.

## Trigonometric Equations and Inequalities Revisited

A specific equivalent form involving trigonometric expressions can make information more accessible. Equivalent trigonometric forms may be useful in solving trigonometric equations and inequalities.

**Example 1**

Solve $\tan\theta = \cot\theta$ on the interval $0 \le \theta \le 2\pi$.

Solution: Because $\tan\theta = \dfrac{\sin\theta}{\cos\theta}$ and $\cot\theta = \dfrac{\cos\theta}{\sin\theta}$, the original equation can be rewritten as $\dfrac{\sin\theta}{\cos\theta} = \dfrac{\cos\theta}{\sin\theta}$. Multiplying each side of this equation by $\cos\theta \sin\theta$ yields $(\cos\theta \sin\theta)\dfrac{\sin\theta}{\cos\theta} = \dfrac{\cos\theta}{\sin\theta}(\cos\theta \sin\theta)$. Simplifying results in the equation $\sin^2\theta = \cos^2\theta$. Because $\sin^2\theta + \cos^2\theta = 1$, that means $\cos^2\theta = 1 - \sin^2\theta$. Therefore, $\sin^2\theta = \cos^2\theta$ is equivalent to $\sin^2\theta = 1 - \sin^2\theta$. This is equivalent to $\sin^2\theta = \dfrac{1}{2}$, or $\sin\theta = \pm\dfrac{\sqrt{2}}{2}$. Therefore, $\theta = \dfrac{\pi}{4}, \dfrac{3\pi}{4}, \dfrac{5\pi}{4}$, or $\dfrac{7\pi}{4}$.

**Example 2**

Find all solutions to $\sec^2\theta + \tan\theta = 1$.

Solution: Using the Pythagorean Identity $\tan^2\theta + 1 = \sec^2\theta$, the equation $\sec^2\theta + \tan\theta = 1$ is equivalent to $\tan^2\theta + 1 + \tan\theta = 1$. Subtracting 1 from each side of this equation yields $\tan^2\theta + \tan\theta = 0$. Factoring results in the equation $\tan\theta(\tan\theta + 1) = 0$. The zero-product property tells us that $\tan\theta = 0$ or $\tan\theta + 1 = 0$. If $\tan\theta = 0$, then $\theta = 0 + k\pi$, where $k$ is an integer. If $\tan\theta + 1 = 0$, then $\tan\theta = -1$. Therefore, $\theta = \dfrac{3\pi}{4} + k\pi$. The complete solution is $\theta = 0 + k\pi$ or $\theta = \dfrac{3\pi}{4} + k\pi$.

**Example 3**

Solve $2\cos(2\theta) + 2\sin^2\theta = 1$ on the interval $0 \le \theta \le 2\pi$.

Solution: Using the double angle formula for cosine, $\cos(2\theta) = 1 - 2\sin^2\theta$, this is equivalent to $2(1 - 2\sin^2\theta) + 2\sin^2\theta = 1$, or $2 - 4\sin^2\theta + 2\sin^2\theta = 1$. Combining like terms yields $2 - 2\sin^2\theta = 1$. This is equivalent to $\sin^2\theta = \dfrac{1}{2}$, or $\sin\theta = \pm\dfrac{\sqrt{2}}{2}$. Therefore, $\theta = \dfrac{\pi}{4}, \dfrac{3\pi}{4}, \dfrac{5\pi}{4}$, or $\dfrac{7\pi}{4}$.

## Polar Coordinates

The polar coordinate system is based on a grid of circles centered at the origin and on lines through the origin. Polar coordinates are defined as an ordered pair, $(r, \theta)$, such that $r$ represents the radius of the circle on which the point lies, and $\theta$ represents the measure of an angle in standard position whose terminal ray includes the point. In the polar coordinate system, the same point can be represented many ways because the terminal rays of an angle and the same angle $\pm 2k\pi$, where $k$ is an integer, are the same.

**Example 1**

Graph the polar coordinate $\left(2, \dfrac{\pi}{3}\right)$.

Solution: The terminal ray of the angle $\theta = \dfrac{\pi}{3}$ in standard position is in the first quadrant. From the origin, move two units along the terminal ray.

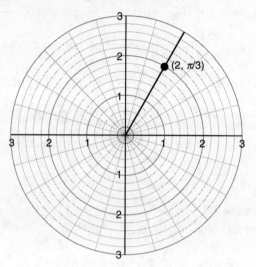

**Example 2**

Graph the polar coordinate $\left( 3, \dfrac{5\pi}{4} \right)$.

Solution: The terminal ray of the angle $\theta = \dfrac{5\pi}{4}$ in standard position is in the third quadrant. From the origin, move three units along the terminal ray.

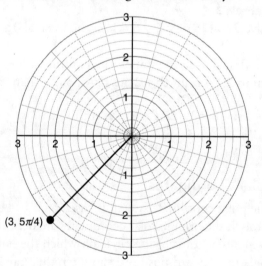

**Example 3**

Graph the polar coordinate $\left( -\dfrac{3}{2}, \dfrac{5\pi}{6} \right)$.

Solution: The terminal ray of the angle $\theta = \dfrac{5\pi}{6}$ in standard position is in the second quadrant. Because $r < 0$, from the origin we move one and a half units *backward* from the terminal ray. Note that this is the same point as $\left( \dfrac{3}{2}, \dfrac{11\pi}{6} \right)$ by moving one and a half steps along the terminal ray $\theta = \dfrac{5\pi}{6}$.

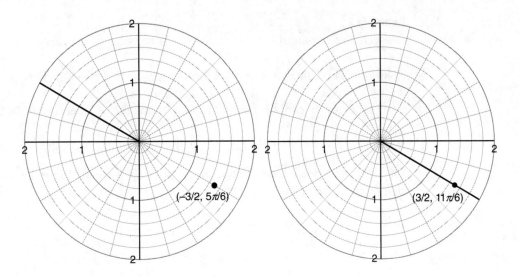

## Converting Between Coordinate Systems

The coordinates of a point in the polar coordinate system, $(r, \theta)$, can be converted to coordinates in the rectangular coordinate system, $(x, y)$, using $x = r\cos\theta$ and $y = r\sin\theta$. The coordinates of a point in the rectangular coordinate system, $(x, y)$, can be converted to coordinates in the polar coordinate system, $(r, \theta)$, using $r = \sqrt{x^2 + y^2}$ and $\theta = \arctan\left(\dfrac{y}{x}\right)$ for $x > 0$ or $\theta = \arctan\left(\dfrac{y}{x}\right) + \pi$ for $x < 0$.

**Example 1**

Convert the polar coordinate $\left(2, \dfrac{\pi}{3}\right)$ to rectangular coordinates.

Solution: The rectangular coordinates can be found using $x = r\cos\theta$ and $y = r\sin\theta$. Substituting 2 for $r$ and $\dfrac{\pi}{3}$ for $\theta$ yields $x = 2\cos\dfrac{\pi}{3}$ and $y = 2\sin\dfrac{\pi}{3}$. This is equivalent to $x = 2\left(\dfrac{1}{2}\right)$ and $y = 2\left(\dfrac{\sqrt{3}}{2}\right)$, which is approximately $(1, 1.732)$.

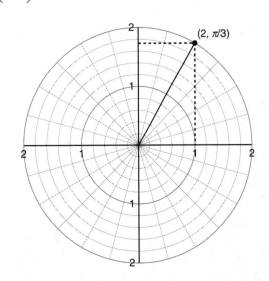

**Example 2**
Convert the rectangular coordinate (3, −4) to polar coordinates.

Solution: The value of $r$ can be found using $r = \sqrt{x^2 + y^2}$. This is equivalent to $r = 5$. The value of $\theta$ can be found using $\theta = \arctan\left(\dfrac{y}{x}\right)$ because $x > 0$. This means that $\theta = \arctan\left(\dfrac{-4}{3}\right) \approx -0.927$. Therefore, the rectangular coordinate (3, −4) is approximately (5,−0.927) in polar coordinates. Note: another form of the polar coordinate is approximately (5,5.356) by adding $2\pi$ to $\theta$.

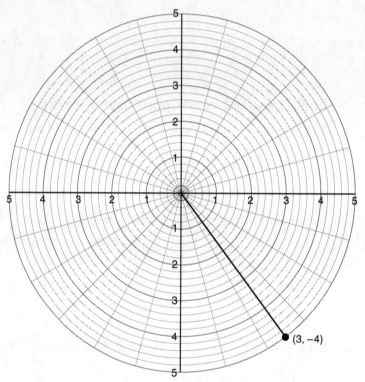

**Example 3**
Convert the rectangular coordinate (−2,−2) to polar coordinates.

Solution: The value of $r$ can be found using $r = \sqrt{x^2 + y^2}$. This is equivalent to $r = 2\sqrt{2}$. The value of $\theta$ can be found using $\theta = \arctan\left(\dfrac{y}{x}\right) + \pi$ because $x < 0$. This means that $\theta = \arctan\left(\dfrac{-2}{-2}\right) + \pi$, or $\theta = \arctan(1) + \pi$, which is $\dfrac{\pi}{4} + \pi$, or $\dfrac{5\pi}{4}$. Therefore, the rectangular coordinate (−2,−2) is approximately $\left(2\sqrt{2}, \dfrac{5\pi}{4}\right)$ in polar coordinates, or approximately (2.828,3.927).

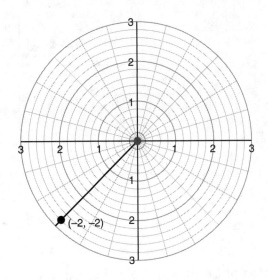

(–2, –2)

## Complex Numbers

A complex number can be understood as a point in the complex plane and can be determined by its corresponding rectangular or polar coordinates. When the complex number has rectangular coordinates $(a, b)$, it can be expressed as $a + bi$. When the complex number has polar coordinates $(r, \theta)$, it can be expressed as $(r\cos\theta) + i(r\sin\theta)$ because $x = r\cos\theta$ and $y = r\sin\theta$.

### Example

Find the polar form of the complex number $-5 + 12i$.

Solution: The value of $a$ is $-5$ and $b$ is 12. Therefore $r = \sqrt{(-5)^2 + 12^2}$, or $r = 13$. The value of $\theta$ can be found using $\theta = \arctan\left(\dfrac{y}{x}\right) + \pi$ because $x < 0$. Therefore, $\theta = \tan^{-1}\left(\dfrac{12}{-5}\right) + \pi$, which is equivalent to $\theta \approx 1.966$.

## Graphing Polar Functions

The graph of the function $r = f(\theta)$ in polar coordinates consists of input-output pairs of values where the input values are angle measures and the output values are radii. When graphing polar functions in the form of $r = f(\theta)$, changes in input values correspond to changes in angle measure from the positive $x$-axis, and changes in output values correspond to changes in distance from the origin.

Note: You are not expected to memorize the shape or names of the polar graphs. Instead, you are expected to be able to use common angles to generate the basic shape.

### Example

Graph of $r = 2 - 2\sin\theta$.

Solution:
As shown in the graph, when $\theta = 0$, $r = 2$. As $\theta$ increases from 0 to $\dfrac{\pi}{2}$, $r$ decreases from 2 down to 0. As $\theta$ increases from $\dfrac{\pi}{2}$ to $\pi$, $r$ increases from 0 to 2. As $\theta$ increases from $\pi$ to $\dfrac{3\pi}{2}$, $r$ increases from 2 to 4. Finally, as $\theta$ increases from $\dfrac{3\pi}{2}$ to $2\pi$, $r$ decreases from 4 to 2.

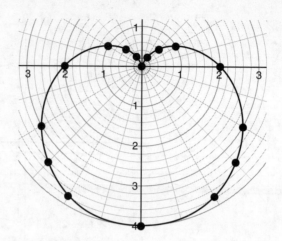

## Rates of Change in Polar Functions

If a polar function, $r = f(\theta)$, is positive and increasing or negative and decreasing, then the distance between $f(\theta)$ and the origin is increasing. If a polar function, $r = f(\theta)$, is positive and decreasing or negative and increasing, then the distance between $f(\theta)$ and the origin is decreasing. For a polar function, $r = f(\theta)$, if the function changes from increasing to decreasing or decreasing to increasing on an interval, then the function has a relative extremum on the interval corresponding to a point relatively closest to or farthest from the origin.

### Example

For the graph of $r = 2 - 2\sin\theta$, identify the relative extremum on the interval $0 \le \theta \le 2\pi$.

Solution: As shown in the previous graph, on the interval $0 < \theta < \dfrac{\pi}{2}$, $r$ is positive and decreasing. On the interval $\dfrac{\pi}{2} < \theta < \pi$, $r$ is positive and increasing. Therefore, there is a relative minimum at $\theta = \dfrac{\pi}{2}$. On the interval $\pi < \theta < \dfrac{3\pi}{2}$, $r$ is positive and increasing. On the interval $\dfrac{3\pi}{2} < \theta < 2\pi$, $r$ is positive and decreasing. Therefore, there is a relative maximum at $\theta = \dfrac{3\pi}{2}$.

The average rate of change of $r$ with respect to $\theta$ over an interval of $\theta$ is the ratio of the change in the radius values to the change in $\theta$ over an interval of $\theta$, or average rate of change $= \dfrac{f(\theta_2) - f(\theta_1)}{\theta_2 - \theta_1}$. Graphically, the average rate of change indicates the rate at which the radius is changing per radian. The average rate of change of $r$ with respect to $\theta$ over an interval of $\theta$ can be used to estimate values of the function within the interval.

### Example

For the graph of $r = 2 - 2\sin\theta$, what is the average rate of change of $r$ on the interval $\pi \le \theta \le \dfrac{3\pi}{2}$?

Solution: Average rate of change $= \dfrac{f\left(\frac{3\pi}{2}\right) - f(\pi)}{\frac{3\pi}{2} - \pi}$, or average rate of change $= \dfrac{4 - 2}{\frac{\pi}{2}}$. This is equivalent to $\dfrac{4}{\pi}$.

# 〉 Rapid Review

## Sine, Cosine, and Tangent

- An angle in standard position has one ray on the positive x-axis and rotates counterclockwise as the angle measure, in radians, increases from 0.
- The ratio of degrees to radians is equal to the ratio of $360°$ to $2\pi$ radians.
- The sine of an angle in standard position is the ratio of the vertical displacement to the distance from the origin.
- The cosine of an angle in standard position is the ratio of the horizontal displacement to the distance from the origin.
- The tangent of an angle in standard position is the ratio of the vertical displacement to the horizontal displacement.
- Special angles, from isosceles right triangles and halves of equilateral triangles are $\dfrac{\pi}{6}, \dfrac{\pi}{4}, \dfrac{\pi}{3}, \dfrac{\pi}{2}$, and integer multiples of these angles.
- The coordinates of a point on a circle centered at the origin where the terminal ray of an angle in standard position are $(r\cos\theta, r\sin\theta)$.
- An angle is coterminal to an angle $\pm 2k\pi$, where $k$ is an integer.
- The sine values of coterminal angles are equal. Similarly for cosine and tangent values of coterminal angles.
- Because the values of the sine, cosine, and tangent repeat, these functions are periodic.

## Sinusoidal Function

- A sinusoidal function is a function that involves additive and multiplicative transformations of $f(\theta) = \sin\theta$.
- The cosine function is a translation left $\dfrac{\pi}{2}$ units, which is equivalent to $\cos(\theta) = \sin\left(\theta + \dfrac{\pi}{2}\right)$.
- The sine functions oscillate between −1 and 1, taking every value in between and tracking the vertical distance of points on the unit circle from the x-axis.
- The cosine functions oscillate between −1 and 1, taking every value in between and tracking the horizontal distance of points on the unit circle from the y-axis.
- The sine and cosine functions are periodic, with period $2\pi$.
- The amplitude of a sinusoidal function is half the distance between the maximum and minimum values.
- The midline is the horizontal line between the maximum and minimum values.
- The graph of the sine function is odd, and the graph of the cosine function is even.
- Transformations of sinusoidal functions behave the same way as they behave for other functions.
- For the functions $f(\theta) = a\sin(b(\theta + c)) + d$ and $g(\theta) = a\cos(b(\theta + c)) + d$, $|a|$ is a vertical dilation, so the amplitude is $|a|$.
- For the functions $f(\theta) = a\sin(b(\theta + c)) + d$ and $g(\theta) = a\cos(b(\theta + c)) + d$, $\dfrac{1}{|b|}$ is a horizontal dilation so the period is $\dfrac{2\pi}{|b|}$.
- For the functions $f(\theta) = a\sin(b(\theta + c)) + d$ and $g(\theta) = a\cos(b(\theta + c)) + d$, $c$ represents a horizontal translation of $-c$ units.
- For the functions $f(\theta) = a\sin(b(\theta + c)) + d$ and $g(\theta) = a\cos(b(\theta + c)) + d$, $d$ represents a vertical translation of $d$ units.

- Sinusoidal functions that model a data set are frequently only useful over their contextual domain and can be used to predict values of the dependent variable from a value of the independent variable.

## Tangent Functions

- The slope of the terminal ray of an angle in standard position is equal to the tangent of the angle.
- The tangent function is a rational function represented as a quotient of the sine function and the cosine function. It can be represented as $f(\theta) = \tan\theta = \dfrac{\sin\theta}{\cos\theta}$, where $\cos\theta \neq 0$.
- Because the denominator of the tangent function is $\cos\theta$, the tangent function has vertical asymptotes at input values $\theta = \dfrac{\pi}{2} + k\pi$.
- The period of the tangent function is $\pi$.
- The tangent function is always increasing.
- Halfway between consecutive vertical asymptotes, the tangent function has an inflection point and changes from concave down to concave up.
- Transformations of the tangent function behave the same way as they behave for other functions.
- For the function $f(\theta) = a\tan(b(\theta + c)) + d$, $|a|$ is a vertical dilation. If $a < 0$, the transform involves a reflection over the $x$-axis.
- For the function $f(\theta) = a\tan(b(\theta + c)) + d$, $\dfrac{1}{|b|}$ is a horizontal dilation so the period is $\dfrac{\pi}{|b|}$. If $b < 0$, the transform involves a reflection over the $y$-axis.
- For the function $f(\theta) = a\tan(b(\theta + c)) + d$, $c$ represents a horizontal translation of $-c$ units.
- For the function $f(\theta) = a\tan(b(\theta + c)) + d$, $d$ represents a vertical translation of $d$ units.

## Inverse Trigonometric Functions

- The inverse functions are labeled either $\arcsin x$ or $\sin^{-1}x$, $\arccos x$ or $\cos^{-1}x$, $\arctan x$ or $\tan^{-1}x$.
- The domains of the sine, cosine, and tangent functions can be restricted in order for the inverse sine, inverse cosine, and inverse tangent to exist.
- The domain of the sine function must be restricted to $\left[-\dfrac{\pi}{2}, \dfrac{\pi}{2}\right]$ for the inverse sine to exist.
- The domain of the cosine function must be restricted to $[0, \pi]$ for the inverse cosine to exist.
- The domain of the tangent function must be restricted to $\left(-\dfrac{\pi}{2}, \dfrac{\pi}{2}\right)$ for the inverse tangent to exist.
- The inverse functions are useful in solving equations and inequalities.
- Depending on the context, more answers may exist because sine, cosine, and tangent are periodic.

## Secant, Cosecant, and Cotangent Functions

- The reciprocal of the cosine function is the secant function. This means that $\sec\theta = \dfrac{1}{\cos\theta}$.
- Because the denominator of the secant function is $\cos\theta$, the secant function has vertical asymptotes at input values $\theta = \dfrac{\pi}{2} + k\pi$.

- The range of the secant function is $(-\infty, -1] \cup [1, \infty)$.
- The reciprocal of the sine function is the cosecant function. This means that $\csc\theta = \dfrac{1}{\sin\theta}$.
- Because the denominator of the cosecant function is $\sin\theta$, the cosecant function has vertical asymptotes at input values $\theta = 0 + k\pi$.
- The range of the cosecant function is $(-\infty, -1] \cup [1, \infty)$.
- The reciprocal of the tangent function is the cotangent function. This means that $\cot\theta = \dfrac{1}{\tan\theta}$, or $\cot\theta = \dfrac{\cos\theta}{\sin\theta}$.
- Because the denominator of the cotangent function is $\sin\theta$, the cotangent function has vertical asymptotes at input values $\theta = \dfrac{\pi}{2} + k\pi$.
- The range of the cotangent function is all real numbers.

## Identities and Equivalent Forms

- The Pythagorean Identity is $\sin^2\theta + \cos^2\theta = 1$.
- The sum identity for sine is $\sin(\alpha + \beta) = \sin\alpha\cos\beta + \cos\alpha\sin\beta$.
- The sum identity for cosine is $\cos(\alpha + \beta) = \cos\alpha\cos\beta - \sin\alpha\sin\beta$.
- These and other identities can be used to create new identities, such as $\tan^2\theta + 1 = \sec^2\theta$ and $\sin(2\theta) = 2\sin\theta\cos\theta$.
- Equivalent trigonometric forms may be useful in solving trigonometric equations and inequalities.

## Polar Coordinates

- The rectangular coordinate $(x, y)$ can be represented as $(r, \theta)$, where $r$ measures the distance from the origin and $\theta$ is an angle in standard position.
- The equations $x = r\cos\theta$ and $y = r\sin\theta$ can be used to convert from polar to rectangular coordinates.
- The equations $r = \sqrt{x^2 + y^2}$ and $\theta = \tan^{-1}\left(\dfrac{y}{x}\right)$ for $x > 0$ or $\theta = \tan^{-1}\left(\dfrac{y}{x}\right) + \pi$ for $x < 0$ can be used to convert from rectangular to polar coordinates.
- A complex number in rectangular coordinates, $a + bi$ with $a = x$ and $b = y$, can be converted to the polar form of a complex number by $(r\cos\theta) + i(\sin\theta)$.

## Graphs of Polar Functions

- The graph of the function $r = f(\theta)$ in polar coordinates consists of input-output pairs of values where the input values are angle measures, and the output values are radii.
- There is no need to memorize the graphs of polar functions.
- If a polar function, $r = f(\theta)$, is positive and increasing or negative and decreasing, then the distance between $f(\theta)$ and the origin is increasing.
- If a polar function, $r = f(\theta)$, is positive and decreasing or negative and increasing, then the distance between $f(\theta)$ and the origin is decreasing.
- For a polar function, $r = f(\theta)$, if the function changes from increasing to decreasing or decreasing to increasing on an interval, then the function has a relative extremum on the interval corresponding to a point relatively closest to or farthest from the origin.

# › Review Questions

## Basic Level

1. Find the values of all six trigonometric functions when $\theta = \dfrac{5\pi}{3}$.

2. Describe the graph of $f(x) = \sin x$.

3. Find the period, frequency, amplitude, phase shift, and vertical translation for the given sine function.

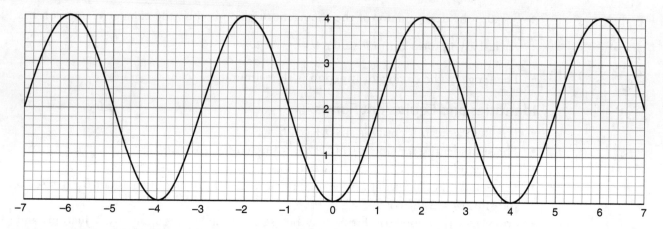

4. Find three equivalent expressions to $\cos(2x)$.

5. Find $\sin^{-1}\left(-\dfrac{1}{2}\right)$ and $\cos^{-1}\left(-\dfrac{1}{2}\right)$.

6. Describe one period of the tangent function.

7. Convert the rectangular coordinate $(-3, -4)$ to polar coordinates.

## Advanced Level

8. Solve for $\theta$ on the interval $0 \leq \theta \leq 2\pi$ for the equation $2\sin\theta + \sqrt{3} = 0$.

9. Solve for $\theta$ on the interval $0 \leq \theta \leq 2\pi$ for the equation $\sin(2\theta) - \cos\theta = 0$.

10. Find the equation of the following graph.

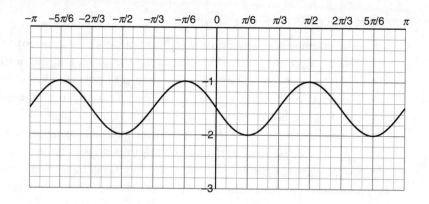

**11.** Which of the following is the graph of $r = 4\sin(3\theta)$? Explain.

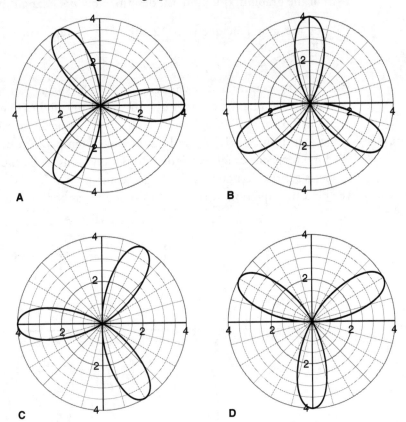

A          B

C          D

**12.** The graph of $r = a + b\sin\theta$ is shown as follows. Assuming they are positive, what are the values of $a$ and $b$?

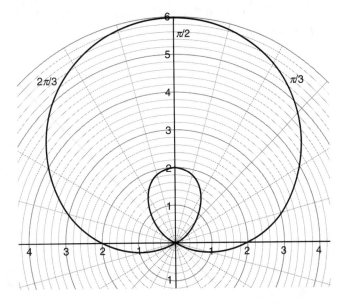

**13.** For the graph in question 12, find the values of $\theta$ in the interval $0 < \theta < 2\pi$ for which $r = 0$.

**14.** For the graph in question 12, describe how $r$ is changing on the interval $\dfrac{7\pi}{6} < \theta < \dfrac{3\pi}{2}$.

**15.** For the graph in question 12, find the average rate of change of $r$ on the interval $\dfrac{7\pi}{6} \le \theta \le \dfrac{3\pi}{2}$.

**16.** The temperature in a certain city during the spring can be modeled using a sinusoidal model. Let $t$ be the number of hours since midnight. The low temperature is predicted to be 55° at 4:30 a.m., $t = 4.5$. The high temperature each day is predicted to be 79° at 4:30 p.m., $t = 16.5$. Find the predicted temperature at noon, $t = 12$.

**17.** Find the value of all six trigonometric functions when the terminal ray of angle $\theta$ intersects a circle centered at the origin at the point $(7, -24)$.

**18.** Find the equation of the secant function graphed as follows.

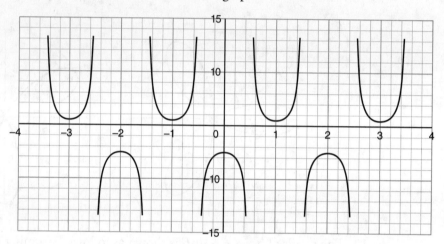

**19.** Simplify the following to a single trigonometric function $\csc\theta\sec\theta - \tan\theta$.

**20.** Solve for $\theta$: $\sin(2\theta) = \sqrt{2}\cos\theta$.

**21.** Solve for $\theta$: $\cos(2\theta) = \sin\theta$.

**22.** Find the average rate of change of the tangent function on the interval $\left[0, \dfrac{\pi}{4}\right]$.

**23.** Let $p$ be a value in the interval $\dfrac{\pi}{4} < p < \dfrac{\pi}{2}$. Are the average rates of change from $\pi/2$ to $p$ less than or greater than the average rate of change from $\theta = 0$ to $\theta = \dfrac{\pi}{4}$ found in question 22? Explain your reasoning.

## 〉 Answers and Explanations

1. • $\sin\left(\dfrac{5\pi}{3}\right) = -\dfrac{\sqrt{3}}{2}$

   • $\cos\left(\dfrac{5\pi}{3}\right) = \dfrac{1}{2}$

   • $\tan\left(\dfrac{5\pi}{3}\right) = -\sqrt{3}$

   • $\csc\left(\dfrac{5\pi}{3}\right) = -\dfrac{2\sqrt{3}}{3}$

   • $\sec\left(\dfrac{5\pi}{3}\right) = 2$

   • $\cot\left(\dfrac{5\pi}{3}\right) = -\dfrac{\sqrt{3}}{3}$

2. • The graph passes through the origin.
   • The midline of the graph is $y = 0$.
   • The amplitude of the graph is 1.
   • The period of the graph is $2\pi$.
   • The frequency of the graph is 1.
   • The graph oscillates between a maximum of 1 and a minimum of $-1$.
   • The graph alternates between increasing and decreasing for an interval of length $\pi$.
   • The graph is concave down on the interval $0 < x < \pi$ and concave up on $\pi < x < 2\pi$.
   • The graph repeats this pattern.

3. • The period is 4.
   • The frequency is $\dfrac{\pi}{2}$.
   • The amplitude is 2.
   • The phase shift is 1 unit right. The answer could also be $1 \pm 4k$, where $k$ is an integer.
   • The vertical translation is 2 units up.

4. • $\cos^2 x - \sin^2 x$
   • $1 - 2\sin^2 x$
   • $2\cos^2 x - 1$

5. • $\sin^{-1}\left(-\dfrac{1}{2}\right) = -\dfrac{\pi}{6}$

   • $\cos^{-1}\left(-\dfrac{1}{2}\right) = \dfrac{2\pi}{3}$

6. • The tangent function has vertical asymptotes at $x = -\dfrac{\pi}{2}$ and $x = \dfrac{\pi}{2}$.

   • The tangent function has period $\pi$.
   • The tangent function is always increasing. Therefore, the tangent function does not oscillate and has no amplitude.
   • The tangent function has an inflection point at $(0, 0)$.

   • The tangent function is concave down on $\left(-\dfrac{\pi}{2}, 0\right)$ and concave up on $\left(0, \dfrac{\pi}{2}\right)$.

**7.** • The value of $r$ can be found by the equation $r = \sqrt{(-3)^2 + (-4)^2}$, which is equivalent to $r = 5$.

   • Because $x < 0$, the value of $\theta$ can be found by the equation $\theta = \arctan\left(\dfrac{-4}{-3}\right) + \pi$, which is approximately 4.069.

   • Therefore, the rectangular coordinate $(-3, -4)$ is approximately the polar coordinate $(5, 4.069)$.

   • Other forms of possible answers include but are not limited to $(-5, 0.927)$, $(5, -2.214)$, or $(5, 10.352)$.

**8.** • By subtracting $\sqrt{3}$ from each side of the equation, $2\sin\theta + \sqrt{3} = 0$ is equivalent to $2\sin\theta = -\sqrt{3}$.

   • Dividing both sides of this equation by 2 yields $\sin\theta = -\dfrac{\sqrt{3}}{2}$.

   • Therefore, $\theta = \dfrac{4\pi}{3}$ or $\theta = \dfrac{5\pi}{3}$.

**9.** • The expression $\sin(2\theta)$ is equivalent to $2\sin\theta\cos\theta$.

   • Therefore, $\sin(2\theta) - \cos\theta = 0$ is equivalent to $2\sin\theta\cos\theta - \cos\theta = 0$.

   • Factoring yields $\cos\theta(2\sin\theta - 1) = 0$.

   • The zero product property states that $\cos\theta = 0$ or $2\sin\theta - 1 = 0$.

   • This is equivalent to $\cos\theta = 0$ or $\sin\theta = \dfrac{1}{2}$.

   • $\cos\theta = 0$ implies $\theta = \dfrac{\pi}{2}$ or $\theta = \dfrac{3\pi}{2}$ and $\sin\theta = \dfrac{1}{2}$ implies $\theta = \dfrac{\pi}{6}$ or $\theta = \dfrac{5\pi}{6}$.

**10.** • The function is either of the form $y = a\sin(b(x + c)) + d$ or $y = a\cos(b(x + c)) + d$.

   • The amplitude is the average distance between maximum values and minimum values. Because the maximum is $y = -1$ and the minimum is $y = -2$, the amplitude is $\dfrac{1}{2}$. Assuming there is no reflection about the $x$-axis, $a = \dfrac{1}{2}$.

   • The period is the distance between consecutive maximums or consecutive minimums. Because there is a maximum $x = -\dfrac{\pi}{6}$ and the next maximum is $x = \dfrac{\pi}{2}$, the period is $\dfrac{\pi}{2} - \left(-\dfrac{\pi}{6}\right)$, which is $\dfrac{2\pi}{3}$.

   • Also, the period is given by $\dfrac{2\pi}{|b|}$. Therefore, $\dfrac{2\pi}{3} = \dfrac{2\pi}{|b|}$. Assuming there is no reflection about the $y$-axis, $b = 3$.

   • The sine function crosses a midline as it passes through the origin. A corresponding point is located at $\left(-\dfrac{\pi}{3}, -\dfrac{3}{2}\right)$. Therefore, the phase shift is $\dfrac{\pi}{3}$ units left and the vertical translation is $\dfrac{3}{2}$ units down. Therefore, $c = \dfrac{\pi}{3}$ and $d = \dfrac{-3}{2}$.

   • The equation is given by $y = \dfrac{1}{2}\sin\left(3\left(x + \dfrac{\pi}{3}\right)\right) - \dfrac{3}{2}$.

   • Similarly, it can be shown that $y = \dfrac{1}{2}\cos\left(3\left(x + \dfrac{\pi}{6}\right)\right) - \dfrac{3}{2}$ or $y = \dfrac{1}{2}\sin\left(3\left(x - \dfrac{\pi}{3}\right)\right) - \dfrac{3}{2}$.

**11.** • When you substitute $\theta = 0$ into the equation, $r = 4\sin(3\theta)$, $r = 0$.

    • When you substitute $\theta = \dfrac{\pi}{2}$ into the equation, $r = 4\sin(3\theta)$, $r = -4$.

    • The only graph that contains the polar coordinates $(0, 0)$ and $\left(-4, \dfrac{\pi}{2}\right)$ is graph (D).

**12.** • The graph contains the polar coordinate $(2,0)$.

    • Substituting 0 for $\theta$ and 2 for $r$ in the equation $r = a + b\sin\theta$ yields $2 = a + b\sin 0$. This is equivalent to $2 = a$.

    • The graph also contains the polar coordinate $\left(6, \dfrac{\pi}{2}\right)$.

    • Substituting $\dfrac{\pi}{2}$ for $\theta$ and 6 for $r$ in the equation $r = a + b\sin\theta$ yields $6 = a + b\sin\dfrac{\pi}{2}$. This is equivalent to $6 = a + b$.

    • It was determined that $a = 2$, therefore, $6 = 2 + b$. This is equivalent to $b = 4$.

    • The equation is $r = 2 + 4\sin\theta$.

**13.** • If $r = 0$, then $0 = 2 + 4\sin\theta$.

    • Therefore, $\sin\theta = -\dfrac{1}{2}$.

    • Applying the arcsin to each side of this equation yields $\theta = \arcsin\left(-\dfrac{1}{2}\right)$.

    • This is equivalent to $\theta = -\dfrac{\pi}{6}$, which is the acute angle made between the terminal ray in the fourth quadrant.

    • That value is not in the desired interval. To find the first value, adding $2\pi$ yields $\theta = \dfrac{11\pi}{6}$.

    • The second value by symmetry of the graph is $\theta = \dfrac{7\pi}{6}$.

**14.** • At $\theta = \dfrac{7\pi}{6}$, $\sin\dfrac{7\pi}{6} = -\dfrac{1}{2}$, therefore $4\sin\dfrac{7\pi}{6} = -2$.

    • Substituting $-2$ for $4\sin\theta$ in the equation $r = 2 + 4\sin\theta$ yields $r = 2 - 2$, which is equivalent to $r = 0$.

    • As $\theta$ increases from $\theta = \dfrac{7\pi}{6}$ to $\theta = \dfrac{3\pi}{2}$, the value of $4\sin\theta$ decreases from $-2$ to $-4$.

    • Therefore, $r$ decreases from 0 to $-2$.

    • On the interval $\dfrac{7\pi}{6} < \theta < \dfrac{3\pi}{2}$, $r$ is negative and decreasing.

**15.** • The average rate of change of (AROC) $r$ is found using $\text{AROC} = \dfrac{f(\theta_2) - f(\theta_1)}{\theta_2 - \theta_1}$.

    • $f\left(\dfrac{7\pi}{6}\right) = 0$ and $f\left(\dfrac{3\pi}{2}\right) = -2$, therefore, $\text{AROC} = \dfrac{-2 - 0}{\frac{3\pi}{2} - \frac{7\pi}{6}}$.

    • This simplifies to $\text{AROC} = \dfrac{-2}{\frac{\pi}{3}}$, or $\text{AROC} = -\dfrac{6}{\pi}$.

**16.** • The function is either of the form $y = a\sin(b(x + c)) + d$ or $y = a\cos(b(x + c)) + d$.

    • The midline is the average of the maximum and minimum temperatures. Because the maximum is $79°$ and the minimum is $55°$, the average is $67°$. Therefore, the midline is $y = 67$ and $d = 67$.

- The amplitude is the distance from the midline to the maximum or minimum. The maximum is 79° and the midline is 67°. Therefore, $a = 79 - 67$, or $a = 12$.
- The period is twice the distance between consecutive maximum and minimum values. Because a minimum occurs at $t = 4.5$ and the maximum occurs at $t = 16.5$, the period is $2(16.5 - 4.5)$, which is 24.

- Also, the period is given by $\frac{2\pi}{|b|}$. Therefore, $24 = \frac{2\pi}{|b|}$. Assuming there is no reflection about the $y$-axis, $b = \frac{\pi}{12}$.
- The sine function crosses the midline as it passes through the origin. A corresponding point is the average of the minimum values and maximum values, which is located at (10.5,67). Therefore, the phase shift is 10.5 units right and the vertical translation is 67 units up. Therefore, $c = -10.5$ and $d = 67$.

- The equation is given by $y = 12\sin\left(\frac{\pi}{12}(x - 10.5)\right) + 67$.

- Substituting 12 for $x$ in the preceding equation yields $y = 12\sin\left(\frac{\pi}{12}(12 - 10.5)\right) + 67$ or $y = 71.592°$.

17. • The graph shows the terminal ray passing through (7,−24) of a circle centered at the origin.
- The hypotenuse can be found using the Pythagorean Theorem, $a^2 + b^2 = c^2$. Specifically, $(7)^2 + (-24)^2 = c^2$. This is equivalent to $c^2 = 625$, or $c = 25$.

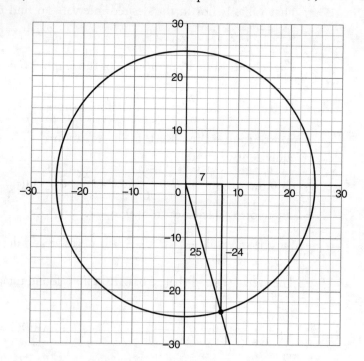

- $\sin\theta = -\dfrac{24}{25}$

- $\cos\theta = \dfrac{7}{25}$

- $\tan\theta = -\dfrac{24}{7}$

- $\csc\theta = -\dfrac{25}{24}$

- $\sec\theta = \dfrac{25}{7}$

- $\cot\theta = -\dfrac{7}{24}$

**18.** • First, it is suggested that you graph the reciprocal function, the cosine, in order to help determine the values of $a$, $b$, $c$, and $d$ in the equation $y = a\,\sec(b(x + c)) + d$.

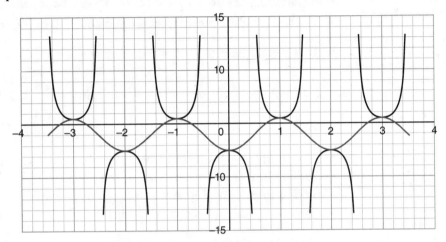

- The midline is the average of the maximum and minimum of the cosine function. Because the maximum is 1 and the minimum is −5, the average is −2. Therefore, the midline is $y = -2$ and $d = -2$.
- The amplitude is the distance from the midline to the maximum or minimum. The maximum is 1 and the midline is −2. Therefore, $|a| = 3$.
- Because the $y$-intercept of the cosine function is a maximum at $(0,1)$ and the $y$-intercept of this cosine function is a minimum, I will choose $a = -3$ because of the reflection about the $x$-axis.
- The period is the distance between consecutive maximums or consecutive minimums. Because a minimum occurs at $x = 0$ and the next minimum is at $x = 2$, the period is 2.
- Also, the period is given by $\dfrac{2\pi}{|b|}$. Therefore, $2 = \dfrac{2\pi}{|b|}$. Assuming there is no reflection about the $y$-axis, $b = 2$.
- The cosine function has a maximum at $x = 0$ and this graph is a reflection about the $x$-axis with a minimum at $x = 0$. Therefore, the phase shift is 0, or $c = 0$.
- The cosine function is given by $y = -3\cos(\pi x) - 2$.
- Therefore, the secant graph has equation $y = -3\sec(\pi x) - 2$.

**19.** • The expression $\csc\theta\sec\theta - \tan\theta$ is equivalent to $\dfrac{1}{\sin\theta\cos\theta} - \dfrac{\sin\theta}{\cos\theta}$.

- The common denominator is $\sin\theta\cos\theta$, so multiplying the second fraction by $\sin\theta/\sin\theta$ yields $\dfrac{1}{\sin\theta\cos\theta} - \dfrac{\sin^2\theta}{\sin\theta\cos\theta}$.

- This is equivalent to $\dfrac{1 - \sin^2\theta}{\sin\theta\cos\theta}$.

- The Pythagorean Identity is $\sin^2\theta + \cos^2\theta = 1$, or $\cos^2\theta = 1 - \sin^2\theta$.

- Therefore, $\dfrac{1-\sin^2\theta}{\sin\theta\cos\theta}=\dfrac{\cos^2\theta}{\sin\theta\cos\theta}$.
- Dividing out the common factor of $\cos\theta$ yields $\dfrac{\cos\theta}{\sin\theta}$, which is $\cot\theta$.
- Therefore, $\csc\theta\sec\theta-\tan\theta=\cot\theta$.

20.
- Substituting $2\sin\theta\cos\theta$ for $\sin(2\theta)$ in the equation yields $2\sin\theta\cos\theta=\sqrt{2}\cos\theta$.
- Subtracting $\sqrt{2}\cos\theta$ from each side of this equation yields $2\sin\theta\cos\theta-\sqrt{2}\cos\theta=0$.
- Important: Do not divide each side of the equation by a function of $\theta$, as you may be dividing out possible solutions!
- By factoring, $2\sin\theta\cos\theta-\sqrt{2}\cos\theta=0$ can be rewritten as $\cos\theta\left(2\sin\theta-\sqrt{2}\right)=0$.
- The zero product property states that $\cos\theta=0$ or $2\sin\theta-\sqrt{2}=0$.
- This is equivalent to $\cos\theta=0$ or $\sin\theta=\dfrac{\sqrt{2}}{2}$.
- $\cos\theta=0$ implies $\theta=\dfrac{\pi}{2}$ or $\theta=\dfrac{3\pi}{2}$ and $\sin\theta=\dfrac{\sqrt{2}}{2}$ implies $\theta=\dfrac{\pi}{4}$ or $\theta=\dfrac{3\pi}{4}$.
- Therefore, $\theta=\dfrac{\pi}{2}+k\pi,\ \dfrac{\pi}{4}+2k\pi,$ or $\dfrac{3\pi}{4}+2k\pi$, where $k$ is any integer.

21.
- Substituting $1-2\sin^2\theta$ for $\cos(2\theta)$ in the equation yields $1-2\sin^2\theta=\sin\theta$.
- Adding $2\sin^2\theta-1$ to each side of this equation yields $2\sin^2\theta+\sin\theta-1=0$.
- By factoring, $2\sin^2\theta+\sin\theta-1=0$ can be rewritten as $(2\sin\theta-1)(\sin\theta+1)=0$.
- The zero product property states that $2\sin\theta-1=0$ or $\sin\theta+1=0$.
- This is equivalent to $\sin\theta=\dfrac{1}{2}$ or $\sin\theta=-1$.
- $\sin\theta=\dfrac{1}{2}$ implies $\theta=\dfrac{\pi}{6}$ or $\theta=\dfrac{5\pi}{6}$ and $\sin\theta=-1$ implies $\theta=\dfrac{3\pi}{2}$.
- Therefore, $\theta=\dfrac{\pi}{6}+2k\pi,\ \dfrac{5\pi}{6}+2k\pi,$ or $\dfrac{3\pi}{2}+2k\pi$, where $k$ is any integer.

22.
- The average rate of change (AROC) is given by $\text{AROC}=\dfrac{f(\theta_2)-f(\theta_1)}{\theta_2-\theta_1}$.
- $f\left(\dfrac{\pi}{4}\right)=1$ and $f(0)=0$.
- Therefore, $\text{AROC}=\dfrac{1-0}{\frac{\pi}{4}-0}$.
- This is equivalent to $\text{AROC}=\dfrac{4}{\pi}$.

23.
- The average rates of change of the tangent function on the interval $\dfrac{\pi}{4}<\theta<\dfrac{\pi}{2}$ are greater than the average rate of change from $\theta=0$ to $\theta=\dfrac{\pi}{4}$.
- On the interval $\dfrac{\pi}{4}<\theta<\dfrac{\pi}{2}$, the tangent function is concave up.
- Therefore, the average rates of change are increasing over equal-length input-value intervals as $\theta$ increases.
- For example, if $\theta=\dfrac{\pi}{3}$, because $f\left(\dfrac{\pi}{4}\right)=1$ and $f\left(\dfrac{\theta}{3}\right)=\sqrt{3}$, $\text{AROC}=\dfrac{\sqrt{3}-1}{\frac{\pi}{3}-\frac{\pi}{4}}$.
- This is equivalent to $\text{AROC}=\dfrac{\sqrt{3}-1}{\frac{4\pi}{12}-\frac{3\pi}{12}}=\dfrac{\sqrt{3}-1}{\frac{\pi}{12}}$, or $\dfrac{\left(\sqrt{3}-1\right)12}{\pi}$.
- $\dfrac{4}{\pi}\approx1.273$ and $\dfrac{\left(\sqrt{3}-1\right)12}{\pi}\approx2.796$, so $\dfrac{\left(\sqrt{3}-1\right)12}{\pi}>\dfrac{4}{\pi}$.

STEP **5**

# Build Your Test-Taking Confidence

AP Precalculus Practice Exam 1
AP Precalculus Practice Exam 2

# AP Precalculus Practice Exam 1

## ANSWER SHEET FOR SECTION I

### Part A

1 (A) (B) (C) (D)
2 (A) (B) (C) (D)
3 (A) (B) (C) (D)
4 (A) (B) (C) (D)
5 (A) (B) (C) (D)
6 (A) (B) (C) (D)
7 (A) (B) (C) (D)
8 (A) (B) (C) (D)
9 (A) (B) (C) (D)
10 (A) (B) (C) (D)
11 (A) (B) (C) (D)
12 (A) (B) (C) (D)
13 (A) (B) (C) (D)
14 (A) (B) (C) (D)
15 (A) (B) (C) (D)

16 (A) (B) (C) (D)
17 (A) (B) (C) (D)
18 (A) (B) (C) (D)
19 (A) (B) (C) (D)
20 (A) (B) (C) (D)
21 (A) (B) (C) (D)
22 (A) (B) (C) (D)
23 (A) (B) (C) (D)
24 (A) (B) (C) (D)
25 (A) (B) (C) (D)
26 (A) (B) (C) (D)
27 (A) (B) (C) (D)
28 (A) (B) (C) (D)

### Part B

76 (A) (B) (C) (D)
77 (A) (B) (C) (D)
78 (A) (B) (C) (D)
79 (A) (B) (C) (D)
80 (A) (B) (C) (D)
81 (A) (B) (C) (D)

82 (A) (B) (C) (D)
83 (A) (B) (C) (D)
84 (A) (B) (C) (D)
85 (A) (B) (C) (D)
86 (A) (B) (C) (D)
87 (A) (B) (C) (D)

# Section I Part A (Multiple-Choice)

Directions:
Time – 80 minutes
Number of Questions – 28
No calculator is allowed for this part of the exam.

Tear out the answer sheet provided on the previous page and mark your answers on it. All questions are given equal weight. Points are *not* deducted for incorrect answers, and no points are given to unanswered questions. Unless otherwise specified, the domain of a function $f$ is assumed to be the set of all real numbers $x$ for which $f(x)$ is a real number. Angle measures for trigonometric functions are assumed to be in radians.

1. Which of the following is the location of the hole in the graph of the function
$$f(x) = \frac{(x-2)^2(x-4)(x-6)}{(x+3)(x-2)(x-4)^2}?$$

| (A) | $(-3,0)$ | (B) | $(2,0)$ | (C) | $(4,0)$ | (D) | $(6,0)$ |
|---|---|---|---|---|---|---|---|

2.

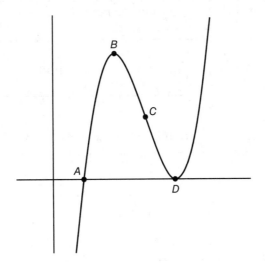

The figure shows the graph of a cubic function $f$, with several points labeled. Let $A$, $B$, $C$, and $D$ represent the $x$-coordinates of those points. Which of the following represents the $x$-coordinate of the point of inflection for $f$?

| (A) | $A$ | (B) | $B$ | (C) | $C$ | (D) | $D$ |
|---|---|---|---|---|---|---|---|

3. The function $f$ is given by $f(x) = 2x^3 - 3x^5$. Which of the following describes the end behavior of $f$?

| (A) | $\lim\limits_{x \to -\infty} f(x) = -\infty$ and $\lim\limits_{x \to \infty} f(x) = -\infty$. | (B) | $\lim\limits_{x \to -\infty} f(x) = \infty$ and $\lim\limits_{x \to \infty} f(x) = -\infty$. |
|---|---|---|---|
| (C) | $\lim\limits_{x \to -\infty} f(x) = -\infty$ and $\lim\limits_{x \to \infty} f(x) = \infty$. | (D) | $\lim\limits_{x \to -\infty} f(x) = \infty$ and $\lim\limits_{x \to \infty} f(x) = \infty$. |

**4.**

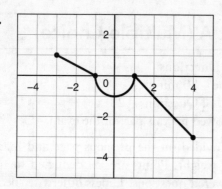

The graph of $y = f(x)$, consisting of two-line segments and a semicircle, is shown for $-3 \le x \le 4$. Which of the following describes the domain and range of the transformed graph for $y = f(2x) + 3$?

| | |
|---|---|
| (A) | The domain is $[-6, 6]$ and the range is $[-2, -6]$. |
| (B) | The domain is $[-6, 6]$ and the range is $[0, 4]$. |
| (C) | The domain is $\left[-\dfrac{3}{2}, 2\right]$ and the range is $[-2, -6]$. |
| (D) | The domain is $\left[-\dfrac{3}{2}, 2\right]$ and the range is $[0, 4]$. |

**5.** The polynomial function $p$ is given by $p(x) = x^3 - 3x^2 + 4x - 12$ and has a real zero at $x = 3$. Which of the following describes the zeros of $p$?

| | |
|---|---|
| (A) | $p$ has exactly two distinct real zeros. |
| (B) | $p$ has exactly three distinct real zeros. |
| (C) | $p$ has exactly one distinct real zero and no nonreal zeros. |
| (D) | $p$ has exactly one distinct real zero and two nonreal zeros. |

**6.** Let $g$ be a geometric sequence. If $g_2 = 36$ and $g_4 = 16$, which of the following could be a formula for $g_n$?

| | | | |
|---|---|---|---|
| (A) | $g_n = 56 - 10d$ | (B) | $g_n = (8 - n)^2$ |
| (C) | $g_n = 81\left(\dfrac{2}{3}\right)^n$ | (D) | $g_n = \dfrac{80 - 4n}{n}$ |

7.

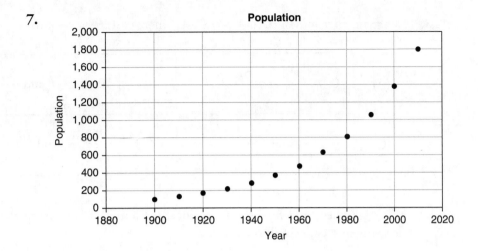

Every 10 years, a local city takes a census of the residents. The preceding figure shows the data from 1900 to 2010. Which of the following graphs displays the data indicating that the population is growing exponentially?

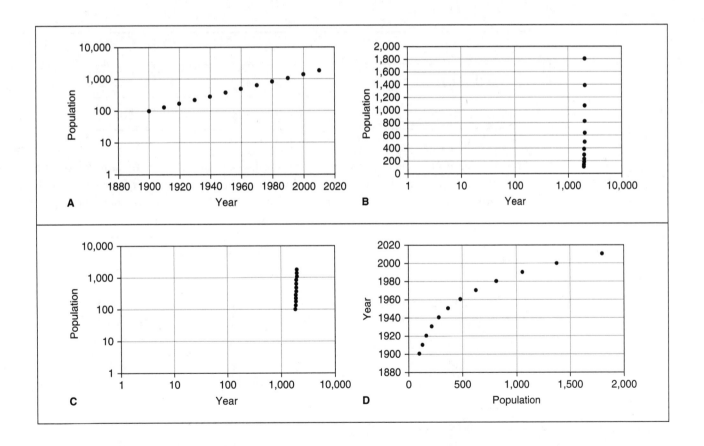

**8.** What are all values of $\theta$, for $0 \le \theta \le 2\pi$, where $\cos(2\theta) = 1 - \sin\theta$?

| | | | |
|---|---|---|---|
| (A) | $0, \pi, \dfrac{\pi}{6},$ and $\dfrac{5\pi}{6}$ | (B) | $0, \pi, \dfrac{\pi}{3},$ and $\dfrac{5\pi}{3}$ |
| (C) | $\dfrac{\pi}{2}, \dfrac{\pi}{6},$ and $\dfrac{5\pi}{6}$ | (D) | $\dfrac{\pi}{2}, \dfrac{\pi}{3},$ and $\dfrac{5\pi}{3}$ |

**9.** When graphed, which of the following functions is an exponential function that is decaying and concave up?

| | | | |
|---|---|---|---|
| (A) | $f(x) = 7\left(\dfrac{1}{3}\right)^{2x}$ | (B) | $g(x) = \dfrac{1}{5}(4)^x$ |
| (C) | $h(x) = -\dfrac{1}{4}(0.2)^x$ | (D) | $j(x) = -5(9)^{\frac{1}{2}x}$ |

**10.**

| $t$ (hours) | 1 | 2 | 4 | 7 | 8 |
|---|---|---|---|---|---|
| distance (miles) | 53 | 115 | 240 | 410 | 468 |

The table shows the distance from home, in miles, a family is after the family left on a road trip at selected values of $t$, the time in hours since the family left home. At which of the following intervals is the average rate of change the smallest for these data?

| (A) | [1, 2] | (B) | [2, 4] | (C) | [4, 7] | (D) | [7, 8] |
|---|---|---|---|---|---|---|---|

**11.** Let $f$ be the function given by $f(x) = 4^x$. The function $g$ is a transformation of $f$ with a horizontal dilation 2. Which of the following is the correct expression for $g$?

| | | | |
|---|---|---|---|
| (A) | $g(x) = 2^x$ | (B) | $g(x) = \dfrac{1}{2}(4^x)$ |
| (C) | $g(x) = 2(4^x)$ | (D) | $g(x) = 16^x$ |

**12.** Which of the following is the graph of $f(\theta) = \dfrac{\cos(\pi\theta)}{\sin(\pi\theta)}$?

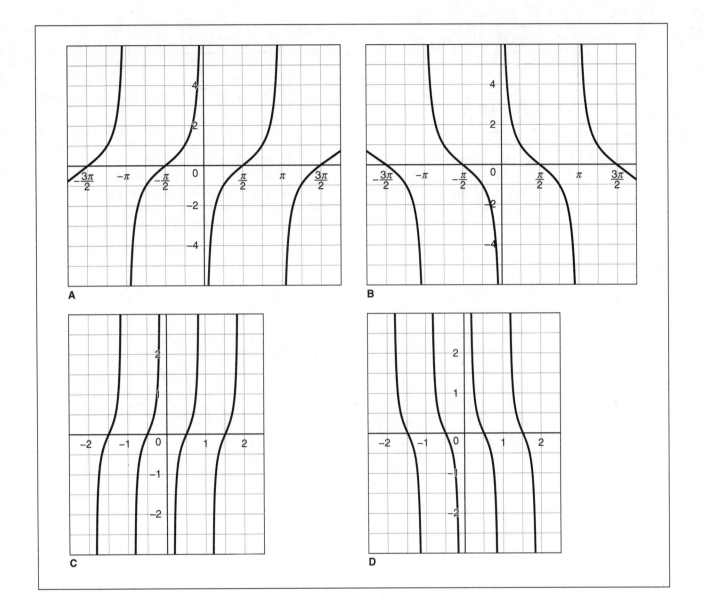

A

B

C

D

**13.**

| $x$ | $-2$ | $-1$ | $0$ | $1$ | $2$ |
|-----|------|------|-----|-----|-----|
| $f(x)$ | $3$ | $1$ | $-1$ | $-2$ | $0$ |

The table shown gives values for the function $f$ at selected values of $x$. The function $f$ is defined for all real numbers. What is the value of $f(f(1))$?

| (A) | $-2$ | (B) | $0$ | (C) | $3$ | (D) | $4$ |
|-----|------|-----|-----|-----|-----|-----|-----|

**14.** An amphitheater has rows that are in the shape of an arc. The first row contains 14 seats, the second row contains 17 seats, the third row contains 20 seats, and so on. How many rows of seats are there if the last row contains 50 seats?

| (A) | 11 | (B) | 12 | (C) | 13 | (D) | 14 |
|-----|----|-----|----|-----|----|-----|----|

**15.** The function $g$ is given by $g(t) = \dfrac{\sin(2\theta)}{\cos^2(\theta)}$. Which of the following is an equivalent form for $g(t)$?

| (A) | $g(t) = 2\cot(\theta)$ | (B) | $g(t) = 2\tan(\theta)$ |
|-----|-----|-----|-----|
| (C) | $g(t) = \tan(\theta)\sec(\theta)$ | (D) | $g(t) = 2\tan(\theta)\sec(\theta)$ |

**16.** The graph of a function $g$ is given as follows. What is the period of $g$?

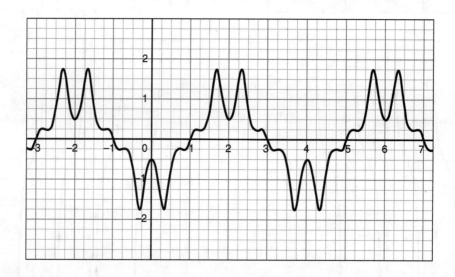

| (A) | 1.75 | (B) | 2 | (C) | 3.5 | (D) | 4 |
|-----|------|-----|---|-----|-----|-----|---|

**17.** Let $f$ be a rational function $f(x) = \dfrac{x^2 - 6x + 8}{x^3 - 4x^2 + 4x}$. When $f$ is graphed in the $xy$-plane, which of the following statements is true?

| (A) | The graph of $f$ has a vertical asymptote at both $x = 0$ and $x = 2$. |
|-----|-----|
| (B) | The graph of $f$ has a vertical asymptote at $x = 0$ and a hole at $x = 2$. |
| (C) | The graph of $f$ has a hole at $x = 0$ and a vertical asymptote at $x = 0$. |
| (D) | The graph of $f$ has a hole at both $x = 0$ and $x = 2$. |

**18.** Which of the following polar coordinates is NOT equal to the rectangular coordinate $(-1, \sqrt{3})$?

| (A) | $\left(2, \dfrac{2\pi}{3}\right)$ | (B) | $\left(-2, -\dfrac{\pi}{3}\right)$ | (C) | $\left(2, \dfrac{5\pi}{3}\right)$ | (D) | $\left(-2, -\dfrac{7\pi}{3}\right)$ |
|---|---|---|---|---|---|---|---|

**19.** Evaluate $\sin\left(\dfrac{7\pi}{6}\right)$.

| (A) | $-\dfrac{1}{2}$ | (B) | $\dfrac{1}{2}$ | (C) | $-\dfrac{\sqrt{3}}{2}$ | (D) | $\dfrac{\sqrt{3}}{2}$ |
|---|---|---|---|---|---|---|---|

**20.** Consider the function $f$ given by $f(x) = \log_4(x^2 - 4) - \log_4(x^2 + 2x - 15)$. Of the following, what are all coordinates of the $x$-intercepts of the graph of $f(x)$ in the $xy$-plane?

| (A) | $x = -5$ | (B) | $x = 2$ |
|---|---|---|---|
| (C) | $x = 3$ | (D) | $x = \dfrac{11}{2}$ |

**21.** The graph of $r = 3\cos(4\theta)$ is shown as follows in the $xy$-plane. As $\theta$ increases from $\theta = 0$ to $\theta = 2\pi$, which labeled point will be traced first?

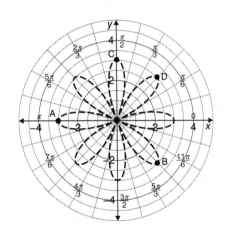

| (A) | $A$ | (B) | $B$ | (C) | $C$ | (D) | $D$ |
|---|---|---|---|---|---|---|---|

**22.** Consider the function $r$ given by $r(x) = \dfrac{x - 2}{x^2 - x - 12}$. Which of the following is true about the graph of $r(x)$ in the $xy$-plane?

| (A) | $\lim\limits_{x \to 3^+} r(x) = -\infty$ | (B) | $\lim\limits_{x \to 4^-} r(x) = \infty$ | (C) | $\lim\limits_{x \to \infty} r(x) = \dfrac{1}{2}$ | (D) | $\lim\limits_{x \to -\infty} r(x) = 0$ |
|---|---|---|---|---|---|---|---|

**23.** The mean monthly high temperature throughout the year for a city periodically increases and decreases. The average time between consecutive maximum mean monthly high temperatures in the city is 12 months, with a minimum mean monthly high temperature occurring at the midpoint of that time interval. The average change in the mean monthly high temperatures in the city between maximum mean monthly high temperature and the minimum mean monthly high temperature is 26.1° Fahrenheit. The mean monthly high temperatures, in degrees Fahrenheit, during a month of the year can be modeled by a sinusoidal function of the form $y = A\sin(B(t-C)) + D$, where $A$, $B$, $C$, and $D$ are constants. Which of the following statements involving $A$ is true?

| (A) | $A = \dfrac{26.1}{2}$ | (B) | $A = 26.1 \cdot 2$ | (C) | $\dfrac{2\pi}{A} = 6$ | (D) | $\dfrac{2\pi}{A} = 6 \cdot 2$ |
|-----|----|-----|----|-----|----|-----|----|

**24.** The following graph is the sinusoidal function $f(\theta) = a\cos(b(\theta + c)) + d$, where $a$, $b$, $c$, and $d$ are constants. Which of the following represents the correct value of a constant?

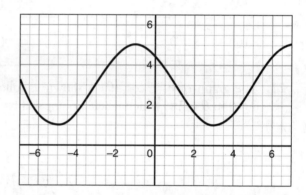

| (A) | $a = 7$ | (B) | $b = 8$ | (C) | $c = -1$ | (D) | $d = 3$ |
|-----|----|-----|----|-----|----|-----|----|

**25.** A concert is scheduled to begin at 8:00 p.m. and the doors to the concert hall open at 5:00 p.m. Let $t$ be the minutes after the concert hall opens. The number of people inside the concert hall at 5:30 p.m. was 24, and there were 48 people in the concert hall at 6:00 p.m. If the number of people in the concert hall is increasing exponentially, which of the following models $n$, the number of people in the concert hall as a function $t$, the number of minutes after 5:00 p.m.?

| (A) | $n(t) = 12(2)^{30t}$ | (B) | $n(t) = 12(2)^{t/30}$ |
|-----|----|-----|----|
| (C) | $n(t) = 24(2)^{30t}$ | (D) | $n(t) = 24(2)^{t/30}$ |

**26.** Which of the following is NOT equivalent to $\log_4 10$?

| (A) | $\dfrac{1}{\log 4}$ | (B) | $\log_2 \sqrt{10}$ | (C) | $\dfrac{1}{2}\log_8 10$ | (D) | $\log_{16} 100$ |
|---|---|---|---|---|---|---|---|

**27.** Let $f(\theta) = \tan\theta$ and $g(\theta) = 3f\left(\pi x - \dfrac{\pi}{2}\right) - 1$. The $x$-coordinate of the point $\left(\dfrac{\pi}{4}, 1\right)$ on the graph of $f$ is mapped to what $x$-coordinate on the graph of $g$?

| (A) | $-\dfrac{1}{4}$ | (B) | $\dfrac{3}{4}$ | (C) | $\dfrac{\pi^2}{4} - \dfrac{\pi}{2}$ | (D) | $\dfrac{\pi^2}{4} + \dfrac{\pi}{2}$ |
|---|---|---|---|---|---|---|---|

**28.** What is the equation of the slant asymptote for the rational function $r(x) = \dfrac{x^3 - 4x^2 + 5x - 15}{x^2 + 4}$?

| (A) | $y = x + 1$ | (B) | $y = x - 4$ |
|---|---|---|---|
| (C) | $y = x - 31$ | (D) | $y = 9x - 31$ |

# Section I Part B (Multiple-Choice)

Directions:
Time – 40 minutes
Number of Questions – 12
A graphing calculator is required for some questions on this part of the exam.

Continue to use the same answer sheet. Please note that the questions begin with number 76. This is not an error; it was done to be consistent with the numbering system of the actual AP Precalculus Exam. All questions are given equal weight. Points are *not* deducted for incorrect answers, and no points are given to unanswered questions. Unless otherwise specified, the domain of a function $f$ is assumed to be the set of all real numbers $x$ for which $f(x)$ is a real number. Angle measures for trigonometric functions are assumed to be in radians. Make sure your calculator is in radian mode. The exact numerical value does not always appear among the choices given. When this happens, select from among the choices the number that best approximates the exact numerical value.

**76.** There were 125 bacteria at the beginning of an experiment in a lab culture. The bacteria were growing exponentially, and after one week the number of bacteria was 250. Which of the following is the approximate growth rate per day?

| (A) | 10.4% | (B) | 28.6% | (C) | 110.4% | (D) | 128.6% |
|---|---|---|---|---|---|---|---|

**77.** Which of the following is the same as $\sin \alpha \cos \beta$?

| (A) | $\dfrac{\cos(\alpha - \beta) + \cos(\alpha + \beta)}{2}$ | (B) | $\dfrac{\sin(\alpha + \beta) + \sin(\alpha - \beta)}{2}$ |
|---|---|---|---|
| (C) | $\dfrac{\cos(\alpha - \beta) - \cos(\alpha + \beta)}{2}$ | (D) | $\dfrac{\cos(\alpha + \beta) + \sin(\alpha + \beta)}{2}$ |

**78.** The terminal side of an angle in standard position intersects a circle at the point $(-6, -8)$. What is the angle measure of the angle?

| (A) | 0.644 | (B) | 0.927 | (C) | 3.785 | (D) | 4.069 |
|---|---|---|---|---|---|---|---|

**79.** The following table displays selected values of a polynomial function.

| $x$ | 0 | 1 | 2 | 3 | 4 | 5 | 6 | 7 |
|---|---|---|---|---|---|---|---|---|
| $f(x)$ | 5 | −1 | −17 | −31 | −31 | −5 | 59 | 173 |

Find the value of $f(-1)$.

| (A) | −11 | (B) | 15 | (C) | 64 | (D) | 88 |
|---|---|---|---|---|---|---|---|

**80.** The amount of time it takes to complete a transaction at the grocery store varies based on the number of items in an order. Data was collected on the number of items in a randomly selected transaction and the time it took to complete the order. The data was graphed, and a linear, quadratic, and exponential model were fit to the data. The following residual plots were created for each of the three models. Which of the following is an appropriate conclusion based on the residual plots?

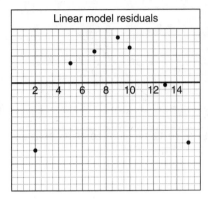 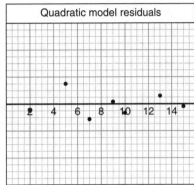 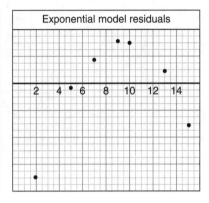

| (A) | The linear model is appropriate. |
|-----|----------------------------------|
| (B) | The quadratic model is appropriate. |
| (C) | The exponential model is appropriate. |
| (D) | Based on the residual plots, none of the models are appropriate. |

**81.** Which of the following is the restricted domain of the function $r = 2 + 3\cos\theta$ to graph only the inner loop?

| (A) [0.841,5.442] | (B) [0.841,3.983] | (C) [2.301,3.983] | (D) [2.301,5.442] |
|---|---|---|---|

**82.** Consider the functions $f(x) = \dfrac{x-7}{x+2}$ and $g(x) = x^2 - 2x - 15$. For what values of $x$ does $f(g(x)) = 0$?

| (A) | $x = 7$ | (B) | $x = -3$ and $x = 5$ |
|-----|---------|-----|----------------------|
| (C) | $x = -5.5$ and $x = -0.5$ | (D) | $x = -3.796$ and $x = 5.796$ |

**83.** A student lives 6 miles from school. One day the student decided to ride their bike to school. The student was riding very slowly at first when they realized they forgot their homework, so they turned around and rode their bike home twice as quickly as they were originally riding. They searched their home for two minutes until they found their homework and then had to ride just as fast as they had ridden home to make up the lost time. While going to school, they were also stopped at a train crossing for one minute. Which of the following graphs depicts this situation, where time, in minutes, is the independent variable, and distance from home, in miles, is the dependent variable?

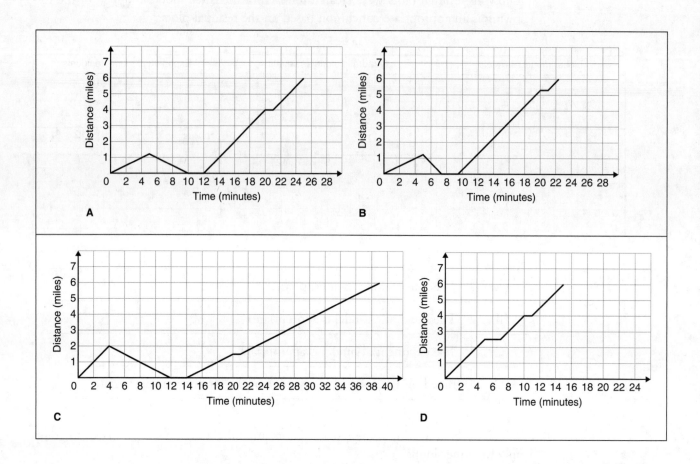

**84.** Over what interval(s) is the polynomial function defined by $p(x) = 2x^3 + 3x^2 - 5x - 6$ decreasing?

| | | | |
|---|---|---|---|
| (A) | $(-1.541, 0.541)(-2, -1)$ and $\left(\dfrac{3}{2}, \infty\right)$ | (B) | $(-\infty, -2)$ and $\left(-1, \dfrac{3}{2}\right)$ |
| (C) | $(-1.541, 0.541)$ | (D) | $(-7.510, 1.510)$ |

**85.** Which of the following functions is even?

| | | | |
|---|---|---|---|
| (A) | $f(x) = \tan x$ | (B) | $f(x) = \cos x$ |
| (C) | $f(x) = x^2 - x + 1$ | (D) | $f(x) = (e^x)^2$ |

**86.** The figure shows a portion of the graph of a function *f*. The function *g* is defined as a vertical dilation by a factor of 2 of *f* and a translation to the left of 2 units. Which of the following is the solution to $g(x) = \sqrt{2}$?

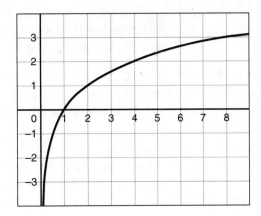

| (A) | −0.367 | (B) | 2.665 | (C) | 3.633 | (D) | 5.103 |
|-----|--------|-----|-------|-----|-------|-----|-------|

**87.** The following table displays the recorded time, adjusted for daylight savings time, of sunrise on the 15th day of each month in Seattle, Washington. The time was recorded as $hour + \dfrac{minutes}{60}$, so 6:15 a.m. would be recorded as 6.25, and the month was recorded as the month number since the beginning of the year, so June was recorded as 6.

| Month | 1 | 2 | 3 | 4 | 5 | 6 | 7 | 8 | 9 | 10 | 11 | 12 |
|-------|------|------|------|------|------|------|------|------|------|------|------|------|
| Time | 7.87 | 7.23 | 6.37 | 5.33 | 4.52 | 4.18 | 4.45 | 5.08 | 5.77 | 6.47 | 7.23 | 7.85 |

Based on a sinusoidal regression, find the residual for the month of May (fifth month) and determine if the model overestimates or underestimates the sunrise on May 15th.

| (A) | The residual is 0.146, meaning the model underestimates the time of sunrise on May 15th. |
|-----|------------------------------------------------------------------------------------------|
| (B) | The residual is 0.146, meaning the model overestimates the time of sunrise on May 15th. |
| (C) | The residual is − 0.146, meaning the model underestimates the time of sunrise on May 15th. |
| (D) | The residual is − 0.146, meaning the model overestimates the time of sunrise on May 15th. |

## Section II Part A (Free-Response)

Directions:
Time – 30 minutes
Number of Questions – 2
A graphing calculator is required for these questions.

*Show all work.* You may *not* receive any credit for correct answers without supporting work. You may use an approved calculator to help solve the problem. However, you must clearly indicate the setup of your solution using mathematical notations and not calculator syntax. A calculator may be used to solve an equation or graph a function. Unless otherwise indicated, you may assume the following: (a) the numeric or algebraic answers need not be simplified; (b) your answer, if expressed in approximation, should be correct to three places after the decimal point; and (c), the domain of a function $f$ is the set of all real numbers $x$ for which $f(x)$ is a real number. Angle measures for trigonometric functions are assumed to be in radians.

**Part A**
A graphing calculator is required for these questions.

1.

| $x$ | 0 | 1 | 2 | 3 | 4 | 5 |
|-----|-----|------|-----|---|---|---|
| $f(x)$ | 0.125 | 0.25 | 0.5 | 1 | 2 | 4 |

Let $f$ be an increasing function defined for all $x$. The table gives values of $f$ at selected values of $x$. The function $g$ is given by $g(x) = \dfrac{x^3 - 1}{x - 2}$.

(A) (i) The function $h$ is defined by $h(x) = (g \circ f)(x)$. Find the value of $h(2)$ as a decimal approximation, or indicate that it is not defined.

  (ii) Find the value of $f^{-1}(2)$, or indicate that it is not defined.

(B) (i) Find all values of $x$, as decimal approximations, for which $g(x) = 1$, or indicate there are no such values.

  (ii) Determine the end behavior of $g$ as $x$ increases without bound. Express your answer using mathematical notation of a limit.

(C) (i) Use the table of values of $f(x)$ to determine if $f$ is best modeled by a linear, quadratic, exponential, or logarithmic function.

  (ii) Give a reason for your answer based on how the output values of $f$ change with respect to the input values of $f$.

2. Students in a biology class were studying the rate at which certain items change temperature when placed in an environment with constant temperature. For one experiment, the students filled a glass with tap water and placed the glass in a refrigerator that was set to 37 degrees Fahrenheit (°F). Fifteen minutes after placing the glass in the refrigerator, the temperature of the water was 71°F and 30 minutes after placing the glass in the refrigerator, the temperature of the water was 66°F.

The temperature of the water in the glass can be modeled by the function $T$ given by $T(t) = 37 + Ae^{kt}$, where $T(t)$ is the temperature of the water, in degrees Fahrenheit, and $t$ is the number of minutes since placing the glass in the refrigerator.

(A) (i) Use the given data to write two equations that can be used to find the values for constants $A$ and $k$ in the expression for $T(t)$.
   (ii) Find the values of $A$ and $k$.

(B) (i) Use the given data to find the average rate of change of the temperature of the water, in degrees Fahrenheit per minute, from $t = 15$ to $t = 30$. Express your answer as a decimal approximation. Show the computations that lead to your answer.
   (ii) Interpret the meaning of your answer from (i) in the context of the problem.
   (iii) Consider the average rates of change of $T$ from $t = 30$ to $t = p$ minutes, where $p > 30$. Are the average rates of change less than or greater than the average rate of change from $t = 15$ to $t = 30$ minutes found in (i)? Explain your reasoning.

(C) The students noted that the model for $T$ is an appropriate model until the temperature of the water was less than 50°F. Based on this information, for how many minutes was model $T$ an appropriate model? Give a reason for your answer.

# Section II Part B (Free-Response)

Directions:
Time – 30 minutes
Number of Questions – 2
No calculator is allowed for these questions.

The use of a calculator is *not* permitted in this part of the exam. You should *show all work*. You may *not* receive any credit for correct answers without supporting work. Unless otherwise indicated, the numeric or algebraic answers need not be simplified, and the domain of a function $f$ is the set of all real numbers $x$ for which $f(x)$ is a real number. Angle measures for trigonometric functions are assumed to be in radians. When you finish this part of the exam, you may return to the problems in Part A of Section II and continue to work on them. However, you may not use a calculator.

3. A buoy is placed in a bay near the ocean to measure the height of the water. On a randomly selected day, the buoy first records the maximum height of water in the bay as 5.2 feet at 4:15 a.m. The buoy first records the minimum height of water in the bay as 1.8 feet at 10:30 a.m.

   The sinusoidal function $h$ represent the height, in feet, of the water in the bay at time $t$ hours after midnight after the buoy was placed in the bay.

   (A) The graph of $h$ and the dashed midline for two full cycles of tides is shown as follows. Five points, $F$, $G$, $J$, $K$, and $P$, are labeled on the graph. No scale is indicated, and no axes are presented. Determine possible coordinates $(t, h(t))$ for the five points $F$, $G$, $J$, $K$, and $P$.

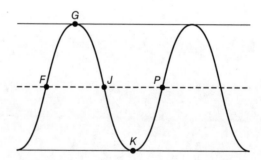

   (B) The function $h$ can be written in the form $h(t) = a\sin(b(t+c)) + d$. Find the values of constants $a$, $b$, $c$, and $d$.

   (C) Refer to the graph of $h$ in part (A). The $t$-coordinate coordinate of $J$ is $t_1$ and the $t$-coordinate coordinate of $K$ is $t_2$.
   (i) On the interval $(t_1, t_2)$, which of the following is true about $h$?
   a. $h$ is positive and increasing.
   b. $h$ is positive and decreasing.
   c. $h$ is negative and increasing.
   d. $h$ is negative and decreasing.
   (ii) Describe the rate of change of $h$ on the interval $(t_1, t_2)$.

4. Directions:

- Unless otherwise specified, the domain of a function $f$ is assumed to be the set of all real numbers $x$ for which $f(x)$ is a real number. Angle measures for trigonometric functions are assumed to be in radians.
- Solutions to equations must be real numbers. Determine the exact value of any expression that can be obtained without a calculator. For example, $\log_2 8$, $\cos\left(\dfrac{\pi}{2}\right)$, and $\sin^{-1}(1)$ can be evaluated without a calculator.
- Unless otherwise specified, combine terms using algebraic methods and rules for exponents and logarithms, where applicable. For example, $2x + 3x$, $5^2 \cdot 5^3$, $\dfrac{x^5}{x^2}$ and $\ln 3 + \ln 5$ should be rewritten in equivalent forms.
- For each part of the question, show the work that leads to your answers.

(A) The functions $g$ and $h$ are given by

$$g(x) = 3\log_2 x + \log_4 x$$

$$h(x) = \frac{\sin(2x)}{1 - \sin^2 x}$$

    (i) Rewrite $g(x)$ as a single logarithmic expression without negative exponents in any part of the expression. Your result should be of the form $\log_2(\text{expression})$.

    (ii) Rewrite $h(x)$ as an expression in which only one trigonometric function appears once and no other trigonometric functions are involved.

(B) The functions $j$ and $k$ are given by

$$j(x) = 2\cos^2 x + \cos x - 1$$
$$k(x) = e^{2x+1} + e$$

    (i) Solve $j(x) = 0$ for values of $x$ in the interval $[0, 2\pi]$.

    (ii) Solve $k(x) = e^3$ for values of $x$ in the domain of $k$.

(C) The function $m$ is given by

$$m(x) = \sin(3x) + 2$$

Find all input values in the domain of $m$ that yield an output value of $\dfrac{3}{2}$.

# Answer Key

| Part A | |
|---|---|
| 1. | B |
| 2. | C |
| 3. | B |
| 4. | D |
| 5. | D |
| 6. | C |
| 7. | A |
| 8. | A |
| 9. | A |
| 10. | C |
| 11. | A |
| 12. | D |
| 13. | C |
| 14. | C |
| 15. | B |
| 16. | D |
| 17. | A |
| 18. | C |
| 19. | A |
| 20. | D |
| 21. | C |
| 22. | D |
| 23. | A |
| 24. | D |
| 25. | B |
| 26. | C |
| 27. | B |
| 28. | B |

| Part B | |
|---|---|
| 76. | A |
| 77. | B |
| 78. | D |
| 79. | A |
| 80. | B |
| 81. | C |
| 82. | D |
| 83. | B |
| 84. | C |
| 85. | B |
| 86. | A |
| 87. | D |

# ❯ Solutions and Explanations

## Section I Part A (Multiple-Choice)

1. The correct answer is (B).
   The multiplicity of the real zero 2 in the numerator is greater than the multiplicity in the denominator; therefore, the graph of the rational function has a hole at the corresponding input value. The output value can be determined by substituting 2 into the simplified expression $f(x) = \dfrac{(x-2)(x-6)}{(x+3)(x-4)}$.

2. The correct answer is (C).
   Points of inflection of a polynomial function occur at input values where the rate of change of the function changes from increasing to decreasing or from decreasing to increasing. This occurs where the graph of a polynomial function changes from concave up to concave down or from concave down to concave up.

3. The correct answer is (B).
   The degree and sign of the leading term of a polynomial determines the end behavior of the polynomial function, in this case $-3x^5$. As $x$ decreases without bound, $-3x^5$ increases without bound, and as $x$ increases without bound, $-3x^5$ decreases without bound.

4. The correct answer is (D).
   The graph of the function $f(bx)$ is a horizontal dilation of the graph of $f$ by a factor of $\left|\dfrac{1}{b}\right|$, so the domain of $g$ is $\left[-\dfrac{3}{2}, 2\right]$. The graph of the function $f(x) + k$ is a vertical translation of the graph of $f$ by $k$ units, so the range of $g$ is $[0, 4]$.

5. The correct answer is (D).

   Because $x = 3$ is a zero of the function, $(x - 3)$ is a linear factor of $p$. Therefore, $p(x) = x^3 - 3x^2 + 4x - 12$ is the same as $p(x) = (x - 3)(x^2 + 4)$. The non-real zeros of $x^2 + 4$ are $\pm 2i$.

6. The correct answer is (C).

   The general form of a geometric sequence is $g_n = g_0 r^n$. The given information indicates that $36 = g_0 r^2$ and $16 = g_0 r^4$. Dividing these equations yields $\dfrac{16}{36} = \dfrac{g_0 r^4}{g_0 r^2}$, or $r^2 = \dfrac{16}{36}$, which means $r = \dfrac{2}{3}$. Substituting $\dfrac{2}{3}$ for $r$ in the equation $36 = g_0 r^2$ yields $36 = g_0 \left(\dfrac{2}{3}\right)^2$, which is equivalent to $36 = \dfrac{4}{9} g_0$. Therefore, $g_0 = 81$.

7. The correct answer is (A).

   When the $y$-axis of a semi-log plot is logarithmically scaled, data or functions that demonstrate exponential characteristics will appear linear.

8. The correct answer is (A).

   $\cos(2\theta) = 1 - \sin\theta \Rightarrow 1 - 2\sin^2\theta = 1 - \sin\theta$, or $0 = 2\sin^2\theta - \sin\theta$. Factoring this expression yields $0 = \sin\theta(2\sin\theta - 1)$. The zero product property states that if two quantities are multiplied and the result is zero, at least one of the quantities must be zero. Therefore $\sin\theta = 0$ or $2\sin\theta - 1 = 0$. $\sin\theta = 0$ for $\theta = 0$ and $\theta = \pi$. $2\sin\theta - 1 = 0$ is equivalent to $\sin\theta = \dfrac{1}{2}$, which occurs at $\theta = \dfrac{\pi}{6}$ and $\theta = \dfrac{5\pi}{6}$.

9. The correct answer is (A).

   An exponential function is decaying if $0 < b < 1$, and an exponential function is growing if $b > 1$. A graph is concave up if the rate of change is increasing, and a graph is concave down if the rate of change is decreasing.

   Note the following:

   | FUNCTION | $b$ | RATE OF CHANGE |
   | --- | --- | --- |
   | $f(x) = 7\left(\dfrac{1}{3}\right)^{2x}$ | $\dfrac{1}{9}$ | increasing |
   | $g(x) = \dfrac{1}{5}(4)^x$ | $4$ | increasing |
   | $h(x) = -\dfrac{1}{4}(0.2)^x$ | $0.2$ | decreasing |
   | $j(x) = -5(9)^{\frac{1}{2}x}$ | $3$ | decreasing |

10. The correct answer is (C).

    The average rate of change on the interval $[a, b]$ is the slope of the secant line from $(a, f(a))$ to $(b, f(b))$. The average rate of change on $[1, 2]$ is $\dfrac{115 - 53}{2 - 1} = 62$. The average rate of change on [2, 4] is $\dfrac{240-115}{4-2}=\dfrac{125}{2}=62.5$. The average rate of change on [4, 7]

is $\dfrac{410-240}{7-4}=\dfrac{170}{3}\approx 56.667$. The average rate of change on [7, 8] is $\dfrac{468-410}{8-7}=58$.

Therefore, the interval [4, 7] is the interval with the smallest average rate of change.

11. The correct answer is (A).

The function $f(bx)$ has a horizontal dilation by a factor of $\left|\dfrac{1}{b}\right|$. A horizontal dilation

of 2 is equivalent to $f\left(\dfrac{x}{2}\right)$, so $g(x)=4^{\frac{x}{2}}$. Using the power rule, this is equivalent

to $g(x)=\left(4^{1/2}\right)^{x}=2^{x}$.

12. The correct answer is (D).

$f(\theta)=\dfrac{\cos(\pi\theta)}{\sin(\pi\theta)}=\cot(\pi\theta)$. The period of the cotangent function is $\pi$, so the period

of $f(\theta)=\cot(\pi\theta)$ is 1. Also, the cotangent is decreasing between consecutive vertical asymptotes.

13. The correct answer is (C).

From the table, $f(1)=-2$, so $f(f(1))=f(-2)$. From the table, $f(-2)=3$.

14. The correct answer is (C).

The sequence given is arithmetic with a common difference $d=3$ and an initial value $a_1=14$. For an arithmetic sequence $a_n=a_1+d(n-1)$. In this case, $50=14+3(n-1)$ or $50=11+3n$. Solving yields $n=13$.

15. The correct answer is (B).

$g(t)=\dfrac{\sin(2\theta)}{\cos^2(\theta)}=\dfrac{2\sin(\theta)\cos(\theta)}{\cos^2(\theta)}=\dfrac{2\sin\theta}{\cos\theta}=2\tan\theta$

16. The correct answer is (D).

The period of the function is the smallest positive value $k$ such that $f(x+k)=f(x)$ for all $x$ in the domain. A local minimum occurs $(0, -0.5)$ and the corresponding local minimum first occurs again at $(4, -0.5)$

17. The correct answer is (A).

The graph of a rational function has a vertical asymptote when $a$ is a real zero of the denominator and not the numerator or when the multiplicity of the real zero in the denominator is greater than the multiplicity of the real zero in the numerator.

Factoring $f$ yields $f(x)=\dfrac{(x-2)(x-4)}{x(x-2)^2}=\dfrac{x-4}{x(x-2)}$. Therefore, the graph of $f$ has verti-

cal asymptotes at $x=0$ and $x=2$.

18. The correct answer is (C).

The Cartesian coordinate $\left(-1,\sqrt{3}\right)$ lies in the second quadrant. The polar coordinate

$\left(2,\dfrac{5\pi}{3}\right)$ lies in the fourth quadrant. Also, the formulas $x=r\cos\theta$ and $y=r\sin\theta$ can

be used to convert between polar and Cartesian coordinates. For answer choice (A),

$-1 = 2\cos\left(\dfrac{2\pi}{3}\right)$ and $\sqrt{3} = 2\sin\left(\dfrac{2\pi}{3}\right)$. For answer choice (B), $-1 = -2\cos\left(-\dfrac{\pi}{3}\right)$ and $\sqrt{3} = -2\sin\left(-\dfrac{\pi}{3}\right)$. For answer choice (D), $-1 = -2\cos\left(-\dfrac{7\pi}{3}\right)$ and $\sqrt{3} = -2\sin\left(-\dfrac{7\pi}{3}\right)$.

However, for answer choice (C), $1 = 2\cos\left(\dfrac{5\pi}{3}\right)$ and $-\sqrt{3} = 2\sin\left(\dfrac{5\pi}{3}\right)$.

**19.** The correct answer is (A).

The terminal side of $\theta = \dfrac{7\pi}{6}$ lies in the third quadrant. The reference angle in the right triangle made with the terminal side of the angle intersecting the unit circle is $\theta = \dfrac{\pi}{6} = 30°$. The sine is the ratio of the opposite side and the hypotenuse, which is $\dfrac{1}{2} : 1$. Because the angle is in the third quadrant, the value is negative.

**20.** The correct answer is (D).

The intercepts occur when $f(x) = 0$, or $\log_4(x^2 - 4) - \log_4(x^2 + 2x - 15) = 0$, which is equivalent to $\log_4 \dfrac{x^2 - 4}{x^2 + 2x - 15} = 0$, or $\dfrac{x^2 - 4}{x^2 + 2x - 15} = 1 \Rightarrow x^2 - 4 = x^2 + 2x - 15 \Rightarrow 11 = 2x$, or $x = \dfrac{11}{2}$.

**21.** The correct answer is (C).

The tips of the petals for the rose curve $r = 3\cos(4\theta)$ occur at multiples of $\dfrac{\pi}{4}$, with $\theta > 0$. The following table shows the polar coordinates of the tips in order with the corresponding letter where applicable.

| PETAL ORDER FOR $\theta > 0$ | 1 | 2 | 3 | 4 | 5 | 6 | 7 | 8 |
|---|---|---|---|---|---|---|---|---|
| Coordinate | $\left(-3, \dfrac{\pi}{4}\right)$ | $\left(3, \dfrac{\pi}{2}\right)$ | $\left(-3, \dfrac{3\pi}{4}\right)$ | $(3, \pi)$ | $\left(-3, \dfrac{5\pi}{4}\right)$ | $\left(3, \dfrac{3\pi}{2}\right)$ | $\left(-3, \dfrac{7\pi}{4}\right)$ | $(3, 2\pi)$ |
| Label | | C | B | A | D | | | |

**22.** The correct answer is (D).

The polynomial in the denominator has a larger degree than the polynomial in the numerator; therefore, the rational function has a horizontal asymptote at $y = 0$.

**23.** The correct answer is (A).

The amplitude is half the distance between the maximum value and the minimum value. It is given that the difference between maximums and minimums is 26.1°F, so $A = \dfrac{26.1}{2}$.

**24.** The correct answer is (D).

The amplitude is $|a|$, which is the vertical distance from the midline to the maximum or minimum, which is 2. The period is $\left|\dfrac{1}{b}\right| 2\pi$, which is the horizontal distance between consecutive minimums, which is 8. Therefore, $b = \dfrac{\pi}{4}$. The maximum of the cosine is at

(0, 1), which has been shifted left one unit. The phase shift is $-c$, therefore $c = 1$. The midline of the cosine function is $y = 0$. The midline of the graph has shifted upward to $y = 3$, therefore, $d = 3$.

**25.** The correct answer is (B).

It is given that $n(30) = 24$ and $n(60) = 48$. Because $n(t) = a(b)^t$, the given information results in the equations $24 = a(b)^{30}$ and $48 = a(b)^{60}$. Dividing these equations yields $2 = b^{30}$ or $b = 2^{1/30}$. Plugging $b = 2^{1/30}$ into the first equation $24 = a(b)^{30}$ results in $a = 12$.

**26.** The correct answer is (C).

Using the change of base formula, $\log_4 10 = \dfrac{\log 10}{\log 4} = \dfrac{1}{\log 4}$. Using the change of base

formula, $\log_4 10 = \dfrac{\log_2 10}{\log_2 4} = \dfrac{\log_2 10}{2} = \dfrac{1}{2}\log_2 10 = \log_2 \sqrt{10}$. Using the change of base

formula, $\log_4 10 = \dfrac{\log_{16} 10}{\log_{16} 4} = \dfrac{\log_{16} 10}{\dfrac{1}{2}} = 2\log_{16} 10 = \log_{16} 10^2 = \log_{16} 100$.

**27.** The correct answer is (B).

$g(\theta) = 3f\left(\pi x - \dfrac{\pi}{2}\right) - 1 = 3f\left(\pi\left(x - \dfrac{1}{2}\right) - 1\right)$. Therefore, there is a horizontal dilation

of $\dfrac{1}{\pi}$ and then a translation of $\dfrac{1}{2}$ units to the right. This is equivalent to taking the

$x$-coordinate and multiplying by $\dfrac{1}{\pi}$ and then adding $\dfrac{1}{2}$, or $\left(\dfrac{\pi}{4}\right)\dfrac{1}{\pi} + \dfrac{1}{2} = \dfrac{3}{4}$.

**28.** The correct answer is (B).

Using long division, $x^3 - 4x^2 + 5x - 15 = (x^2 + 4)(x - 4) + (x + 1)$, where the quotient, $q$, is $q(x) = x - 4$ and the slant asymptote is the quotient, $q$, which is $q(x) = x - 4$.

# Section I Part B (Multiple-Choice)

**76.** The correct answer is (A).

The rate of growth can be modeled by $P(w) = 125(2)^w$, where $p$ is the number of bacteria and $w$ is the number of weeks. This is equivalent to $P(d) = 125(2)^{d/7}$, where $p$ is the number of bacteria and $d$ is the number of days. This is approximately $P(d) \approx 125(1.104)^d$, so each day, there are about 10.4% more bacteria.

**77.** The correct answer is (B).

It is known that $\sin(\alpha + \beta) = \sin\alpha\cos\beta + \cos\alpha\sin\beta$ and $\sin(\alpha - \beta) = \sin\alpha\cos\beta - \cos\alpha\sin\beta$. Adding these equations yields $\sin(\alpha + \beta) + \sin(\alpha - \beta) = 2\sin\alpha\cos\beta$, or

$\sin\alpha\cos\beta = \dfrac{\sin(\alpha + \beta) + \sin(\alpha - \beta)}{2}$.

**78.** The correct answer is (D).

The terminal side of the angle goes through $(-6, -8)$, which is in the third quadrant.

Therefore, $\theta = \tan^{-1}\left(\dfrac{-8}{-6}\right) + \pi$.

**79.** The correct answer is (A).

When examining successive differences from the output values, it can be shown that the least value $n$ for which the $n$th difference is constant is 3. Therefore, the polynomial is degree 3. Using technology to calculate a cubic regression model yields $f(x) = 2x^3 - 11x^2 + 3x + 5$. Plugging in $-1$ for $x$ yields $f(-1) = (-1)^3 - 11(-1)^2 + 3(-1) + 5$, which is equivalent to $f(-1) = -11$.

**80.** The correct answer is (B).

A model is justified as appropriate for a data set if the graph of the residuals of a regression appear without a pattern. The quadratic model is the only model that does not show a pattern.

**81.** The correct answer is (C).

The inner loop of $r = 2 + 3\cos\theta$ is when $2 + 3\cos\theta = 0$, which means $\theta = \cos^{-1}\left(-\dfrac{2}{3}\right)$ and $\theta = 2\pi - \cos^{-1}\left(-\dfrac{2}{3}\right)$.

**82.** The correct answer is (D).

The function $f(g(x))$ is obtained by substituting $g(x)$ for $x$ in the equation of $f(x)$. Therefore, $f(g(x)) = \dfrac{(x^2 - 2x - 15) - 7}{(x^2 - 2x - 15) + 2}$. Using technology, the graph of $f(g(x))$ is shown as follows.

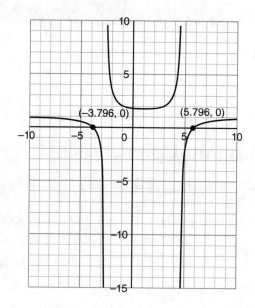

**83.** The correct answer is (B).

The slope of the line returning to home is twice the magnitude of the slope of the line when the student first left. Also, the slopes of the lines when leaving for the second time should be the same in magnitude as when the student returned home.

**84.** The correct answer is (C).

On the interval $(-1.541, 0.541)$ in the graph that follows, for $a < b$ in the interval, $f(a) > f(b)$.

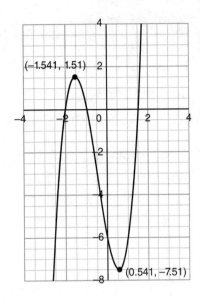

**85.** The correct answer is (B).

The graph of $f(x) = \cos x$ is the only function with the property $f(-x) = f(x)$.

**86.** The correct answer is (A).

The graph shown is $f(x) = \log_2 x$. Therefore, $g(x) = 2\log_2(x+2)$. Therefore, the equation

$$2\log_2(x+2) = \sqrt{2} \Rightarrow \log_2(x+2) = \frac{\sqrt{2}}{2}, \text{ or } x+2 = 2^{\sqrt{2}/2} \Rightarrow x = 2^{\sqrt{2}/2} - 2 \approx -0.367.$$

**87.** The correct answer is (D).

Using technology to obtain a sinusoidal regression model, the time of sunrise on the 15th day of the month can be approximated by $\hat{t} = 1.845944908 \sin(0.5002275417 (x + 1.543449224)) + 6.115736178$. The predicted time on May 15th is 4.66633. The residual is given by observed minus predicted, or $4.52 - 4.66633 = -0.14633$. The time predicted is larger than the time observed.

# Section II Free-Response Answer Key

**1.** (A) (i) $h(2) = \dfrac{7}{12} \approx 0.583$    1 point

      (ii) $f^{-1}(2) = 4$    1 point

   (B) (i) $x \approx -1.325$    1 point

      (ii) $\lim\limits_{x \to \infty} g(x) = \infty$    1 point

   (C) (i) exponential    1 point

      (ii) See full solution.    1 point

**2.** (A) (i) $71 = 37 + Ae^{15k}$ and $66 = 37 + Ae^{30k}$        1 point

    (ii) $k = \dfrac{1}{15}\ln\left(\dfrac{29}{34}\right)$, $A = \dfrac{1{,}156}{29}$        1 point

  (B) (i) $\dfrac{T(30) - T(15)}{30 - 15} \approx -0.333$ degrees Fahrenheit per minute        1 point

    (ii) See full solution.        1 point

    (iii) greater than        1 point

  (C) approximately 116.239 minutes        1 point

**3.** (A) $F$ has coordinates $(1.125, 3.5)$        1 point for $h(t)$
       $G$ has coordinates $(4.25, 5.2)$        coordinates
       $J$ has coordinates $(7.375, 3.5)$
       $K$ has coordinates $(10.5, 1.8)$        1 point for $t$
       $P$ has coordinates $(13.625, 3.5)$        coordinates

  (B) $h(t) = 1.7\sin\left(\dfrac{4\pi}{25}(t - 1.125)\right) + 3.5$        2 points

    1 point for values of $a$ and $d$ and 1 point for values of $b$ and $c$

  (C) (i) b        1 point

    (ii) See full solution.        1 point

**4.** (A) (i) $g(x) = \log_2 x^{\frac{7}{2}}$ for $x > 0$        1 point

    (ii) $h(x) = 2\tan x$, $\cos x \neq 0$        1 point

  (B) (i) $x = \dfrac{\pi}{3}$, $x = \pi$, or $x = \dfrac{5\pi}{3}$        1 point

    (ii) $x = \dfrac{1}{2}\ln(e^2 - 1)$ or $x = \ln\sqrt{e^2 - 1}$        1 point

  (C) value $\theta$ in $0 \leq \theta \leq 2\pi$ with $\sin\theta = -\dfrac{1}{2}$        1 point
      general solution        1 point

# Section II Free-Response Full Solutions

**1.** (A) (i) $h(2) = (g \circ f)(2)$, which is equivalent to $g(f(2))$. The table shows that when $x = 2$, the function $f$ is equal to 0.5. Therefore, $g(f(2))$ is equivalent to $g(0.5)$. Using the defined function for $g$, $g(0.5) = \dfrac{(0.5)^3 - 1}{0.5 - 2}$, which is $g(0.5) = \dfrac{0.125 - 1}{0.5 - 2}$, or $g(0.5) = \dfrac{-0.875}{-1.5} = \dfrac{7}{12} \approx 0.583$.

    (ii) Because $f$ is increasing for all values of $x$, $f^{-1}$ exists. Algebraically, the inverse function results from interchanging the input values and output values. Therefore, the value of $f^{-1}(2)$, or the inverse function with an input value of 2, is equivalent to asking what input value $x$, does $f(x)$ have an output of 2. From the table, $f(x) = 2$ when $x = 4$.

(B) (i) To find when $g(x) = 1$, we need to solve the equation $\dfrac{x^3 - 1}{x - 2} = 1$. Multiplying both sides of this equation by $x - 2$ yields $x^3 - 1 = x - 2$. This is equivalent to $0 = x^3 - x + 1$. To find the approximate root, examine the graph of $y = x^3 - x + 1$. Use technology to determine that the graph crosses the $x$-axis at $x \approx -1.325$.

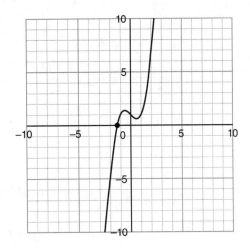

(ii) As $x$ increase without bound, eventually $g(x)$ increases without bound. For example, $g(5) \approx 41.333$, $g(10) \approx 124.875$, and $g(20) \approx 444.389$. As shown in the graph of $g(x)$, $\lim\limits_{x \to \infty} g(x) = \infty$.

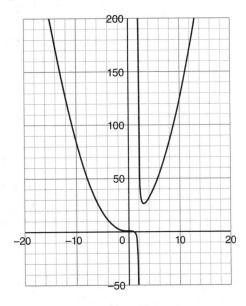

(C) (i) $f$ is best modeled by an exponential function.

(ii) Over equal-length input-value intervals, if the output values of a function change proportionally, then the function is exponential. Each input-value interval differs by 1, so they are equal-length intervals. Each output value is twice the size of the previous output value. Because the output values are changing multiplicatively as input values change additively, the function is exponential.

2. (A) (i) The first given data is that when the time, $t$, is 15 minutes, the temperature of the water, $T(15)$, is 71°F. Therefore, the first equation that can be used to find the values of the constants is $71 = 37 + Ae^{15k}$. The second given data is that when $t = 30$, $T(30) = 66°$. Therefore, the second equation that can be used to find the values of the constants is $66 = 37 + Ae^{30k}$.

   (ii) The first equation, $71 = 37 + Ae^{15k}$, is equivalent to $34 = Ae^{15k}$, and the second equation, $66 = 37 + Ae^{30k}$, is equivalent to $29 = Ae^{30k}$. Dividing the second equation by the first equation yields $\dfrac{29}{34} = \dfrac{Ae^{30k}}{Ae^{15k}}$, or $\dfrac{29}{34} = e^{15k}$. Taking the natural logarithm of both sides of this equation yields $\ln\left(\dfrac{29}{34}\right) = 15k$.

   Therefore $k = \dfrac{1}{15}\ln\left(\dfrac{29}{34}\right)$, or $k \approx -0.0106$. Plugging $k = \dfrac{1}{15}\ln\left(\dfrac{29}{34}\right)$ into the equation $34 = Ae^{15k}$ yields $34 = Ae^{15 \cdot \frac{1}{15}\ln\left(\frac{29}{34}\right)}$, which is equivalent to $34 = Ae^{\ln\left(\frac{29}{34}\right)}$, or $34 = A\left(\dfrac{29}{34}\right)$. Therefore, $A = \dfrac{34^2}{29} = \dfrac{1{,}156}{29} \approx 39.862$. The equation $T(t) = 37 + \dfrac{1{,}156}{29}\left(\dfrac{29}{34}\right)^{\frac{t}{15}}$ models the temperature, in °F, based on the time, in minutes, since placing the glass of tap water in the refrigerator.

   (B) (i) The average rate of change is given as the slope of the secant line between $(a, T(a))$ and $(b, T(b))$, or the slope of the line between $(15, 71)$ and $(30, 66)$. Therefore, the average rate of change from $t = 15$ to $t = 30$ is $\dfrac{T(30) - T(15)}{30 - 15} = \dfrac{66 - 71}{15} = -\dfrac{5}{15} = -\dfrac{1}{3} \approx -0.333$ degrees Fahrenheit per minute.

   (ii) For the water in the glass in the 37°F refrigerator, on average, there is a loss or decrease of 0.333 degrees Fahrenheit per minute when the time is between 15 minutes and 30 minutes.

   (iii) The average rates of change of $T$ from $t = 30$ to $t = p$ minutes are greater than the average rate of change from $t = 15$ to $t = 30$ minutes. The function $T$ is modeled by $T(t) = 37 + \dfrac{1{,}156}{29}\left(\dfrac{29}{34}\right)^{\frac{t}{15}}$. Because $T$ is an exponential function with base, $b = \dfrac{29}{34} < 1$, $T$ is a decreasing function that is concave up. Therefore, the average rates of change, in degrees Fahrenheit per minute, are increasing over equal-length input-value intervals as $t$ increases.

   (C) The model satisfies the equation $37 + \dfrac{1{,}156}{29}\left(\dfrac{29}{34}\right)^{\frac{t}{15}} > 50$, which is equivalent to $\dfrac{1{,}156}{29}\left(\dfrac{29}{34}\right)^{\frac{t}{15}} > 13$. Multiplying both sides of this equation by $\dfrac{29}{1{,}156}$ yields $\left(\dfrac{29}{34}\right)^{\frac{t}{15}} > \dfrac{337}{1{,}156}$. Taking the natural log of both sides of this equation yields $\dfrac{t}{15}\ln\left(\dfrac{29}{34}\right) > \ln\left(\dfrac{337}{1{,}156}\right)$. Because $\ln\left(\dfrac{29}{34}\right) < 0$, this is equivalent to

$t < 15 \cdot \ln\left(\frac{337}{1{,}156}\right) \div \ln\left(\frac{29}{34}\right)$, or $t < 116.239$. The model is only appropriate for approximately the first 116.239 minutes.

3. (A) The maximum height of water is recorded as 5.2 feet, so the highest points of the sinusoidal function, like point $G$, represent the maximum height. The minimum height is recorded as 1.8 feet, so the lowest points of the sinusoidal function, like point $K$, represent the minimum height. This means that points on the dashed midline represent times when the height of the water is $\frac{1.8 + 5.2}{2}$, or 3.5 feet. The time between the maximum height and the minimum height is 6.25 hours. So the time to move from the maximum height to the minimum height, represented by points going from $G$ to points $K$, takes 6.25 hours and the time to move from the dashed midline takes half that, or 3.125 hours. The first time the maximum height is reached is 4:15 a.m., or time $t = 4.25$. Therefore, $F$ has coordinates $(1.125, 3.5)$, $G$ has coordinates $(4.25, 5.2)$, $J$ has coordinates $(7.375, 3.5)$, $K$ has coordinates $(10.5, 1.8)$, and $P$ has coordinates $(13.625, 3.5)$.

(B) The amplitude, $a$, is the vertical distance, in feet, between the dashed midline and the highest or lowest point on the sinusoidal graph. Therefore, $a = 5.2 - 3.5 = 1.7$ feet. The period is the horizontal distance, in seconds, where the sinusoidal pattern repeats and can be presented by the distance between points $F$ and $P$. Thus, the period is $13.625 - 1.125 = 12.5$ hours. The period of a sinusoidal function is $\left|\frac{1}{b}\right| 2\pi$ seconds, so $\left|\frac{1}{b}\right| 2\pi = 12.5$, or $\left|\frac{1}{b}\right| 2\pi = \frac{25}{2}$. Thus, $b = \frac{4\pi}{25}$. The additive transformations, $c$ and $d$, are the horizontal and vertical translations respectively of the sine function and can be represented by the location of the point $F$. There is a horizontal translation of 1.125 units and a vertical translation of 3.5 units. Therefore, $c = -1.125$ and $d = 3.5$. The function $h$ can be written as

$$h(t) = 1.7 \sin\left(\frac{4\pi}{25}(t - 1.125)\right) + 3.5.$$

(C) (i) Between the points $J$ and $K$, the value of $h$ is in the interval $1.8 < h(a) < 3.5$; therefore, $h$ is positive. Also, for $a$ and $b$ in the interval $(t_1, t_2)$, if $a < b$, then $h(a) > h(b)$, so the graph of $h$ is decreasing.

(ii) Because the graph of $h$ is concave up on the interval $(t_1, t_2)$, the rate of change of $h$ is increasing on the interval $(t_1, t_2)$.

4. (A) (i) The function $g$ is defined as $g(x) = 3\log_2 x + \log_4 x$. The change of base property for logarithms states that $\log_b x = \frac{\log_a x}{\log_a b}$. Therefore, $g$ can be written as $g(x) = 3\log_2 x + \frac{\log_2 x}{\log_2 4}$, or $g(x) = 3\log_2 x + \frac{\log_2 x}{2}$. Consequently, $g$ can be rewritten as $g(x) = 3\log_2 x + \frac{1}{2}\log_2 x$. Because the power property for logarithms states that $\log_b x^n = n\log_b x$, $g$ can now be rewritten as $g(x) = \log_2 x^3 + \log_2 x^{\frac{1}{2}}$. Finally, the product property of logarithms states

that $\log_b(xy) = \log_b x + \log_b y$, so $g(x) = \log_2\left(x^3 \cdot x^{\frac{1}{2}}\right)$, which is equivalent to $g(x) = \log_2 x^{\frac{7}{2}}$ for $x > 0$.

(ii) The function $h$ is defined as $h(x) = \dfrac{\sin(2x)}{1 - \sin^2 x}$. The sum identity for sine states that $\sin(\alpha + \beta) = \sin\alpha\cos\beta + \cos\alpha\sin\beta$. Therefore, $\sin(x + x) = \sin(2x) = \sin x \cos x + \cos x \sin x$, which is equivalent to $\sin(2x) = 2\sin x \cos x$. Hence, $h$ can be written as $h(x) = \dfrac{2\sin x \cos x}{1 - \sin^2 x}$. The Pythagorean Identity states that $\sin^2 x + \cos^2 x = 1$, which is equivalent to $\cos^2 x = 1 - \sin^2 x$. Therefore, $h$ can be rewritten as $h(x) = \dfrac{2\sin x \cos x}{\cos^2 x}$. Dividing out a factor of $\cos x$ yields $h(x) = \dfrac{2\sin x}{\cos x}$. The tangent function is the ratio of the sine function to the cosine function, or $\tan x = \dfrac{\sin x}{\cos x}$. Therefore, when $\cos x \neq 0$, $h(x) = 2\tan x$.

(B) (i) Setting the function $j$ equal to zero yields $2\cos^2 x + \cos x - 1 = 0$. Factoring this equation results in the equation $(2\cos x - 1)(\cos x + 1) = 0$. The zero product property states that when $x \cdot y = 0$, either $x = 0$ or $y = 0$, or both equal zero. Therefore, either $2\cos x - 1 = 0$ or $\cos x + 1 = 0$. The first equation is equivalent to $\cos x = \dfrac{1}{2}$ and the second equation is equivalent to $\cos x = -1$. Based on the unit circle for angles in the interval $[0, 2\pi]$, $\cos x = \dfrac{1}{2}$ when $x = \dfrac{\pi}{3}$ or $x = \dfrac{5\pi}{3}$ and $\cos x = -1$ when $x = \pi$.

(ii) Setting the function $k$ equal to $e^3$ yields the equation $e^{2x+1} + e = e^3$. Subtracting $e$ from both sides of this equation yields $e^{2x+1} = e^3 - e$. Dividing both sides of this equation by $e$ results in $e^{2x} = e^2 - 1$. Taking the natural logarithm of both sides of this equation yields $\ln(e^{2x}) = \ln(e^2 - 1)$, which is equivalent to $2x = \ln(e^2 - 1)$. Dividing both sides of this equation by 2 results in $x = \dfrac{1}{2}\ln(e^2 - 1)$, which is equivalent to $x = \ln\sqrt{e^2 - 1}$.

(C) Setting the function $m$ equal to $\dfrac{3}{2}$ produces the equation $\sin(3x) + 2 = \dfrac{3}{2}$. Subtracting 2 from both sides of this equation yields $\sin(3x) = -\dfrac{1}{2}$. Based on the unit circle for angles in the interval $[0, 2\pi]$, $\sin x = -\dfrac{1}{2}$ when $x = \dfrac{7\pi}{6}$ or $x = \dfrac{11\pi}{6}$. Therefore, $3x = \dfrac{7\pi}{6} + 2\pi n$ or $3x = \dfrac{11\pi}{6} + 2\pi n$. Dividing each of these equations by 3 results in $x = \dfrac{7\pi}{18} + \dfrac{2\pi n}{3}$ or $x = \dfrac{11\pi}{18} + \dfrac{2\pi n}{3}$, which is equivalent to $x = \dfrac{7\pi + 12\pi n}{18}$ or $x = \dfrac{11\pi + 12\pi n}{18}$, where $n$ is any integer.

# AP Precalculus Practice Exam 2

## ANSWER SHEET FOR SECTION I

### Part A

1 (A) (B) (C) (D)
2 (A) (B) (C) (D)
3 (A) (B) (C) (D)
4 (A) (B) (C) (D)
5 (A) (B) (C) (D)
6 (A) (B) (C) (D)
7 (A) (B) (C) (D)
8 (A) (B) (C) (D)
9 (A) (B) (C) (D)
10 (A) (B) (C) (D)
11 (A) (B) (C) (D)
12 (A) (B) (C) (D)
13 (A) (B) (C) (D)
14 (A) (B) (C) (D)
15 (A) (B) (C) (D)

16 (A) (B) (C) (D)
17 (A) (B) (C) (D)
18 (A) (B) (C) (D)
19 (A) (B) (C) (D)
20 (A) (B) (C) (D)
21 (A) (B) (C) (D)
22 (A) (B) (C) (D)
23 (A) (B) (C) (D)
24 (A) (B) (C) (D)
25 (A) (B) (C) (D)
26 (A) (B) (C) (D)
27 (A) (B) (C) (D)
28 (A) (B) (C) (D)

### Part B

76 (A) (B) (C) (D)
77 (A) (B) (C) (D)
78 (A) (B) (C) (D)
79 (A) (B) (C) (D)
80 (A) (B) (C) (D)
81 (A) (B) (C) (D)

82 (A) (B) (C) (D)
83 (A) (B) (C) (D)
84 (A) (B) (C) (D)
85 (A) (B) (C) (D)
86 (A) (B) (C) (D)
87 (A) (B) (C) (D)

# Section I Part A (Multiple-Choice)

Directions:
Time—80 minutes
Number of Questions—28
No calculator is allowed for this part of the exam.

Tear out the answer sheet provided on the previous page and mark your answers on it. All questions are given equal weight. Points are *not* deducted for incorrect answers, and no points are given to unanswered questions. Unless otherwise specified, the domain of a function $f$ is assumed to be the set of all real numbers $x$ for which $f(x)$ is a real number. Angle measures for trigonometric functions are assumed to be in radians.

1. Let $f$ be defined as $f(x) = \dfrac{x^2 + 3x + 2}{x^2 - 1}$. Which of the following best describes the graph of $f$?

| (A) | $\lim\limits_{x \to -1^-} f(x) = -\infty$ |
|-----|-------------------------------------------|
| (B) | $\lim\limits_{x \to -1^-} f(x) = \infty$ |
| (C) | $\lim\limits_{x \to -1^-} f(x) = -\dfrac{1}{2}$ |
| (D) | $\lim\limits_{x \to -1^-} f(x) = \dfrac{1}{2}$ |

2.

| $x$ | $-2$ | $-1$ | $0$ | $1$ | $2$ |
|-----|------|------|-----|-----|-----|
| $f(x)$ | 11 | 2 | $-1$ | $-3$ | 8 |

The table gives selected values of function $f$. What is the average rate of change of $f$ over the interval $[-1, 2]$?

| (A) | $-3$ | (B) | $\dfrac{1}{2}$ | (C) | 2 | (D) | 6 |
|-----|------|-----|----------------|-----|---|-----|---|

3. Let $f$ be the logarithmic function defined as $f(x) = \log_4 x$. The function $g$ is vertical dilation of $f$ by a factor of 2. Which of the following is NOT a formula for $g(x)$?

| (A) | $\dfrac{2 \cdot \log_{16} x}{\log_{16} 4}$ | (B) | $2 + \log_4 x$ |
|-----|--------------------------------------------|-----|----------------|
| (C) | $\log_4(x^2)$ | (D) | $\log_4 x + \log_4 x$ |

**4.**

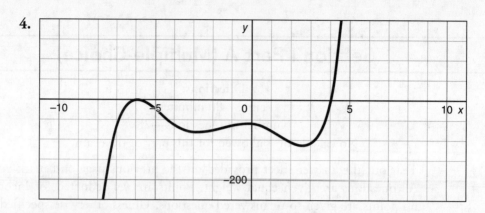

The graph shows the polynomial function $p$. Which of the following describes the real zeros of $p$?

| (A) | Both $x = -6$ and $x = 4$ have even multiplicity. |
|---|---|
| (B) | Both $x = -6$ and $x = 4$ have odd multiplicity. |
| (C) | $x = -6$ has even multiplicity and $x = 4$ has odd multiplicity. |
| (D) | $x = -6$ has odd multiplicity and $x = 4$ has even multiplicity. |

**5.** The graph of the rational function $f$ has a hole at $(2, -1)$. Let $g$ be defined as $g(x) = f(2x)$. What is the coordinate of the hole for $g$?

| (A) | $(4, -1)$ | (B) | $(1, -1)$ | (C) | $(2, -2)$ | (D) | $\left(2, -\dfrac{1}{2}\right)$ |
|---|---|---|---|---|---|---|---|

**6.**

| $x$ | $-3$ | $-2$ | $-1$ | 0 | 1 | 2 | 3 |
|---|---|---|---|---|---|---|---|
| $p(x)$ | 18 | 20 | 12 | 0 | $-10$ | $-12$ | 0 |

The table gives selected values of a polynomial function $p$. Which of the following must be true about $p$?

| (A) | $p$ has exactly two distinct real zeros. |
|---|---|
| (B) | $p$ has a global maximum of 20. |
| (C) | $p$ is concave down on the interval $0 < x < 3$. |
| (D) | $p$ has a local minimum in the interval $0 < x < 3$. |

**7.** If $f(x) = 4 \cdot 2^{x-1} + 3$, then which of the following is $f^{-1}(x)$?

| (A) | $\log_2(x - 3) - 1$ | (B) | $\log_2\left(\dfrac{x-3}{4}\right) - 1$ |
|---|---|---|---|
| (C) | $\log_2\left(\dfrac{x}{4} - 3\right) + 1$ | (D) | $\dfrac{1}{4 \cdot 2^{x-1} + 3}$ |

8.  Which of the following is true about the graph of $y = \cos\theta$?

| (A) | The graph is identical to the graph of $y = \sin\left(\theta + \dfrac{\pi}{2}\right)$. |
|-----|--------------------------------------------------------------------------------|
| (B) | As the input value increase without bound, the graph increases without bound. |
| (C) | The graph has rotational symmetry and is therefore odd. |
| (D) | The frequency of the graph is $2\pi$. |

9.  If $f(x) = \dfrac{x+1}{x-2}$, which of the following represents $f^{-1}(x)$, the inverse function of $f$?

| (A) | $\dfrac{x-2}{x+1}$ | (B) | $\dfrac{2x+1}{x-1}$ |
|-----|--------------------|-----|---------------------|
| (C) | $\dfrac{x-1}{x+2}$ | (D) | $\dfrac{1-2x}{x-1}$ |

10. Which of the following is true about the graph of $f(\theta) = \tan\theta$?

| (A) | The period of the graph is $2\pi$. |
|-----|-------------------------------------|
| (B) | The graph has vertical asymptotes when $\sin\theta = 0$. |
| (C) | The graph is increasing between consecutive asymptotes. |
| (D) | The graph is concave up on the domain. |

11.

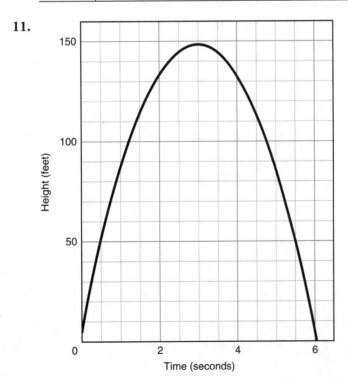

The graph of $h(t)$ shows the height, $h$, of a ball, in feet, $t$ seconds after the ball was hit. The maximum height of the ball is 148 feet and occurs 3 seconds after the ball is hit. Which of the following describes the graph on the interval $1 < t < 3$?

| (A) | $h$ is increasing and concave up. |
| (B) | $h$ is increasing and concave down. |
| (C) | $h$ is decreasing and concave up. |
| (D) | $h$ is decreasing and concave down. |

**12.** Consider the equation $\log_b c = a$. Which of the following statements is true?

| (A) | The value of $a$ can be negative. | (B) | The value of $b$ can be negative. |
| (C) | The value of $c$ can be negative. | (D) | The values of $a$, $b$, and $c$ must be positive. |

**13.** Which of the following is true about the graph of $f(x) = -2e^{-x}$?

| (A) | $\lim\limits_{x \to -\infty} f(x) = \infty$ | (B) | $\lim\limits_{x \to \infty} f(x) = \infty$ |
| (C) | $\lim\limits_{x \to -\infty} f(x) = 0$ | (D) | $\lim\limits_{x \to \infty} f(x) = 0$ |

**14.** As the input values of a nonconstant polynomial function, $p(x)$, increase without bound, the output values decrease without bound. As the input values of $p(x)$ decrease without bound, the output values also decrease without bound. Which of the following best describes the degree and the sign of the leading term of $p(x)$?

| (A) | The degree is odd, and the leading term is negative. |
| (B) | The degree is odd, and the leading term is positive. |
| (C) | The degree is even, and the leading term is negative. |
| (D) | The degree is even, and the leading term is positive. |

**15.** Which of the following equations is true?

| (A) | $\sin^{-1}\left(\dfrac{\sqrt{3}}{2}\right) = \dfrac{2\pi}{3}$ | (B) | $\tan^{-1}(-1) = \dfrac{3\pi}{4}$ |
| (C) | $\cos^{-1}\left(-\dfrac{\sqrt{3}}{2}\right) = \dfrac{5\pi}{6}$ | (D) | $\tan^{-1}\left(\dfrac{\sqrt{3}}{3}\right) = \dfrac{7\pi}{6}$ |

16. The angle $\theta$ is an angle in standard position and has measure $\theta = \dfrac{2\pi}{7}$. Which of the following angles is coterminal with $\theta$?

| (A) | $\dfrac{9\pi}{7}$ | (B) | $\dfrac{4\pi}{7}$ | (C) | $-\dfrac{5\pi}{7}$ | (D) | $-\dfrac{12\pi}{7}$ |
|---|---|---|---|---|---|---|---|

17. Let $f$ be a rational function $f(x) = \dfrac{(x-2)^2(x+3)}{x(x-2)(x-1)}$. When $f$ is graphed in the $xy$-plane, which of the following statements is true?

| (A) | The graph of $f$ has no distinct real roots. |
|---|---|
| (B) | The graph of $f$ has one distinct real root. |
| (C) | The graph of $f$ has two distinct real roots. |
| (D) | The graph of $f$ has three distinct real roots. |

18. Angle $\theta$ is in standard position and intersects the unit circle at $(-0.6, 0.8)$. Which of the following is equal to $\sin\theta$?

| (A) | $-\dfrac{0.6}{0.8}$ | (B) | $-0.6$ | (C) | $-\dfrac{0.8}{0.6}$ | (D) | $0.8$ |
|---|---|---|---|---|---|---|---|

19. Which of the following is the solution to $\sin^2(3x) - \cos^2(3x) + \sin(3x) = 0$?

| (A) | $\dfrac{\pi}{6} + 2k\pi,\ \dfrac{5\pi}{6} + 2k\pi$, and $\dfrac{3\pi}{2} + 2k\pi$ |
|---|---|
| (B) | $\dfrac{\pi}{3} + 2k\pi,\ \dfrac{2\pi}{3} + 2k\pi$, and $\dfrac{3\pi}{2} + 2k\pi$ |
| (C) | $\dfrac{\pi}{18} + \dfrac{2k\pi}{3},\ \dfrac{5\pi}{18} + \dfrac{2k\pi}{3}$, and $\dfrac{\pi}{2} + \dfrac{2k\pi}{3}$ |
| (D) | $\dfrac{\pi}{9} + \dfrac{2k\pi}{3},\ \dfrac{2\pi}{9} + \dfrac{2k\pi}{3}$, and $\dfrac{\pi}{2} + \dfrac{2k\pi}{3}$ |

20. The function $f$ is defined as $f(x) = -2\log_3 x$. Which of the following describes the vertical asymptote and end behavior of $f$?

| (A) | $\lim\limits_{x\to 0^+} f(x) = -\infty$ and $\lim\limits_{x\to\infty} f(x) = -\infty$ |
|---|---|
| (B) | $\lim\limits_{x\to 0^+} f(x) = \infty$ and $\lim\limits_{x\to\infty} f(x) = -\infty$ |
| (C) | $\lim\limits_{x\to 0^+} f(x) = -\infty$ and $\lim\limits_{x\to\infty} f(x) = \infty$ |
| (D) | $\lim\limits_{x\to 0^+} f(x) = \infty$ and $\lim\limits_{x\to\infty} f(x) = \infty$ |

**21.** The function $g$ is a transformation of the function $f(\theta) = \cos(\theta)$. The transformation is a vertical translation of 3 units up and a horizontal translation of 4 units to the right. Which of the following could represent the function $g(x)$?

| (A) | $g(\theta) = \cos(\theta + 4) + 3$ | (B) | $g(\theta) = \cos(\theta - 4) + 3$ |
|---|---|---|---|
| (C) | $g(\theta) = \cos(\theta + 3) + 4$ | (D) | $g(\theta) = \cos(\theta - 3) + 4$ |

**22.** Consider the function $r$ given by $r(x) = \dfrac{x^2 - 4}{x^2 + 13x - 30}$. Which of the following is true about the graph of $r(x)$ in the $xy$-plane?

| (A) | $r$ has a horizontal asymptote at $y = 1$. |
|---|---|
| (B) | $r$ has a vertical asymptote at $x = 2$. |
| (C) | $r$ has exactly two distinct real zeros. |
| (D) | $r$ increases without bound as $x$ increase without bound. |

**23.** The graph of $r = 5\sin(4\theta)$, for $0 \le \theta \le 2\pi$ is shown. Which of the following describes $r$ on the interval $\dfrac{3\pi}{4} < \theta < \dfrac{7\pi}{8}$ ?

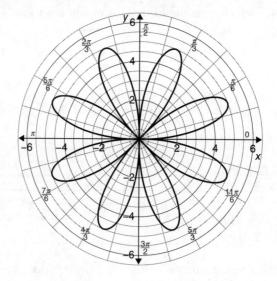

| (A) | $r$ is positive and increasing. | (B) | $r$ is positive and decreasing. |
|---|---|---|---|
| (C) | $r$ is negative and increasing. | (D) | $r$ is negative and decreasing. |

**24.** Which of the following is the graph of $r = 3 - 4\sin(\theta)$?

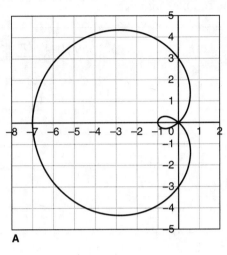

A

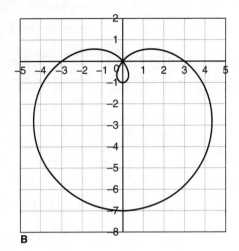

B

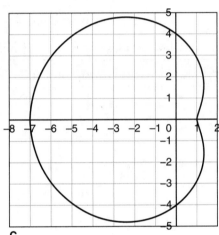

C

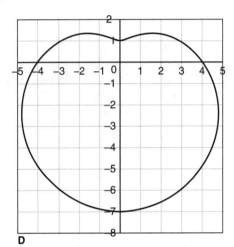

D

**25.** The expression $(3x^2 y)^{-2} \cdot (18x^{-3} y^5)$ is equivalent to which of the following?

| | | | |
|---|---|---|---|
| (A) | $\dfrac{2y^3}{x^7}$ | (B) | $\dfrac{3y^4}{x^3}$ |
| (C) | $\dfrac{-162y^4}{x^3}$ | (D) | $\dfrac{-108y^3}{x^7}$ |

**26.** Let $f(x) = 3^x$ and $g(x)$ be the inverse of $f(x)$. Which of the following is equivalent to $g(x)$?

| (A) | $x^3$ | (B) | $\dfrac{1}{3^x}$ | (C) | $\log_x 3$ | (D) | $\log_3 x$ |
|---|---|---|---|---|---|---|---|

27. The complex number $2 - 2i$ is graphed in the complex plane. What is the corresponding trigonometric form of the complex number?

| (A) | $2\sqrt{2}\left(\cos\dfrac{3\pi}{4} + i\sin\dfrac{3\pi}{4}\right)$ | (B) | $2\sqrt{2}\left(\cos\dfrac{7\pi}{4} + i\sin\dfrac{7\pi}{4}\right)$ |
|---|---|---|---|
| (C) | $8\left(\cos\dfrac{3\pi}{4} + i\sin\dfrac{3\pi}{4}\right)$ | (D) | $8\left(\cos\dfrac{7\pi}{4} + i\sin\dfrac{7\pi}{4}\right)$ |

28. Let $a$, $b$, and $c$ be real numbers. Which of the following is true about the graph of the rational function $r(x) = \dfrac{x(x+a)^2(x+b)}{(x+b)(x+c)^2}$?

| | |
|---|---|
| (A) | The graph of $r$ has 2 vertical asymptotes and no holes. |
| (B) | The graph of $r$ has 2 vertical asymptotes and 1 hole. |
| (C) | The graph of $r$ has 1 vertical asymptote and 1 hole. |
| (D) | The graph of $r$ has no vertical asymptotes and 2 holes. |

# Section I Part B (Multiple-Choice)

Directions:
Time – 40 minutes.
Number of Questions – 12
A graphing calculator is required for some questions on this part of the exam.

Continue to use the same answer sheet. Please note that the questions begin with number 76. This is not an error; it was done to be consistent with the numbering system of the actual AP Precalculus Exam. All questions are given equal weight. Points are *not* deducted for incorrect answers, and no points are given to unanswered questions. Unless otherwise specified, the domain of a function $f$ is assumed to be the set of all real numbers $x$ for which $f(x)$ is a real number. Angle measures for trigonometric functions are assumed to be in radians. Make sure your calculator is in radian mode. The exact numerical value does not always appear among the choices given. When this happens, select from among the choices the number that best approximates the exact numerical value.

**76.** What are all values of $x$ for which $2\ln x - \ln(x-1) = 4$?

| (A) | 1.019 only | (B) | 53.579 only |
|---|---|---|---|
| (C) | 1.019 and 53.579 | (D) | No values of $x$ |

**77.** The following graph of $r = 2 + \sin(5\theta)$ is shown for $0 \le \theta \le 2\pi$.

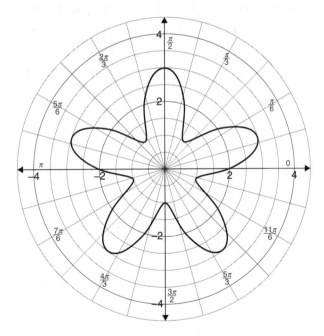

What is the average rate of change on the interval $\dfrac{\pi}{2} \le \theta \le \dfrac{7\pi}{4}$?

| (A) | −0.0746 | (B) | −0.5093 |
|---|---|---|---|
| (C) | −2.5000 | (D) | −13.4076 |

**78.** The angle $\theta$ is in standard position and intersects a circle of radius $r$. If $\theta = 24°$ and $r = 3.6$, which of the following is an approximation for coordinate of the point where the terminal ray of the angle intersects the circle?

| (A) | $(-3.260, 1.527)$ | (B) | $(1.527, -3.260)$ |
|---|---|---|---|
| (C) | $(3.289, 1.464)$ | (D) | $(1.464, 3.289)$ |

**79.** Michelle works as an activities coordinator at a senior living facility. After every six months working at the facility, she receives a 4% raise. When Michelle was hired, she earned $15.00 an hour. Approximately, how much money does Michelle earn per hour after working for the facility for 3 years?

| (A) | $18.24 | (B) | $18.60 |
|---|---|---|---|
| (C) | $18.98 | (D) | $19.74 |

**80.** The functions $f$ and $g$ are defined as $f(x) = \sqrt{x^2 - 11x + 18}$ and $g(x) = \sqrt{x - 3}$ respectively. Which of the following gives the domain of $f(g(x))$?

| (A) | $[3, \infty)$ | (B) | $[7, \infty)$ |
|---|---|---|---|
| (C) | $(-\infty, 2] \cup [9, \infty)$ | (D) | $[3, 7] \cup [84, \infty)$ |

**81.** Which of the following is the equation for the following graph?

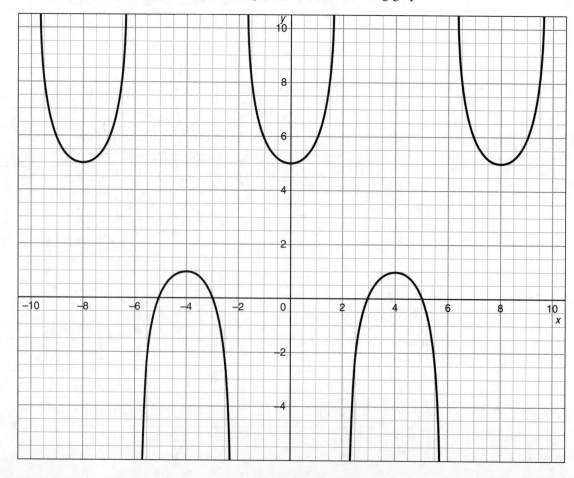

| (A) | $f(x) = 2\sec\left(\dfrac{4}{\pi}x\right) + 3$ | (B) | $f(x) = 4\sec\left(\dfrac{4}{\pi}x\right) + 3$ |
|---|---|---|---|
| (C) | $f(x) = 2\sec\left(\dfrac{\pi}{4}x\right) + 3$ | (D) | $f(x) = 4\sec\left(\dfrac{\pi}{4}x\right) + 3$ |

**82.** The rational function $r$ is defined as $r(x) = \dfrac{x^2 + 7x + 4}{x^2 - 2x - 6}$. For which of the following intervals is $r(x) \geq 0$?

| (A) | $[-6.373, -1.646)$ | (B) | $(-1.646, -0.628]$ |
|---|---|---|---|
| (C) | $[-0.628, 3.646)$ | (D) | $[3.646, \infty)$ |

**83.** The graph of the function $f$ in the $xy$-plane is shown as follows. Point $A\left(4, -\dfrac{4}{3}\right)$ and point $B(8, -2)$ are labeled on the graph of $f$. Which of the following is $f(x)$?

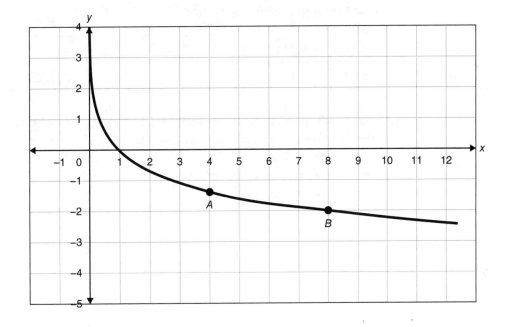

| (A) | $f(x) = -\dfrac{8}{9}(1.107)^x$ | (B) | $f(x) = -0.805\sqrt{x} + 0.276$ |
|---|---|---|---|
| (C) | $f(x) = \dfrac{-3(x - 2.222)}{x}$ | (D) | $f(x) = -\dfrac{1}{3}\log_{1.414}(x)$ |

**84.** For the function $f(x) = \dfrac{1}{4}x^3 - \dfrac{7}{4}x^2 + \dfrac{3}{2}x + 1$, calculate the average rate of change from $x = -1$ to $x = 6$.

| (A) | $-0.3$ | (B) | $0.4$ | (C) | $0.5$ | (D) | $3.5$ |
|---|---|---|---|---|---|---|---|

**85.** Let $r$ be a rational function defined as $r(x) = \dfrac{x^2 + x - 1}{x^2 - 3x - 4}$. Which of the following statements is true about $r(x)$?

| (A) | $\displaystyle\lim_{x \to -1^-} r(x) = \infty$ | (B) | $\displaystyle\lim_{x \to -1^-} r(x) = -\infty$ |
|-----|------|-----|------|
| (C) | $\displaystyle\lim_{x \to \infty} r(x) = 0$ | (D) | $\displaystyle\lim_{x \to \infty} r(x) = \infty$ |

**86.**

| $t$ | 10 | 25 | 40 | 60 | 75 | 100 | 120 |
|-----|----|----|----|----|----|-----|-----|
| $P(t)$ | 6 | 15 | 22 | 50 | 103 | 270 | 625 |

The preceding table shows the number of people, $P(t)$, in a concert hall for select values of $t$, where $t$ represents the number of minutes after 5 p.m. The manager of the concert hall uses an exponential growth model, $y = ab^x$, to estimate the number of people in a concert hall at the beginning of the concert at 7 p.m. Which of the following is closest to the error in the manager's model?

| (A) | −1.722 | (B) | 5.627 |
|-----|--------|-----|-------|
| (C) | 11.364 | (D) | 180.322 |

**87.** The depth of the water in the Long Beach Inner Harbor in California fluctuates during the day. One day in April, the first low tide was 1.45 feet at 1:45 a.m. The first high tide at 4.18 feet occurred at 7:25 a.m. The second low tide was at 1:05 p.m. If the depth of the water can be modeled by a sinusoidal function, which of the following is the best estimate of the period length?

| (A) | 1.365 | (B) | 2.730 |
|-----|-------|-----|-------|
| (C) | 5.667 | (D) | 11.333 |

# Section II Part A (Free-Response)

Directions:
Time – 30 minutes.
Number of Questions – 2
A graphing calculator is required for these questions.

*Show all work.* You may *not* receive any credit for correct answers without supporting work. You may use an approved calculator to help solve the problem. However, you must clearly indicate the setup of your solution using mathematical notations and not calculator syntax. A calculator may be used to solve an equation or graph a function. Unless otherwise indicated, you may assume the following: (a) the numeric or algebraic answers need not be simplified; (b) your answer, if expressed in approximation, should be correct to three places after the decimal point; and (c), the domain of a function $f$ is the set of all real numbers $x$ for which $f(x)$ is a real number. Angle measures for trigonometric functions are assumed to be in radians.

## Part A
A graphing calculator is required for these questions.

1.

| $x$ | 1 | 2 | 4 | 8 | 16 |
|-----|---|---|---|---|----|
| $f(x)$ | 0 | 1 | 2 | 3 | 4 |

Let $f$ be an increasing function defined for all $x > 0$. The table gives values of $f$ at selected values of $x$. The function $g$ is given by $g(x) = \dfrac{x^2 + 8x + 12}{x^2 - 4}$.

(A) (i) The function $h$ is defined by $h(x) = (g \circ f)(x)$. Find the value of $h(2)$ and decimal approximation, or indicate that it is not defined.

    (ii) Find the value of $f^{-1}(4)$, or indicate that it is not defined.

(B) (i) Determine the equation of all horizontal asymptotes of $g$, or indicate that there are no horizontal asymptotes.

    (ii) Find the coordinates of all holes of $g$, or indicate there are no such values. Express your answer using the mathematical notation of a limit.

(C) (i) Use the table of values of $f(x)$ to determine if $f$ is best modeled by a linear, quadratic, exponential, or logarithmic function.

    (ii) Give a reason for your answer based on how the output values of $f$ change with respect to the input values of $f$.

2. An object dropped eventually falls toward the surface of Earth because of the effects of gravity. At time $t = 0$, a ball is dropped off a 550-foot building. Three seconds after dropping the ball, the height of the ball was 405.1 feet.

The height of the ball can be modeled by the function $H$ given by $H(t) = a + bt^2$, where $H(t)$ is the height of the ball in feet, and $t$ is the number of seconds since dropping the ball.

(A) (i) Use the given data to write two equations that can be used to find the values for constants $a$ and $b$ in the expression for $H(t)$.

(ii) Find the values of $a$ and $b$.

(B) (i) Use the given data to find the average rate of change of the ball, in feet per second, from $t = 0$ to $t = 3$. Express your answer as a decimal approximation. Show the computations that lead to your answer.

(ii) Interpret the meaning of your answer from (i) in the context of the problem.

(iii) Consider the average rates of change of $T$ from $t = 3$ to $t = p$ seconds, where $3 < p < 5$. Are these average rates of change less than or greater than the average rate of change from $t = 0$ to $t = 3$ seconds found in (i)? Explain your reasoning.

(C) The model for $H$ is an appropriate model if the height of the ball is positive. Based on this information, for how many seconds is the model for $H$ an appropriate model? Give a reason for your answer.

# Section II Part B (Free-Response)

Directions:
Time – 30 minutes.
Number of Questions – 2
No calculator is allowed for these questions.

The use of a calculator is *not* permitted in this part of the exam. You should *show all work.* You may *not* receive any credit for correct answers without supporting work. Unless other- wise indicated, the numeric or algebraic answers need not be simplified, and the domain of a function *f* is the set of all real numbers *x* for which $f(x)$ is a real number. Angle measures for trigonometric functions are assumed to be in radians. When you finish this part of the exam, you may return to the problems in Part A of Section II and continue to work on them. However, you may not use a calculator.

**3.**

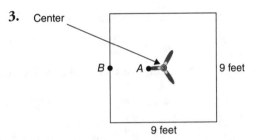

Note: Figure not drawn to scale.

A ceiling fan is in the middle of a 9-foot by 9-foot room as shown in the preceding sketch, with the center of the fan 4.5 feet from each wall. The length from the center of the ceiling fan to the tip of the blade is 1.5 feet. The tip of one of the fan blades, point *A*, is closest to the center of one of the walls, point *B*, at time $t = 0$ seconds, as indicated in the figure. The blades of the fan rotate clockwise and complete 2 rotations every second. As the fan blade turns the point B moves up and down the wall to match point A. As the fan blades rotate at a constant speed, the distance between *A* and *B* periodically increases and decreases.

The sinusoidal function *h* models the distance between *A* and *B*, in feet, as a function of time *t* in seconds.

(A) The graph of *h* and the dashed midline for two full cycles is shown. Five points, *F*, *G*, *J*, *K*, and *P* are labeled on the graph. No scale is indicated, and no axes are presented. Determine possible coordinates $(t, h(t))$ for the five points *F*, *G*, *J*, *K*, and *P*.

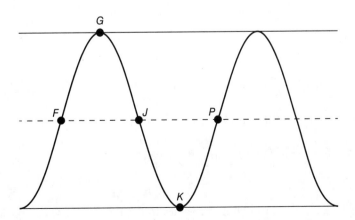

(B) The function $h$ can be written in the form $h(t) = a\sin(b(t+c)) + d$. Find the values of constants $a$, $b$, $c$, and $d$.

(C) Refer to the graph of $h$ in part (A). The $t$-coordinate coordinate of $G$ is $t_1$ and the $t$-coordinate coordinate of $J$ is $t_2$.

  (i) On the interval $(t_1, t_2)$, which of the following is true about $h$?

    a. $h$ is positive and increasing.

    b. $h$ is positive and decreasing.

    c. $h$ is negative and increasing.

    d. $h$ is negative and decreasing.

  (ii) Describe the rate of change of $h$ on the interval $(t_1, t_2)$.

4. Directions:
 • Unless otherwise specified, the domain of a function $f$ is assumed to be the set of all real numbers $x$ for which $f(x)$ is a real number. Angle measures for trigonometric functions are assumed to be in radians.
 • Solutions to equations must be real numbers. Determine the exact value of any expression that can be obtained without a calculator. For example, $\log_2 8$, $\cos\left(\dfrac{\pi}{2}\right)$, and $\sin^{-1}(1)$ can be evaluated without a calculator.
 • Unless otherwise specified, combine terms using algebraic methods and rules for exponents and logarithms, where applicable. For example, $2x+3x$, $5^2 \cdot 5^3$, $\dfrac{x^5}{x^2}$ and $\ln 3 + \ln 5$ should be rewritten in equivalent forms.
 • For each part of the question, show the work that leads to your answers.

(A) The functions $g$ and $h$ are given by
$$g(x) = (e^x + e^{-x})^2$$
$$h(x) = \frac{\cos(2x) - 1}{\sin x}$$

  (i) Rewrite $g(x)$ by expanding it into an exponential expression without negative exponents in any part of the expression.

  (ii) Rewrite $h(x)$ as an expression in which $\sin x$ appears once and no other trigonometric functions are involved.

(B) The functions $j$ and $k$ are given by
$$j(x) = (\tan x)(\cos x) + \sin x + 1$$
$$k(x) = 5(2)^{x-1} + 3$$

  (i) Solve $j(x) = 0$ for values of $x$ in the interval $[0, 2\pi]$.

  (ii) Solve $k(x) = 9$ for values of $x$ in the domain of $k$.

(C) The function $m$ is given by
$$m(x) = \arcsin(3x) + \pi$$

Find all input values in the domain of $m$ that yield an output value of $\dfrac{3\pi}{4}$.

# Answer Key

## Section I, Part A

| | |
|---|---|
| 1. | C |
| 2. | C |
| 3. | B |
| 4. | C |
| 5. | B |
| 6. | D |
| 7. | A |
| 8. | A |
| 9. | B |
| 10. | C |
| 11. | B |
| 12. | A |
| 13. | D |
| 14. | C |
| 15. | C |
| 16. | D |
| 17. | B |
| 18. | D |
| 19. | C |
| 20. | B |
| 21. | B |
| 22. | A |
| 23. | D |
| 24. | B |
| 25. | A |
| 26. | D |
| 27. | B |
| 28. | C |

## Section I, Part B

| | |
|---|---|
| 76. | C |
| 77. | A |
| 78. | B |
| 79. | C |
| 80. | D |
| 81. | C |
| 82. | B |
| 83. | D |
| 84. | C |
| 85. | B |
| 86. | A |
| 87. | D |

**1.** (A) (i) $h(2) \approx -7$                                                                          1 point

       (ii) $f^{-1}(4) = 16$                                                             1 point

  (B) (i) $y = 1$                                                                                       1 point

       (ii) $(-2,-1)$, so $\lim\limits_{x \to -2^{-}} g(x) = \lim\limits_{x \to -2^{+}} g(x) = \lim\limits_{x \to -2} g(x) = -1$     1 point

  (C) (i) logarithmic                                                                           1 point

       (ii) See solution.                                                                    1 point

**2.** (i) $550 = a + b(0)^2$ and $405.1 = a + b(3)^2$                                            1 point

    (ii) $a = 550, b = -16.1$                                                               1 point

  (B) (i) $\dfrac{H(3) - H(0)}{3 - 0} = -48.3$ feet per second                        1 point

       (ii) See solution.                                                                    1 point

       (iii) less than                                                                       1 point

  (C) approximately 5.845 seconds                                                       1 point

**3.** (A) $F$ has coordinates $(0.125, 4.5)$.                                               1 point for $h(t)$

      $G$ has coordinates $(0.25, 6)$.                                                 coordinates

      $J$ has coordinates $(0.375, 4.5)$.

      $K$ has coordinates $(0.5, 3)$.                                                  1 point for $t$

      $P$ has coordinates $(0.625, 4.5)$.                                              coordinates

  (B) $h(t) = 1.5 \sin(4\pi(t - 0.125)) + 4.5$                                          2 points

    1 point for values of $a$ and $d$ and 1 point for values of $b$ and $c$

  (C) (i) Answer b                                                                              1 point

       (ii) See solution.                                                                    1 point

**4.** (A) (i) $g(x) = e^{2x} + 2 + \dfrac{1}{e^{2x}}$ for all $x$                              1 point

       (ii) $h(x) = -2 \sin x,\ \sin x \neq 0$                                             1 point

  (B) (i) $x = \dfrac{7\pi}{6}$ or $x = \dfrac{11\pi}{6}$                                 1 point

       (ii) $x = 1 + \log_2\left(\dfrac{6}{5}\right)$                                       1 point

  (C) $\sin\left(-\dfrac{\pi}{4}\right) = -\dfrac{\sqrt{2}}{2}$                           1 point

    $x = -\dfrac{\sqrt{2}}{6}$                                                              1 point

# › Solutions and Explanations

## Section I Part A (Multiple-Choice)

1.  The correct answer is (C).

    The function $f(x) = \dfrac{x^2 + 3x + 2}{x^2 - 1}$ is equivalent to $f(x) = \dfrac{(x+2)(x+1)}{(x-1)(x+1)} = \dfrac{x+2}{x-1}$.

    Therefore, the graph of $f(x)$ has a hole at $x = -1$. Substituting $-1$ for $x$ in the equation

    $f(x) = \dfrac{x+2}{x-1}$ yields $-\dfrac{1}{2}$. Therefore, $\displaystyle\lim_{x \to -1^-} f(x) = -\dfrac{1}{2}$.

2.  The correct answer is (C).
    The average rate of change over the closed interval $[-1, 2]$ is the slope of the secant

    line. Therefore, the average rate of change is $\dfrac{f(2) - f(-1)}{2 - (-1)} = \dfrac{8 - 2}{2 + 1}$. This is equivalent

    to $\dfrac{6}{3} = 2$.

3.  The correct answer is (B).
    A vertical dilation of a factor of 2 means $g(x) = 2 \cdot f(x)$, which is equivalent to

    $g(x) = 2\log_4 x$. Using the change of base formula, $\log_b a = \dfrac{\log_c a}{\log_c b}$, $f(x) = \log_4 x$ can be

    rewritten as $f(x) = \dfrac{\log_c x}{\log_c 4}$ for any $c > 0$ and $c \neq 1$. Therefore, if $c = 16$, $f(x) = \dfrac{\log_{16} x}{\log_{16} 4}$.

    This means that answer choice (A) is equivalent to $2 \cdot f(x)$, which is a vertical dilation
    of $f$ by a factor of 2. Using the power rule, $\log_b x^k = k\log_b x$ answer choice (C) sim-
    plifies to $2\log_4 x$. This means that answer choice (C) is equivalent to $2 \cdot f(x)$, which
    is a vertical dilation of $f$ by a factor of 2. By adding, answer choice (D) simplifies to
    $2\log_4 x$. This means that answer choice (D) is equivalent to $2 \cdot f(x)$, which is a verti-
    cal dilation of $f$ by a factor of 2. This leaves answer choice (B) as the expression that
    is not a formula for $g(x)$.

4.  The correct answer is (C).
    The graph of a polynomial function with real zeros that have even multiplicity
    are tangent to the $x$-axis. Therefore, $x = -6$ has even multiplicity and $x = 1$ has odd
    multiplicity.

5.  The correct answer is (B).
    The graph of $g(x) = f(2x)$ is a horizontal dilation of $f$ by a factor of $\left|\dfrac{1}{2}\right|$. Therefore,

    the transformed points on the graph of $g$ have $x$-coordinates that are half the value of
    the $x$-coordinate on the graph of $f$. This means the hole on $f$ at $(2, -1)$ corresponds to
    a hole on $g$ at $(1, -1)$.

6.  The correct answer is (D).

    Between every two distinct real zeros of a nonconstant polynomial function, there
    must be at least one input value corresponding to a local maximum or local minimum.
    If the polynomial is degree 3, then there exists a real zero for some value of $x < -3$, $f$
    is concave up on the interval $0 < x < 3$, and $\displaystyle\lim_{x \to \infty} f(x) = \infty$ as shown. Therefore, answer
    choice (A), answer choice (B), and answer choice (C) do not *have* to be true.

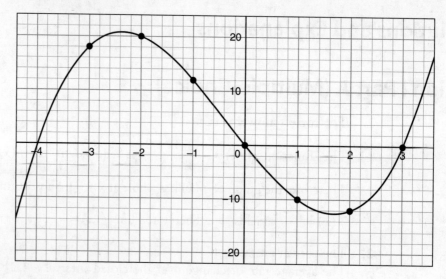

7. The correct answer is (A).

The inverse of $f$ can be found by reversing the roles of $x$ and $y$ and solving for $y$. Therefore,

- $x = 4 \cdot 2^{y-1} + 3$
- $x - 3 = 4 \cdot 2^{y-1}$
- $\dfrac{x-3}{4} = 2^{y-1}$
- $\log_2\left(\dfrac{x-3}{4}\right) = y - 1$
- $\log_2\left(\dfrac{x-3}{4}\right) + 1 = y$
- $\log_2(x-3) - \log_2 4 + 1 = y$
- $\log_2(x-3) - 2 + 1 = y$
- $\log_2(x-3) - 1 = y$

8. The correct answer is (A).

The graph of $y = \cos\theta$ is a horizontal translation of $\dfrac{\pi}{2}$ to the left of the graph of $y = \sin\theta$. This is equivalent to $y = \sin\left(\theta - \left(-\dfrac{\pi}{2}\right)\right)$, or $y = \sin\left(\theta + \dfrac{\pi}{2}\right)$. The graph of $y = \cos\theta$ oscillates between $-1$ and $1$, so answer choice (B) is not correct. The graph of $y = \cos\theta$ is symmetric to the $y$-axis, so it is even. Therefore, answer choice (C) is not correct. The period of the graph of $y = \cos\theta$ is $2\pi$, therefore, the frequency is 1, so answer choice (D) is not correct.

9. The correct answer is (B).

The inverse of $f$ can be found by reversing the roles of $x$ and $y$ and solving for $y$. Therefore,

- $x = \dfrac{y+1}{y-2}$
- $x(y-2) = y + 1$

- $xy - 2x = y + 1$
- $xy - y = 2x + 1$
- $y(x - 1) = 2x + 1$
- $y = \dfrac{2x + 1}{x - 1}$

**10.** The correct answer is (C).

The graph of $f(\theta) = \tan\theta$ is always increasing, so answer (C) is correct. The graph of $f(\theta) = \tan\theta$ has period $\pi$, so answer choice (A) is not correct. The function $f(\theta) = \tan\theta$ is equivalent to $f(\theta) = \dfrac{\sin\theta}{\cos\theta}$. Therefore, the graph has vertical asymptotes whenever $\cos\theta = 0$, so answer choice (B) is not correct. The tangent function changes from concave down to concave up between asymptotes, so answer choice (D) is not correct.

**11.** The correct answer is (B).

For all values in the interval $1 < x < 3$, if $a < b$, then $f(a) < f(b)$. Therefore, the function is increasing. Also, if $a < b < c$, then the rate of change from $a$ to $b$ is larger than the rate of change from $b$ to $c$. Therefore, the function is concave down.

**12.** The correct answer is (A).

$\log_b c = a$ if and only if $b^a = c$, where $a$ and $c$ are constants, $b > 0$, and $b \neq 1$. Because $b^a = c$, the exponent $a$ can be negative, such as $2^{-1} = \dfrac{1}{2}$.

**13.** The correct answer is (D).

The graph of an exponential function $y = ab^{cx}$, with $a > 0$ and $c > 0$ is increasing and concave up as shown in the following graph.

For the given function $f$, $a < 0$ and $c < 0$, resulting in a reflection over the $x$- and $y$-axes, resulting in the following graph. Therefore, $\lim\limits_{x \to \infty} f(x) = 0$.

**14.** The correct answer is (C).

The degree and sign of the leading term of a polynomial determine the end behavior of the polynomial function, because as the input values increase or decrease without bound, the values of the leading term dominate the values of all lower-degree terms. Because the output values decrease without bound when the input values increase without bound, the leading term is less than zero. Also, the polynomial's end behavior is the same as the input values increase or decrease without bound; therefore, the degree is even.

**15.** The correct answer is (C).

In order to have an inverse, the domain of the sine and tangent functions are restricted to $\left[-\dfrac{\pi}{2}, \dfrac{\pi}{2}\right]$, meaning the range of the inverse sine and inverse tangent functions is $\left[-\dfrac{\pi}{2}, \dfrac{\pi}{2}\right]$. Therefore, answer choices (A), (B), and (D) are not correct. In order to have an inverse, the domain of the cosine is restricted to $[0, \pi]$, with $\cos\dfrac{5\pi}{6} = -\dfrac{\sqrt{3}}{2}$; therefore, $\cos^{-1}\left(-\dfrac{\sqrt{3}}{2}\right) = \dfrac{5\pi}{6}$.

**16.** The correct answer is (D).

Angles in standard position that share a terminal ray differ by an integer number of revolutions, with each revolution measuring $2\pi$ radians. Therefore, $\theta = \dfrac{2\pi}{7} + 2k\pi$, where $k$ is an integer, are coterminal. Because $\dfrac{2\pi}{7} - 2\pi = -\dfrac{12\pi}{7}$, $-\dfrac{12\pi}{7}$ is coterminal with $\dfrac{2\pi}{7}$.

**17.** The correct answer is (B).

The real zeros of a rational function correspond to the real zeros of the numerator for such values in its domain. The real zeros of the numerator of $f(x) = \dfrac{(x-2)^2(x+3)}{x(x-2)(x-1)}$ are 2 and $-3$; however, 2 is not in the domain of $f$, because it is a real zero of the denominator. Therefore, the function $f$ has one distinct real zero.

**18.** The correct answer is (D).

Given an angle of measure $\theta$ in standard position and a unit circle centered at the origin, $f(\theta) = \sin\theta$ is given by the $y$-coordinate. Therefore, $\sin\theta = 0.8$.

**19.** The correct answer is (C).

- $\sin^2(3x) - \cos^2(3x) + \sin(3x) = 0$
- $\sin^2(3x) - (1 - \sin^2(3x)) + \sin(3x) = 0$
- $2\sin^2(3x) + \sin(3x) - 1 = 0$
- $(2\sin(3x) - 1)(\sin(3x) + 1) = 0$
- $2\sin(3x) - 1 = 0$ or $\sin(3x) + 1 = 0$
- $\sin(3x) = \dfrac{1}{2}$ or $\sin(3x) = -1$
- $3x = \dfrac{\pi}{6} + 2k\pi$, $3x = \dfrac{5\pi}{6} + 2k\pi$, or $3x = \dfrac{3\pi}{2} + 2k\pi$, where $k$ is an integer
- $x = \dfrac{\pi}{18} + \dfrac{2k\pi}{3}$, $x = \dfrac{5\pi}{18} + \dfrac{2k\pi}{3}$, or $x = \dfrac{\pi}{2} + \dfrac{2k\pi}{3}$, where $k$ is an integer

**20.** The correct answer is (B).

The graph of $f(x) = -2\log_3 x$ is a reflection over the $x$-axis of the graph of $y = \log_3 x$. The vertical asymptote of the graph of $y = \log_3 x$ is described as $\lim\limits_{x \to 0^+} \log_3 x = -\infty$, and the end behavior is $\lim\limits_{x \to \infty} \log_3 x = \infty$. Therefore, the reflection over the $x$-axis means the vertical asymptote can be described as $\lim\limits_{x \to 0^+}(-2\log_3 x) = \infty$ with end behavior $\lim\limits_{x \to \infty}(-2\log_3 x) = -\infty$.

21. The correct answer is (B).

The additive transformation of $g(\theta) = \cos\theta + d$ is a vertical translation by $d$ units. The additive transformation of $g(\theta) = \cos(\theta + c)$ is a horizontal translation by $-c$ units. Therefore, a transformation that is a vertical translation of 3 units up and a horizontal translation of 4 units to the right results in $g(\theta) = \cos(\theta - 4) + 3$.

22. The correct answer is (A).

The numerator and denominator are both polynomials of degree 2. Therefore, the function has a horizontal asymptote at $y = \dfrac{a_2}{b_2}$, where $a_2$ is the coefficient of $x^2$ in the numerator and $b_2$ is the coefficient of $x^2$ in the denominator. Therefore, the function $r(x)$ has a horizontal asymptote at $y = 1$.

23. The correct answer is (D).

When $\theta = \dfrac{3\pi}{4}$, $r = 0$ and when $\theta = \dfrac{7\pi}{8}$, $r = -5$. On the interval $\dfrac{3\pi}{4} < \theta < \dfrac{7\pi}{8}$, $r$ is decreasing from 0 to $-5$, moving from point $a$ to point $b$ in the following graph.

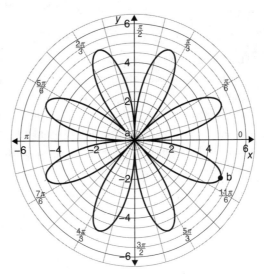

24. The correct answer is (B).

When $\theta = 0$, $r = 3$, and when $\theta = \dfrac{\pi}{2}$, $r = -1$. Therefore, the graph of $r$ passes through the point $(3, 0)$ and $(0, -1)$. The only graph with these points is in answer choice (B).

25. The correct answer is (A).

The negative exponent property states that $b^{-n} = \dfrac{1}{b^n}$; therefore, $(3x^2 y)^{-2} = \dfrac{1}{(3x^2 y)^2}$ and $(18x^{-3} y^5) = \dfrac{18y^5}{x^3}$. The power property for exponents states that $(b^m)^n = b^{(mn)}$; therefore, $\dfrac{1}{(3x^2 y)^2} = \dfrac{1}{9x^4 y^2}$. Therefore, the expression $(3x^2 y)^{-2} \cdot (18x^{-3} y^5) = \dfrac{1}{9x^4 y^2} \cdot \dfrac{18y^5}{x^3}$.

The product property for exponents states that $b^m b^n = b^{(m+n)}$; therefore, $\dfrac{1}{9x^4 y^2} \cdot \dfrac{18y^5}{x^3} = \dfrac{18y^5}{9x^7 y^2}$. This is equivalent to $\dfrac{2y^3}{x^7}$.

**26.** The correct answer is (D).

The inverse of $f$ can be found by reversing the roles of $x$ and $y$ and solving for $y$. Therefore,

- $x = 3^y$
- $\log_3 x = y$

**27.** The correct answer is (B).

When the complex number has the rectangular coordinates $(a, b)$, it can be expressed as $a + bi$.

The corresponding coordinates of a point in the polar coordinate system, $(r, \theta)$, can be converted from coordinates in the rectangular coordinate system, $r = \sqrt{a^2 + b^2}$ and $\theta = \arctan\left(\dfrac{b}{a}\right)$. Therefore, the given complex number $2 - 2i$ has $r = \sqrt{2^2 + (-2)^2} = \sqrt{8}$ and $\theta = \arctan(-1) = -\dfrac{\pi}{4}$. The angle $\theta = -\dfrac{\pi}{4}$ is coterminal with $\theta = \dfrac{7\pi}{4}$. Therefore,

$$2 - 2i = 2\sqrt{2}\left(\cos\frac{7\pi}{4} + i\sin\frac{7\pi}{4}\right).$$

**28.** The correct answer is (C).

A hole occurs when the multiplicity of a real zero in the numerator is greater than or equal to the multiplicity in the denominator. Therefore, there is a hole at $x = -b$. If the real zero of the polynomial function in the denominator of a rational function is not also a real zero of the polynomial function in the numerator, then the graph of the rational function has a vertical asymptote. Therefore, there is a vertical asymptote at $x = -c$.

# Section I Part B (Multiple-Choice)

**76.** The correct answer is (C).

- $2\ln x - \ln(x-1) = 4$

- $\ln x^2 - \ln(x-1) = 4$

- $\ln \dfrac{x^2}{x-1} = 4$

- $e^4 = \dfrac{x^2}{x-1}$

- $e^4(x-1) = x^2$

- $e^4 x - e^4 = x^2$

- $0 = x^2 - e^4 x + e^4$

- $x = \dfrac{e^4 \pm \sqrt{(e^4)^2 - 4(1)(e^4)}}{2(1)}$

- $x \approx 1.109 \text{ or } x \approx 53.579$

Similarly, the points of intersection can be found by looking at the graph of $y = 2\ln x - \ln(x-1)$ and $y = 4$ in the appropriate window as the following shows.

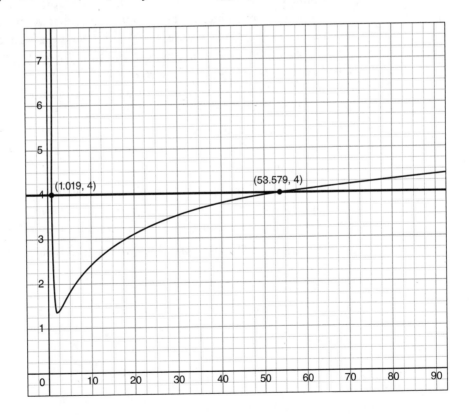

**77.** The correct answer is (A).

The average rate of change over the closed interval $\left[\dfrac{\pi}{2}, \dfrac{7\pi}{4}\right]$ is the ratio of change of $r$ with respect to $\theta$. Therefore, the average rate of change is

$$\dfrac{\left(2+\sin\left(5\cdot\dfrac{7\pi}{4}\right)\right) - \left(2+\sin\left(5\cdot\dfrac{\pi}{2}\right)\right)}{\dfrac{7\pi}{4} - \dfrac{\pi}{2}}. \text{ This is approximately equal to } -0.0746.$$

**78.** The correct answer is (B).

Given an angle measure $\theta$ in standard position and a circle with radius $r$ centered at the origin, there is a point, $P$, where the terminal ray intersects the circle. Recall that the angle measure of $\theta$ is assumed to be in radians and that the coordinates of point $P$ are $(r\cos\theta, r\sin\theta)$. Therefore, the coordinates are $(3.6\cos 24, 3.6\sin 24)$, or $(1.527, -3.260)$.

**79.** The correct answer is (C).

Michelle's pay rate can be modeled by $p_n = p_0(r)^n$, where $p_n$ represents Michelle's pay after completing $n$ six month periods, $p_0$ is the initial pay rate, and $r$ is the increase in pay rate. This is equivalent to $p_n = 15(1.04)^n$. When Michelle has worked for three years, she has completed 6 six-month periods, so $p_6 = 15(1.04)^6 \approx 18.98$.

**80.** The correct answer is (D).

The domain of a composition, $f(g(x))$, is the domain of the intersection of the domain of $g(x)$ and values in the output of $g(x)$ that are in the domain of $f(x)$. The domain of $g(x)$ is $[3,\infty]$ because $x-3\geq 0$ for the square root function. The range of $g(x)$ that is in the domain of $f(x)$ can be found by solving $(g(x))^2 - 11g(x) + 18 \geq 0$. This is equivalent to $(g(x)-9)(g(x)-2)\geq 0$. The product of two numbers is non-negative when both numbers are positive or both numbers are negative or one of the numbers is 0. Therefore, $\sqrt{x-3}-2\leq 0$ or $\sqrt{x-3}-9\geq 0$. Therefore, $\sqrt{x-3}\leq 2$, or $x-3\leq 4$, which is equivalent to $x\leq 7$. Similarly, $\sqrt{x-3}\geq 9$, or $x-3\geq 81$, which is equivalent to $x\geq 84$. This mean the domain of $f(g(x))$ is $[3,7]\cup[84,\infty)$.

**81.** The correct answer is (C).

All of the choices involve the secant function, which is the reciprocal of the cosine function. The underlying cosine function, $y = a\cos(b(x-c))+d$, has a midline at $y=3$, and there is a distance of 2 units between the midline and the maximum of 5 or minimum of 1. Therefore, $a=2$ and $d=3$. The period is 8 units, therefore, $\dfrac{2\pi}{b}=8$, or $b=\dfrac{\pi}{4}$. The cosine function is symmetric to the $y$-axis, and so is the transformed function. Therefore, $c=0$. The correct answer is $y = 2\sec\left(\dfrac{\pi}{4}x\right)+3$.

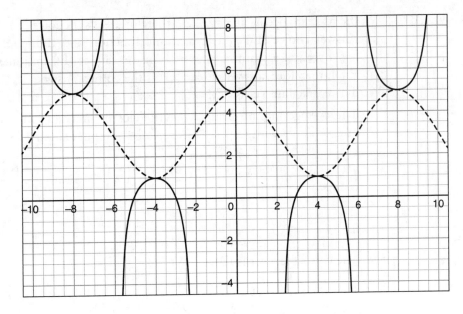

**82.** The correct answer is (B).

The graph of $r(x) = \dfrac{x^2 + 7x + 4}{x^2 - 2x - 6}$ follows. The zeros of $r(x)$ are found by setting the numerator equal to 0, or $x^2 + 7x + 4 = 0$. Therefore, $x = \dfrac{-7 \pm \sqrt{7^2 - 4(1)(4)}}{2(1)}$, or $x \approx -6.373$ and $x \approx -0.628$. The vertical asymptotes of $r(x)$ are found by setting the denominator equal to 0, or $x^2 - 2x - 6 = 0$. Therefore, $x = \dfrac{2 \pm \sqrt{(-2)^2 - 4(1)(-6)}}{2(1)}$, or $x \approx -1.646$ and $x \approx 3.646$, which are not in the domain of $r(x)$. Of the intervals listed, the graph of $r(x) \geq 0$ for $(-1.646, -0.628]$.

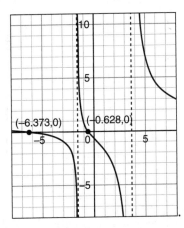

**83.** The correct answer is (D).

The graph shown has a vertical asymptote at $x = 0$ and the real zero occurs at $x = 1$. Answer choice (A) is an exponential equation. Therefore, the graph of answer choice (A) has a horizontal asymptote at $y = 0$ and is not the correct answer. Answer choice (B) is a square root function. Therefore, the graph of answer choice (B) does not have an asymptote and is not the correct answer. Answer choice (C) is a rational function and the denominator equals zero when $x = 0$. Therefore, the graph of answer choice (C) has a vertical asymptote at $x = 0$. However, the numerator of answer choice (C) indicates the real zero occurs at $x = 2.222$; therefore, answer choice (C) is not the correct answer. Answer choice (D) is a logarithmic function and the graph of answer choice (D) has a vertical asymptote at $x = 0$. Answer choice (D) indicates the real zero occurs at $x = 1$; therefore, answer choice (D) is the correct answer.

**84.** The correct answer is (C).

The average rate of change over the closed interval $[-1, 6]$ is the ratio of change of output values with respect to the change of input values. Therefore, the average rate of change is $\dfrac{\left(\dfrac{1}{4}(6)^3 - \dfrac{7}{4}(6)^2 + \dfrac{3}{2}(6) + 1\right) - \left(\dfrac{1}{4}(-1)^3 - \dfrac{7}{4}(-1)^2 + \dfrac{3}{2}(-1) + 1\right)}{6 - (-1)}$. This is equal to $\dfrac{1 + 2.5}{6 + 1} = 0.5$.

**85.** The correct answer is (B).

The graph of $r(x) = \dfrac{x^2 + x - 1}{x^2 - 3x - 4}$ is shown as follows. There is a vertical asymptote at $x = -1$. As the values of $x$ approach $-1$ from values of $x < -1$, the graph decreases without bound.

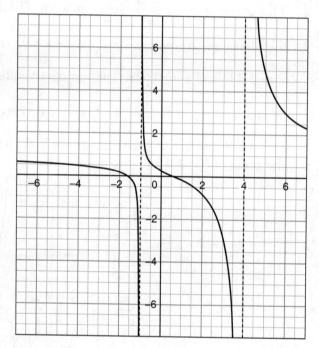

**86.** The correct answer is (A).

Using technology, the exponential regression equation is $y = (4.442911817)(1.042105592)^x$. The predicted number of people at the beginning of the concert is $(4.442911817)(1.042105592)^{120} = 626.722$. Therefore, the error is the observed value minus the predicted value, or $625 - 626.722 = -1.722$.

**87.** The correct answer is (D).

The period length is the time it takes until the pattern repeats. The first low tide occurred at 1:45 a.m., and the second low tide occurred at 1:05 p.m. Therefore, it took 11 hours and 20 minutes for the low tide to repeat. The period length is 11.333 hours.

# Section II Part A (Free-Response)

1. (A) (i) $h(2) = (g \circ f)(2)$, which is equivalent to $g(f(2))$. The table shows that when $x = 2$, the function $f$ is equal to 1. Therefore, $g(f(2))$ is equivalent to $g(1)$. Using the defined function for $g$, $g(1) = \dfrac{(1)^2 + 8(1) + 12}{(1)^2 - 4}$, which is $g(1) = \dfrac{1 + 8 + 12}{1 - 4}$, or $g(1) = -\dfrac{21}{3}$. Therefore, $h(2) = -7$.

   (ii) Because $f$ is increasing for all values of $f$, $f^{-1}$ exists. Algebraically, the inverse function results from interchanging the input values and output values. Therefore, the value of $f^{-1}(4)$, or the inverse function with an input value of 4, is equivalent to what value of $x$ does $f(x)$ have an output of 4. From the table, $f(x) = 4$ when $x = 16$.

   (B) (i) When neither polynomial in a rational function dominates the other, or when the degree of each polynomial is the same, the quotient of the leading terms is the constant that indicates the location of a horizontal asymptote. For the function $g$, both the numerator and denominator have degree 2, so the ratio of the leading terms indicates the location of the horizontal asymptote. In other words, the function $g$ can be approximated by $y = \dfrac{x^2}{x^2}$ for large values $x$. Therefore, $y = 1$ is the equation of the horizontal asymptote.

   (ii) The function $g(x) = \dfrac{x^2 + 8x + 12}{x^2 - 4}$ can be rewritten as $g(x) = \dfrac{(x + 2)(x + 6)}{(x + 2)(x - 2)}$. The multiplicity of the real zero $x = -2$ in the numerator is equal to the multiplicity of the same zero in the denominator. The function $g$ is equivalent to $j(x) = \dfrac{x + 6}{x - 2}$ for all values of $x \neq -2$. Substituting $-2$ for $x$ in the equation $j(x) = \dfrac{x + 6}{x - 2}$ yields $j(-2) = \dfrac{-2 + 6}{-2 - 2} = -1$. Therefore, $\lim\limits_{x \to -2^-} g(x) = \lim\limits_{x \to -2^+} g(x) = \lim\limits_{x \to -2} g(x) = -1$.

   (C) (i) $f$ is best modeled by a logarithmic function.

   (ii) Input values of general-form logarithmic functions change proportionally as output values increase in equal-length intervals. Each output-value interval differs by 1, so they are equal-length intervals. Each input value is twice the size of the previous input value. Because the output values are changing additively as input values are changing multiplicatively, the function is logarithmic.

2. (A) (i) The first given data is that when the time, $t$, is 0 seconds, the height of the ball, $H(0)$, is 550 feet. Therefore, the first equation that can be used to find the values of the constants is $550 = a + b(0)^2$. The second given data is that when $t = 3$, $H(3) = 405.1$. Therefore, the second equation that can be used to find the values of the constants is $405.1 = a + b(3)^2$.

(ii) The first equation, $550 = a + b(0)^2$, is equivalent to $550 = a + 0$, so $a = 550$. The second equation $405.1 = a + b(3)^2$ can be rewritten as $405.1 = a + 9b$. Substituting 550 for $a$ in the second equation, $405.1 = a + 9b$, yields $405.1 = 550 + 9b$. Subtracting 550 from both sides of this equation yields $-144.9 = 9b$. Dividing both sides of this equation by 9 yields $-\dfrac{144.9}{9} = b$, or $b = -16.1$. The equation $H(t) = 550 - 16.1t^2$ models the height of a ball, in feet, based on the time, in seconds, since dropping a ball off a 550-foot building.

(B) (i) The average rate of change is the slope of the secant line between $(a, H(a))$ and $(b, H(b))$, or the slope of the line between $(0, 550)$ and $(3, 405.1)$. Therefore, the average rate of change from $t = 0$ to $t = 3$ is

$$\frac{H(3) - H(0)}{3 - 0} = \frac{405.1 - 550}{3} = -\frac{144.9}{3} = -48.3 \text{ feet per second.}$$

(ii) For a ball dropped from a 550-foot building, on average, the height of the ball decreases or falls 48.3 feet per second when the time is between 0 seconds and 3 seconds.

(iii) The average rates of change of $H$ from $t = 3$ to $t = p$ seconds are less than the average rate of change from $t = 0$ to $t = 3$ seconds. The function $H$ is modeled by $H(t) = 550 - 16.1t^2$. Because $H$ is a quadratic function with a leading coefficient, $a = -16.1 < 0$, $H$ is a decreasing function that is concave down. Therefore, the average rates of change, in feet per second, are decreasing over equal-length input-value intervals as $t$ increases.

(C) The model satisfies the equation $550 - 16.1t^2 > 0$, which is equivalent to $-16.1t^2 > -550$. Because $-16.1 < 0$, dividing both sides of this equation by $-16.1$ yields $t^2 < \dfrac{550}{16.1}$. Taking the square root of both sides of this equation yields $t < \sqrt{\dfrac{550}{16.1}}$, or $t < 5.845$. The model is only appropriate for approximately the first 5.845 seconds, or $0 \le t < 5.845$.

# Section II Part B (Free-Response)

3. (A) The shortest distance between $A$ and $B$ is 3 feet and occurs when point $A$ is closest to the wall, which is shown in the picture and represented by the lowest point on the graph before $F$ in the sinusoidal function. The greatest distance between $A$ and $B$ is 6 feet and occurs when point $A$ is furthest from the wall and is represented by point $G$ in the sinusoidal function. This means that points on the dashed midline represent times when the distance between points $A$ and $B$ is $\dfrac{3 + 6}{2}$, or 4.5 feet.

The blades make 2 complete rotations every second, so the time it takes for point $A$ to move from the closest to point $B$ to the furthest distance from point $B$, represented by points going from $G$ to point $K$, take 0.25 seconds, and the time to move from the closest $A$ is to $B$ to the dashed midline or the dashed midline half that, or 0.125 seconds. Therefore, if time $t = 0$ is the beginning of the sinusoidal graph, $F$ has coordinates $(0.125, 4.5)$, $G$ has coordinates $(0.25, 6)$, $J$ has coordinates $(0.375, 4.5)$, $K$ has coordinates $(0.5, 3)$, and $P$ has coordinates $(0.625, 4.5)$.

(B) The amplitude, $a$, is the vertical distance, in feet, between the dashed midline and the closest or furthest $A$ is from $B$ on the sinusoidal graph. Therefore, $a = 6 - 4.5 = 1.5$ feet. The period is the horizontal distance, in seconds, where the sinusoidal pattern repeats and can be presented by the distance between points $F$ and $P$. Thus, the period is $0.625 - 0.125 = 0.5$ seconds. The period of a sinusoidal function is $\left|\frac{1}{b}\right| 2\pi$ seconds, so $\left|\frac{1}{b}\right| 2\pi = 0.5$, or $b = 4\pi$. The additive transformations, $c$ and $d$, are the horizontal and vertical translations respectively of the sine function and can be represented by the location of point $F$. There is a horizontal translation of $0.125$ units and a vertical translation of $4.5$ units. Therefore, $c = -0.125$ and $d = 4.5$. The function $h$ can be written as $h(t) = 1.5\sin(4\pi(t - 0.125)) + 4.5$.

(C) (i) Between points $G$ and $J$, the value of $h$ is in the interval $4.5 < h(a) < 6$; therefore, $h$ is positive. Also, for $a$ and $b$ in the interval $(t_1, t_2)$, if $a < b$, then $h(a) > h(b)$, so the graph of $h$ is decreasing.

    (ii) Because the graph of $h$ is concave down on the interval $(t_1, t_2)$, the rate of change of $h$ is decreasing on the interval $(t_1, t_2)$.

4. (A) (i) The function $g$ is defined as $g(x) = (e^x + e^{-x})^2$. Therefore, $g(x) = (e^x + e^{-x})(e^x + e^{-x})$, which is equivalent to $g(x) = e^x \cdot e^x + e^x \cdot e^{-x} + e^{-x} \cdot e^x + e^{-x} \cdot e^{-x})$, or $g(x) = e^{x+x} + e^{x-x} + e^{-x+x} + e^{-x-x}$. This is equivalent to $g(x) = e^{2x} + 1 + 1 + e^{-2}x$. Consequently, $g$ can be rewritten as $g(x) = e^{2x} + 2 + \dfrac{1}{e^{2x}}$.

    (ii) The function $h$ is defined as $h(x) = \dfrac{\cos(2x) - 1}{\sin x}$. The sum identity for sine states that $\cos(\alpha + \beta) = \cos\alpha\cos\beta + \sin\alpha\sin\beta$. Therefore, $\cos(x + x) = \cos(2x) = \cos x \cos x - \sin x \sin x$, which is equivalent to $\cos(2x) = \cos^2 x - \sin^2 x$. Hence, $h$ can be written as $h(x) = \dfrac{\cos^2 x - \sin^2 x - 1}{\sin x}$. The Pythagorean Identity states that $\sin^2 x + \cos^2 x = 1$, which is equivalent to $\cos^2 x = 1 - \sin^2 x$. Therefore, $h$ can be rewritten as $h(x) = \dfrac{1 - \sin^2 x - \sin^2 x - 1}{\sin x}$, or $h(x) = \dfrac{-2\sin^2 x}{\sin x}$. Dividing out a factor of $\sin x$ yields $h(x) = -2\sin x$. Therefore, when $\sin x \neq 0$, $h(x) = -2\sin x$.

(B) (i) Setting the function $j$ equal to zero yields $(\tan x)(\cos x) + \sin x + 1 = 0$. The tangent function is the ratio of the sine function to the cosine function, so this equation can be rewritten as $\dfrac{\sin x}{\cos x} \cdot \cos x + \sin x + 1 = 0$. This is equivalent to $\sin x + \sin x + 1 = 0$, or $2\sin x + 1 = 0$. This equation is equivalent to $\sin x = -\dfrac{1}{2}$. Based on the unit circle for angles in the interval $[0, 2\pi]$, $\sin x = -\dfrac{1}{2}$ when $x = \dfrac{7\pi}{6}$ or $x = \dfrac{11\pi}{6}$.

(ii) Setting the function $k$ equal to 9 yields the equation $9 = 5(2)^{x-1} + 3$. Subtracting 3 from both sides of this equation yields $6 = 5(2)^{x-1}$. Dividing both sides of this equation by 5 results in $\frac{6}{5} = (2)^{x-1}$. Taking the log base 2 of both sides of this equation yields $\log_2\left(\frac{6}{5}\right) = \log_2(2)^{x-1}$, which is equivalent to $\log_2\left(\frac{6}{5}\right) - x \quad 1$. Adding 1 to both sides of this equation results in $x = 1 + \log_2\left(\frac{6}{5}\right)$.

(C) Setting the function $m$ equal to $\frac{3\pi}{4}$ produces the equation $\arcsin(3x) + \pi = \frac{3\pi}{4}$. Subtracting $\pi$ from both sides of this equation yields $\arcsin(3x) = -\frac{\pi}{4}$. Taking the sine of both sides of this equation yields $3x = \sin\left(-\frac{\pi}{4}\right)$, or $3x = -\frac{\sqrt{2}}{2}$.

Dividing each of these equations by 3 results in $x = -\frac{\sqrt{2}}{6}$.